TOOLS FOR TEAMS
The Manager's Guide to Building Teams

Harrison D. Snow

Team Building Associates
Falls Church, Virginia

TEAM BUILDING ASSOCIATES
6521 Elmhirst Drive
Falls Church, VA 22043

Library of Congress Cataloging-in-Publication Data
Snow, Harrison
Tools for Teams: The Manager's Guide to Building Teams

Library of Congress Catalogue Number: 00-90190

ISBN: 0-9677329-0-5

BOOKS BY HARRISON SNOW

The Power of Team Building Using Ropes Techniques

Indoor/Outdoor Team Building Games for Trainers

In the early 1950's Werner von Braun, pioneer of America's space program was found standing on the beach at Cape Canaveral, staring out at the waves. One of his colleagues approached and said,

"What are you thinking about Dr. von Braun? Are you planning an innovation in space flight or trying to solve a technical problem?"

"No," Dr. von Braun replied, "I'm thinking about something much more important—my team.

Acknowledgements

As this book was written over a span of eight years it went through numerous rewrites and revisions. During that time the contributions of others were many.

Special thanks to Stephanie Snow, Vickie Worthington, and Susan Reiss for their careful editing and helpful comments and to Cynthia Stock for typesetting this book. Special appreciation and gratitude is due to my fellow trainers and friends, Bill Liggett, Glenda Short, and Donna Bauman, for their valuable ideas and comments in reviewing early versions of the manuscript. Many thanks to the outstanding trainers and friends I've had the good fortune to associate with and benefit from their expertise and ideas. Through discussions, helpful input and/or the opportunity to observe their work I am indebted and grateful to: Jane Bonin, Jeff Boyd, John Buck, Susan Caparaso, Betsy Dalgliesh, Susan Dweck, Dawn Frick, Alan Gilburg, Rhonda Gordon, States Hines, Mike Horne, Craig Imler, Deb Loucks, Colleen Luzier, Matt Minahan, Claudia Phelps, Chris Powers, Mindy Lee Pruss, Ed Quinn, Vicky Simmons, Elinor Spieler, Moses Thompson, Joyce Warner, Wendy Watkins, Tom Wootten, Carol Wzorek, and the many other great trainers I have worked with.

As a trainer and facilitator I also thank every participant in the many teams I have worked with. As one trainer said after a challenging group, "When things go well you learn a lot about the team. When things do not, you learn a lot about yourself." In every training program, large or small, lasting a couple of hours or a couple of weeks, I've had the opportunity to learn something each time I have gotten up in front of a group. Hopefully, those learnings are captured in these pages.

To Mom and Dad

Table of Contents

GRAPHS & PHOTOGRAPHS

Introduction
Why Teamwork?

Team Building Associates

*We know that people who are successful in
life are people who have a positive desire to
achieve rather than a fear of failure.*

RON FIRTH, SPORTS PSYCHOLOGIST

Working with others can be an enjoyable, and even transforming,
experience. It can also be a tribulation of the worst kind. What
separates one experience from the other is more than just the personalities of the people with whom you work. Consciously or unconsciously, there are a number of things a group does to develop
that sense of collective cohesion and commitment we call teamwork. This book covers the range of actions, from informal on-
the-run activities to structured interventions and programs, you
can use to develop your team.

Companies are faced with a dilemma. They want and need the
loyalty and dedication of their employees, but they can no longer
offer job security in return. Workers who feel disillusioned and

disenfranchised are less productive. As a result more jobs are lost to our global competitors. Workers used to stay with one company their entire career. Now people change companies, and even careers, about as often as they change their cars. The bonds that time and tenure built are no longer there. Change, due to turnover and restructuring, is just too fast and unrelenting. In this kind of environment if an organization wants the benefits of teamwork it has to make the effort to build teams.

The production of world-class, quality products and services demands exceptional levels of cooperation and problem solving. Many companies, both large and small, have learned the hard way that the traditional methods of managing a work force are no longer effective. The demand for greater productivity and higher quality, in both the public and private sectors, is forging a new management paradigm. This new paradigm seeks to give every member of an organization a sense of ownership and personal involvement. Real teamwork offers each team member the opportunity to lead as well as follow. Teams often take off like rockets when the members agree to welcome and respect everyone's contribution.

We do not know what the new millennium will hold. Whatever the mix of old and new challenges the only sure bet is that we will have to deal with even more change. The metaphor that summed up the 1990s, *permanent whitewater*, still applies.

We do know that interpersonal communications is key to negotiating the rapids and staying afloat. Teamwork is a competitive advantage. It relies on a group to manage the collective effort for the common good. Leaving this process up to the vicissitudes of idiosyncratic relationships is a luxury few can afford. Appreciating diversity, working as teams, and leveling the organizational hierarchy are trends that are here to stay.

Too often when teamwork does occur, it is more of a "happy accident" than the outcome from a series of conscious decisions. When the effort to reorganize into teams fails, it is most often due

to the lack of training. Good team skills are more than a friendly or positive attitude. Organizations that are successful in building teams invest significant time and resources in developing the team skills of their employees. Too often this common sense approach fails to be common practice.

Tools For Teams offers the manager or team leader a toolkit filled with an assortment of team building skills, activities, and programs. It catalogues and explains what you can do, or hire someone else to do, to help build a better team. It is unique in the range of what it offers. You can improve the performance of your team by selecting the tool that best fits your team's stage of development. If one tool is not right for the job another in the kit might be. Since any tool is only as good as the skill and understanding of the user, this toolkit comes with some of the knowledge you need to develop your "teamcraft."

It is important not to read this as a management cookbook. With most cookbooks, the closer you follow the recipe the better your chances for success. A toolkit differs in that using one requires thinking, experimenting, and taking responsibility for the results. The responsibility for building a high-performance team belongs in every team members' job description. As in any personal relationship, it requires effort on a daily basis. The process can never be delegated to one person or to some once-a-year event.

If you are tackling a serious situation that has been intractable and frustrating for longer than you care to admit, it may be wise to bring in some outside help. Before you can take action you should know the range of resources that are available. This book defines those resources and explains how to use them. Properly applied, these tools will leverage your effectiveness as a manager and team member, and improve the productivity of the people working for you and with you. Programs that build skills and help develop a culture of cooperation cost time and money. By making the required investment, you can unleash the full potential of your work force. Without an investment in the human dimension, the costs of lost opportunity and lower productivity are unavoidable.

Any systematic effort to deal with the problems and challenges confronting your team has to start somewhere. Someone has to take the initiative to close the office door, unplug the phone, and think about the "How?" rather than the "What?" that is pressing to be done. I hope that someone is you.

Section I
Understanding Teamwork

1
Tool List

Maxcomm Associates

Give us the tools and we will do the job.

WINSTON CHURCHILL

In some organizations the topic of teamwork is like the weather. Everyone talks about it but no one does much to improve it. The fact that you have this book in your hands right now shows you are different. You are going to do something that will make a difference. Before you can impact the quality of teams and teamwork it is important to know what "tools" you have to work with. This chapter provides an overview of the theories, skills and programs offered in this book. Each section builds upon the information presented in the previous one. The sections are:

- Section I. Understanding Teamwork
- Section II. Interpersonal Skills
- Section III. Tools for Teamwork
- Section IV. Team-Building Programs
- Section V. The Challenge of Change

UNDERSTANDING TEAMWORK–SECTION I

Using a tool skillfully requires a basic level of understanding about that tool. For some groups forging a common definition of what constitutes a team is the place to start. Theoretical knowledge augments personal knowledge by helping you select the management actions that will influence and motivate people. For example, you can do a better job building trust in your team if you know how trust, or the lack of it, affects the dynamics of a group. By itself, theoretical knowledge seldom changes anyone's behavior. Since action guided by understanding is more likely to hit its mark the first section covers the following topics:

- Tool List (Chapter 1)
- What is Teamwork? (Chapter 2)
- Theories and Models (Chapter 3)

INTERPERSONAL SKILLS–SECTION II

Mastering the technical skills of a professional takes years of education and practice. Interpersonal skills, often called "soft" or "people" skills, are just as essential and tougher to acquire. Many human resource professionals believe that eighty percent of a manager's success comes from communication and other people skills. A manager's job is to manage the interactions between employees and that takes interpersonal skills. Three essential interpersonal skills are discussed in Section Two:

- Communication Skills (Chapter 4)
- Facilitation (Chapter 5)
- Conflict and Negotiation (Chapter 6)

It is doubtful whether anyone ever completely masters these skills. This educational journey is life long. But many of us never take more than a few halting steps. The most basic skill of listening is a good example. Most of us do not even realize just how poorly we listen. Improvement comes when we gain enough self-awareness to catch ourselves being ourselves and comprehend the effect that has on others.

TOOLS FOR TEAMWORK—SECTION III

When people leave their desks and gather in groups of two or more the potential for teamwork can be actualized. Most managers and team members shortchange themselves; not realizing every meeting they have together is a team-building opportunity. Tools for improving team dynamics presented in Section Three are:

- Ground Rules and Agreements (Chapter 7)
- Team Building On-The-Run (Chapter 8)
- Decisions and Problem Solving (Chapter 9)

Some of these tools are informal actions and agreements that create an atmosphere conducive to teamwork, others help to get energy and ideas moving in a group that is bogged down. These processes and others presented in this book for decision making and problem solving are essential team skills.

TEAM-BUILDING PROGRAMS—SECTION IV

Increasingly, major corporations are contracting with providers of team-building programs for their services. The most effective of these programs use action learning. The participants learn by doing instead of sitting through lectures about how to work as a team. Team-building programs in Section Four include:

- Organizational Interventions (Chapter 10)
- Different Work Styles (Chapter 11)
- Ropes Course (Chapter 12)
- Wilderness Adventure (Chapter 13)
- Cross-Cultural Teamwork (Chapter 14)
- Benefiting From Diversity (Chapter 15)
- Business Games (Chapter 16)

THE CHALLENGE OF CHANGE–SECTION V

The corporate world is going through a period of turbulent change driven by technological innovation and an increasingly complex business and social environment. In their efforts to deal with these forces companies are becoming more adaptable and flexible. This section describes how resistance and inertia are overcome, structures developed, and training conducted to mold an organization that can thrive in the global economy. It explains the dynamics and special challenges that arise when the team concept is introduced into a hierarchical organization. Some of the knowledge and skills needed to manage the constant process of change will be found in the following chapters:

- Team Killers (Chapter 17)
- Managing Stress (Chapter 18)
- Managing Change (Chapter 19)
- Team Leadership (Chapter 20)
- Structural Reinforcement (Chapter 21)
- Process Improvement (Chapter 22)
- Forging a Vision (Chapter 23)
- The New Spirit At Work (Postscript)

The following picture shows how each section of this book, represented by a level in the pyramid builds upon the previous, to foster the skills needed to build and run a high-performance organization.

THE REAL CHALLENGE

Ask most senior managers what their biggest challenge is and they might say things like, "keeping the boss off my back", "making this quarter's revenue goals", or "keeping the customer happy". All are worthy goals. However, it is worth considering that there is a challenge even more basic and fundamental to obtaining the results we seek. The bigger challenge is in fostering a sense of

Foundations of Team Building

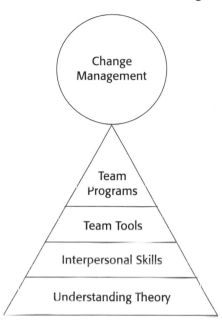

Change
Management

Team
Programs

Team Tools

Interpersonal Skills

Understanding Theory

community around shared goals and values, open communication and collaboration. Teamwork comes closest to summing this up. Build a healthy culture and a healthy bottom line will follow. The techniques and tools offered in this book will help you to meet this essential challenge.

2
What Is Teamwork?

Team Building Associates

When a group of individual brains are coordinated and function in harmony, the increased energy created through that alliance becomes available to every individual brain in the group.

NAPOLEON HILL

A predominant feature of our society is how goods and services are produced through a collective effort. An effort that is the sum of isolated individual efforts will not be as productive as one where the individual efforts are coordinated and mutually reinforcing. The shift from an individual to a collective force is the result of a set of behaviors in a group that is complementary and mutually reinforcing. Individual efforts are magnified geometrically when people energize and assist each other. These behaviors produce products or concepts that could not have been manifested by the same number of individuals working in isolation. We call these behaviors teamwork.

TEAM BUILDING

The application of knowledge, skills, and tools to produce a desired effect is a craft. Team building is the craft of making a team. Teamwork results from effective use of team-building skills. The essence of team building is structuring an environment that enhances the enjoyment and productivity of a group effort. Anyone engaged in crafting a team will use at least some of the knowledge, skills, tools, or programs discussed in this book.

As in any endeavor the better the choices made, the better results achieved. The information provided in this book is here to help you make the choices that will result in a high-performance team.

WHAT IS A TEAM?

A team exists whenever two or more people work together to accomplish a task or achieve a common goal. The potential for synergy results from the impact the team members have upon each other and the work they do. Because of this impact and the goals they hold in common, team members recognize they are dependent upon each other and accountable to each other.

A strong team is one in which the following elements[1] are acknowledged by all the members:

- *Shared Purpose*. We have the same vision, mission, and goals.
- *Interdependence*. What we do affects each other. I need your effort so I can do my job and you need mine.
- *Accountability*. We are responsible to each other because of our interdependence.
- *Common Culture*. We share identities, values, and rituals.

A fifth element is also present in exceptionally productive teams. The members know and care about each other. They look out for each other. There is mutual trust and camaraderie.

When the first four elements are not clearly present in the workplace, instead of a team or a potential team, you will find either a
work group or a number of individuals working on similar tasks.
Depending on the nature of the work and the people involved
one of these two options could be more appropriate than a team.

TYPES OF TEAMS

Teams accomplish as a group what their members could not achieve
by their individual efforts. Teams are defined both by the tasks
assigned to them and how they are put together to perform those
tasks. There are four different types of teams.[2]

- *Production/service* teams make things or provide services.
- *Management/administrative* teams run things.
- *Advisory* teams recommend things.
- *Project* teams are formed for a specific, one-time task.

NO LIMITS

Most of us have felt the enjoyment that comes from working har-
moniously with our coworkers. Teams that have achieved a state
of mutual support and trust are noted not only for their productivity and innovation, but also for the amount of fun everyone
seems to be having. In this environment people become excited
about who they are and what they are doing. The excitement and
the sense of fun that accompanies it are contagious. Observers
have long called this excitement the spirit of teamwork.

When the energy of this spirit is unleashed people become truly
involved in what they are doing. Old limits are surpassed by people
who amaze themselves by achieving exceptional levels of excel-
lence. Accomplishments no one thought possible, like putting a
man on the moon, are done in a surprisingly short amount of time.
In fact, just eight years after President Kennedy declared that goal
in a speech before Congress, it was realized by Neil Armstrong's

historic first step. Between the declaration of that compelling vision and the resulting footprint, high-performance teamwork occurred on a national scale.

BARN RAISING

The Amish have a time-honored practice of "barn raising". Within one day they gather with tools and materials, food and spirits, and raise a barn for one of their neighbors. If a person were to attribute the successful conclusion of that task to good teamwork his audience will nod and say, "Of course, good teamwork." But if pressed to be more specific, the response might be: "They worked together well. You know, teamwork." All of this is true, but just what does it mean? More specifically, what can we do to help a group gain the synergistic benefits of working together as the word, team, suggests? By asking yourself this question you increase the chances of finding the answer that will best help your team.

PRODUCTION VERSUS MAINTENANCE

Rarely is any thought given in an organization to compatibility and working styles. We hire a person or a group of individuals, put them in a room together, and tell them to produce. Until recently, most MBA programs reflected this orientation on task with a near total focus on finance and marketing. The human dimension, such as leadership and team building, was generally neglected; all emphasis was on task performance rather than maintenance. Even racecars make periodic pit stops although nothing is apparently broken. A high-performance team, like a high-performance car, requires periodic fine-tuning.

Team maintenance is any activity that helps build relationships and trust. Regardless of their position in the hierarchy, team members need to know how to manage each other as well as their responsibilities and tasks. Like any other achievement, teamwork does not just happen. It is a collective responsibility that takes training, coaching, and the willingness to reflect on your role within the team.

In any group some members will have more influence than others because of personality or position or both. Sometimes groups, overly swayed by these members, ignore the potential contribution of those less vocal or assertive. Appreciating and encouraging the potential contributions of all members, even those who seem withdrawn at first, enables the group to fully access its resources. A group becomes a team when everyone is "on-board" and invited to participate.

TEAM NETWORK

The life of a team is lived on two levels: the relationships between individual members and the sum of these relationships represented by the identity of the group. Our inter-relatedness touches everything and everyone around us. Give twelve people a collective

Team Network Diagram

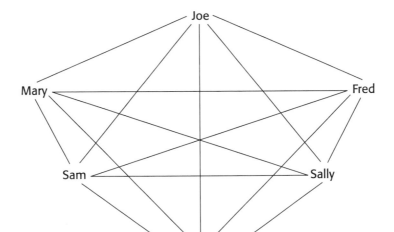

task and you will have 144 different connections occurring simultaneously. The network created by a team is interdependent and dynamic. When one member changes, the entire group changes because of this interconnectedness.

CLEAR COMMUNICATION

Not long ago companies found they could increase the productivity gained from personal computers by connecting them in a network. However, that gain in productivity is eroded if communications between the PC's are hindered by one or more faulty connections. The same is true of teams. The dynamics of the group network draw forth and magnify each member's contribution. Likewise, overall performance suffers, if even just one member is not giving or receiving the information he and others need to know.

Communication is the life-blood of a team effort. As a task becomes more complex, the quality and quantity of communication becomes more important. Information sharing is facilitated when the team has a network of relationships that allows team members to connect with each other in more than one context. In a social situation certain topics can be raised that might never be mentioned in a more formal business environment. Relating to someone in a different context encourages a broader or deeper connection with that person. Conflicts and misunderstandings that hinder the exchange of information are more likely to be resolved.

TAKING TIME TO TAKE STOCK

Before taking action and using one of the team building actions described in this book you need to gather information. Walk through the office front door like it's the first time you have been there. Without preconceptions ask yourself:

- What do you hear in the small talk around you?
- What is the tone in people's voices?

- What does their body language say about their state of mind?
- And most important, how are they treating each other?

WHAT GOES AROUND . . . COMES AROUND

The way members of a group treat each other has a lot to do with the way they are treated by their manager. Remember, *the way employees treat each other will not be that much different from the way they treat their internal or external clients.*

According to a popular adage, "if you continue to do what you always did, you will get what you always got." Taking time to think about how well you are doing is the first step towards improvement. An assessment begins by asking two questions: "What is working?" and "What is not working?" The answers lead to other questions, such as, "Why?" and "What should we do about it?" These questions will not be answered by any epistle on management, including this one. The best answers come from drawing upon the collective resources of your team. Often overlooked is just how much employees at all levels have to contribute and would be glad to contribute if someone took the time to ask.

DEVELOPING YOUR CRAFT

Everyone has the ability to work with others. There are things all of us can do to nurture that ability in ourselves and others. The basic principle of this book is that by taking care of the human element you will better access the human resources of a team. All of us start learning this craft in kindergarten. Hopefully, you will never stop learning. There is always more to understand about ourselves and groups, especially when the two are put together. Take this book with you to work. Practice some of the skills for listening and conflict resolution in Section II. Try some of the team building activities listed in Section III. Develop your craft. Everything you do has an effect. Go back and look at the cause. Measure the results by how you feel when you walk into the office in the morning and leave at night. If you show up with a smile and leave with one, you are doing something right.

HIGH PERFORMANCE

Some teams achieve the seemingly impossible. Teams that developed new products like the Apple IIe computer or the first minivan, or put a man on the moon, achieved at the critical time, a level of genius that can be described as high or peak performance.

High-performance teams have team spirit, which encompasses more than the team and its identity. This "more" is a state that the English language cannot quite define, but here is an analogy. In computer terms you could say that the network created by the team is plugged into a super mainframe that has all the answers as long as you ask the right questions. Being in a high-performance team is often a peak experience. The members describe being on such a team with words like: amazing, fulfilling, uplifting or breakthrough. The descriptions suggest spiritual experiences that transcend "normal" reality.

TEAM SPIRIT

The term "team spirit" implies the presence of something beyond the physical. In both the Old and New Testament references are made to the power of a group when the members are open to the presence of something greater than themselves ("Wherever two or more of you are gathered in My name . . ."). Because of the associations religion has for some, these words can be a turn-off. Fortunately, there are also other words, psychological or metaphysical, that describe this phenomena.

CREATIVE INTELLIGIENCE

Over the ages people have given different names to the reservoir of an endless field of creativity, intelligence, and inspiration. Some of the labels include: Great Spirit, Collective Unconsciousness, Cosmic Consciousness, Unified Field, The Tao, the Way, Christ Consciousness, the Nigual, The Cloud of Unknowing, "E," Creative Intelligence, the Force, Higher Power, the Id, Buddha Nature, the Null State, and the Absolute. The list can go on to the point that it might fill up this book.

THE GATEWAY

What we call the gateway to this reservoir is not important. Words do such a poor job of describing the transcendent power of a group that any description, scientific or religious, is inevitably an approximation. It is not the subscription to a common dogma nor the readiness to engage in "touchy-feely" activities that enables a group to reach the state of high performance.

When a group of individuals comes together anything feels possible. Teams somehow access this field of energy and creativity by getting out of their own way. By accident or design high-performance teams do some of the things described in this book. However, teams, just like the individuals in them, are too idiosyncratic to conform to a pat formula.

The common thread that links groups I have worked with that achieve this state is the basic respect shown by the members for each other's humanity. That respect is reflected in both their commitment to their mission and each other. It shows up in how the members help each other ride out all the turns and bumps encountered in the process of becoming and sustaining a team. There is enough mutual trust to allow the members to have their different and conflicting points of view. They may fight with each other, even vehemently disagree with one another, but the conflict is dealt with in a way that strengthens rather than weakens the team. In this kind of group, being yourself and asking for help if you need it, is not only okay, it is encouraged.

BREAKING BOUNDARIES

A group functioning at a peak level is capable of surpassing the expectations of even its most optimistic supporters. One team building facilitator, Wendy Watkins, sums it up this way.[3]

> *For me it's a spiritual thing. Some groups shouldn't be capable of doing what they do. When they are all charged up there is some unknown piece that gets enlivened. An analogy, for what I've seen groups do, is when there's a car accident and someone who should not be able to lift a car does it in order to save the person underneath. Somehow they do it. Groups in the same way are capable of letting go of their limitations and doing amazing things. Those are the times when I say to myself, I've just seen God.*

3
Theories & Models

Team Building Associates

For the lack of training they lacked knowledge.
For the lack of knowledge they lacked confidence.
For the lack of confidence they lacked victory.

Julius Caesar

No theory can totally explain teamwork; human behavior is too complex. What a theoretical model can offer is a useful framework for discussing the general dynamics of a group and suggest a set of guidelines on what a team needs at each stage of its development.

WHO, WHAT, AND HOW

Three aspects of any team are universal. For a group of people to come together as a team, these three aspects have to be addressed. These aspects, shown in the diagram on the next page, are:

- *Team:* Who is on the team? What are their needs, skills, and expectations?

18

Three Aspects of Every Team

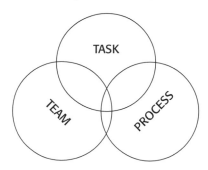

- *Process:* How do the members work together?
- *Task:* What is produced or performed? What results define success?

TEAM

When you first join an organization you want to know about your new associates and what are they like. These concerns need to be answered before you can begin to relax and focus on your work. Even if you are not consciously aware of these concerns they can still have a subtle impact. Along with pertinent questions such as "Where's the bathroom?" or "When do I get paid?" your concerns could be framed as:

- How will I be treated?
- What are the rules?
- Will I be accepted?
- How much influence will I have?

A company that warmly welcomes new employees is acting with a sense of enlightened self-interest. Bringing a new member on board cannot be left up to the tender mercies of the personnel department. The team should have its own set of activities that will help a new member feel welcomed. No matter how long a team has been together it is wise to set aside time for the members to get to know each other better and to recognize the unique contribution and skills that each member brings to the collective effort.

Information that team members need to know about each other can be summed up in two questions:

1) What do I need and expect from my teammates?
2) What do my teammates need and expect from me?

TASK

Teams exist because they have a job to do. Most of a new team's attention is on learning what that job is and figuring out how to do it. Even if the team has a history of success with similar tasks there is usually some anxiety over the possibility of failure. One way teams deal with that anxiety is by rushing to "get on with it" and tackle the job. Getting to know each other and doing some planning are hardly considered. "Outcomes" are forgotten in the rush to produce "outputs." A wise team will invest the time needed to define and measure success. Key questions to ponder are:

- What outcome or results do we want to produce?
- What results are we are responsible for?
- What resources (material and personnel) do we have?
- What is success and how do we measure it?

PROCESS

Once a team knows who is on it and what it has to do, the next step is to figure out how. But unless a team knows how to discuss the question of "how" it will skip this step and jump into task performance. Learning solely by trial and error ends up, as you might predict, producing a surplus of errors. Every team has a process whether it is aware of it or not. A team's process is the approach the members use to exchange information, plan, make decisions, and solve problems. The optimal approach integrates both the human dimension of working with others and the technical requirements of the task.

PLUS/DELTA MODEL

A useful tool for assessing a team's performance is the Plus/Delta model. The team takes a look at its performance and asks these questions:

- What are the pluses?
- What is not working and needs to be changed?

TEAM MAINTENANCE

The things team members do or say to take care of each other emotionally and physically are called team maintenance. These are the rituals and behaviors that strengthen relationships. Some maintenance activities, like the office party, awards ceremony, or coffee break, are mainly social. Others activities, like deciding how information will be exchanged or conflict resolved, are more structured, and may need to be led by a facilitator. Whether it is fifteen minutes or a couple of days, it is useful for a team to take some time away from its primary job and examine the way members relate to each other and the processes and procedures that affect their working relationships.

Team maintenance can take place at the water cooler, during lunch or whenever a few minutes are spent building rapport in a discussion about a mutual interest. It can also take place during a structured exercise used to improve teamwork skills. When people gather in groups of two or more something beneficial can and should happen. Every meeting a manager has with his subordinates is a team-building opportunity. Team maintenance is taking advantage of that opportunity.

THE ASSESSMENT/ADJUSTMENT MODEL

The assessment/adjustment model diagrams the things successful teams do, knowingly or unknowingly, to help them achieve outstanding results. Becoming a high-performance team does not have to be left up to chance. There is nothing inevitable about these

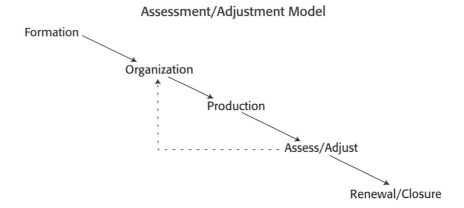

Assessment/Adjustment Model

steps or stages. In fact, unless the team has exceptional leadership or a skilled facilitator, it is not likely to go through all the stages described in the model that lead to optimal performance. The higher the level of teamwork, the more likely it is the team went through most or all of these stages. The assessment/adjustment model has five stages diagrammed on the chart below. These stages and their themes are:

- *Formation:* who we are as a team.
- *Organization:* what we plan to do and how.
- *Performance:* what we resolve, decide, and do.
- *Assessment/Adjustment:* what we should do differently.
- *Renewal/Closure:* how we complete or celebrate what we did.

As shown in the diagram of the model, these stages are not strictly linear. Work groups will fluctuate from one stage to another in response to changes in personnel, mission, and other factors that impact the work environment. Each of the stages of the assessment/adjustment model is discussed below:

FORMATION

In a new group there is a need for strong leadership that informs the group about the nature of the task and the initial approach, and also reassures the members about the viability of the team effort. The two main tasks during formation are getting to know each other both individually and as a group and understanding the work the team will do.

The members of a group relate to each other by discussing work, sports, and other topics that hold a common interest. Sharing who they are through these discussions allows the members to relax and build social relationships. Knowing a person's background and temperament helps you understand what to expect from your teammates and how they might respond to certain situations. The fact that others now know something about you adds to your sense of being a member of the group.

As the team members get to know each other in terms of who they are in relationship to each other and their common task, the bonds of a common identity begin to form. These bonds are expressed through the collective personality of the team—a personality that takes on a life and even a name of its own.

ORGANIZATION

Whether they realize it or not every team has its own approach towards conducting meetings, planning, making decisions, and solving problems. It does take some conscious thinking to decide if the approach being used is best suited to the task.

The ability to conceptually process large amounts of time sensitive and seemingly unrelated information is key to organizing complex activities and making the best use of available resources. Effective teams organize their approach by recognizing inherent trade-offs and selecting priorities that maximize the greatest return on resources for a given level of risk.

Major tasks require that data be gathered and analyzed, resources identified and requested, and a plan of action developed. The team brainstorms to both define the problems and to think of potential solutions. Roles and responsibilities are clarified and decisions made that all team members agree to support or at least not block.

Roles: The level of synergy created by the team effort depends on the extent to which the team members have clarified and structured their individual roles around the results the team must produce. Role clarity is not to be confused with a rigidity in who does what. Who does what role is less important than the understanding that the role will be performed when needed.

Ground Rules: An important part of getting organized is the ground rules that everyone understands and agrees to support. Often these ground rules or norms are produced almost unconsciously and never stated. A better approach is to hold a meeting devoted to defining how the members will work with each other and resolve conflict. Information flows more freely in groups that adopt the norm of respect for each person's ideas and contribution. In broad terms the group is addressing the questions:

- What kind of group do we want to be?
- What values will we live and work by?
- How will we treat each other?

PRODUCTION

Teams often grapple with one or more dilemmas as the work is performed. The pressures of time, data overload, and performance anxiety make it difficult to develop the most optimal strategy. Spending more time to get organized means less time for production; a trade-off many teams fail to even consider. Between the two extremes of "just-do-it" and "analysis paralysis" the team has to find that happy medium where capable planning produces good results. Sometimes the only way to make headway is to accept mistakes as part of the price for making progress and get on with it.

ASSESSMENT/ADJUSTMENT

No matter how much planning has been conducted, unanticipated problems will arise during task performance. The difficulties encountered by the team, with their work or with each other, affect the level of group participation and satisfaction. The team's ability to meet these challenges and maintain a high level of commitment depends, in part, on the extent the previous stages have been successfully completed. The adjustment can be as simple as one small act of continuous improvement or it could involve the complete reengineering of a major system along with the vision and values that guide the organization. Successful teams share a common trait in their skill at making mid-course adjustments and corrections. The inevitable conflicts and miscalculations have to be addressed before improvement can occur.

Postponing an assessment is easy to rationalize. The process can be painful, consume valuable time, and offer no sure fix while all manners of urgent details are demanding attention. The inability to put the problems on the table and discuss them with honesty and respect keeps things stuck. Leadership, or more precisely that particular mixture of gumption and insight on the part of any team member, means posing the central questions that need to be asked when the overriding tendency is to do rather than think.

During the assessment/adjustment process the team should pull out the Plus/Delta Model and ask itself at least three questions:

- What is working?
- What is not working?
- What should we do differently?

To gain the maximum benefits from an assessment, stop working on the task and devote some time to a discussion. Effective leaders know they do not have to have all the answers. They do need to have the right questions because it takes the right question to get the right answer. Reactive teams ricochet from one crisis to the next, never stopping to consider what they might be doing wrong or could do better. Proactive teams conduct assessments and make adjustments to their approach on a continuous basis. Often the problem is resolved by clarifying roles, revising work methods, or establishing new norms and procedures. Whatever the solution the first step to finding it comes from linking one pertinent question with another.

RENEWAL/CLOSURE

At certain points in any collective effort it is useful to celebrate what has been accomplished by the individual members and by the team as a whole. Honoring a person's contribution fosters individual pride and commitment. Acknowledging the team effort also fosters pride and strengthens the sense of belonging. The power of renewal and team pride is found in the stories people tell each other about the work place. The stories the newcomers hear about previous exploits and trials enhance the socialization process between old and new members.

Harrison Owen discusses the dynamics of corporate myth making in shaping the culture of an organization in his book, *Spirit: Transformation and Development in Organizations.*[1] According to Owen, recounting or just referring to these "war" stories can renew the sense of membership and common purpose.

Military organizations, because they experience a steady turnover, have formalized this ritual of story telling in monthly "command performances" known as "Hail and Farewells." The stories of recent or past exploits helps the service members find closure when their team is disbanded or an individual member leaves.

There is something that takes place in a workplace ceremony that reduces stress, repairs relationships, and lifts morale. An important part of a senior leader's job is conducting a ceremony that has that beneficial impact.

DYNAMIC PROCESS

The team-building process has to be continuous to be effective. It is not a one-time, one-shot affair. Teams are dynamic creations. There is no guarantee a team will always stay at a certain performance level. As the environment, membership, leadership, and task change the team will also change. Even one member who changes in some way can alter the dynamics of a group requiring it to revisit one or more stages of development.

ACHIEVING INTERDEPENDENCE

Members who have just formed or joined a group are usually very polite towards each other. Caution is the norm because so much is unknown about how the others think and behave. The group looks for strong leadership to set the initial direction and tell everyone what to do. As the team members become more familiar with how they impact each other's work and confident in each other's abilities, the reliance on a strong leader decreases. The more you trust someone the more you will rely on them and they on you. That mutual reliance leads to greater interdependence.

As interdependence grows, performance improves, generating the sense of excitement and power known as team spirit. The relationship between these forces is presented here graphically in the Performance Model of Interdependence.

Groups that are dependent on a highly controlling leader may perform adequately, but the members will be unable to develop their ability for independent thought or action. The debilitating effects of "group think" are more likely.

Colleagues who are separated by distrust and inertia miss the benefits of cooperation and collaboration. The results are a sort of

Performance Model of Interdependence

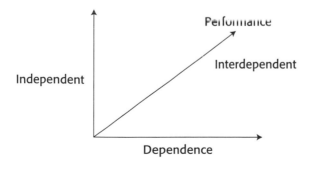

negative synergy where the collective effort is less than the sum of the individual efforts.

IT'S JUST A STAGE

There are numerous models that define the life cycle and stages of group development. B.W. Tuckman called these stages: forming, storming (referring to conflict), norming, performing, and adjourning.[2] As a team gets organized, does its job, and finally disbands, it goes through each of these stages.

JACK GIBB

Jack Gibb saw group development as a matter of trust.[3] Without trust there can be no free flow of ideas and opinions essential to productivity and problem solving. Gibb defined four stages of group development based on the questions the group must resolve at that particular time: membership, data flow, goal formation, and control. At each stage team members have personal needs for inclusion, control, influence, and trust particular to that stage. If the needs at one stage of development are not met the team will stay stuck at that level and exhibit behaviors of rebelliousness or dependency.

R.B. LACOURSIERE

R.B. Lacoursiere published a similar theory that work groups go through four stages of development that encompass differing levels of morale and productivity.[4] These stages are orientation, dissatisfaction, resolution, and production. Issues arise during the life of the group that must be addressed so the group can move from dissatisfaction to resolution and task performance.

KEN BLANCHARD

Ken Blanchard developed the model of situational leadership.[5] According to this model the most effective leaders will align their style of management with the level of development of those they are leading. New groups require an authoritarian style of management to succeed. More developed teams perform better under a democratic style of management. As the team members become familiar with their tasks and more confident in each other, leadership functions can be shared or rotated. Good coaching by a leader helps move her direct reports from dependence to interdependence.

These models, each with its own perspective, present the stages teams go through that are considered more or less inevitable. The assessment/adjustment performance model draws from the work done by the men listed above and the personal experience of the author in working with a large number of teams.

Section II
Interpersonal Skills

4
Communication Skills

Broderbund

*If you would persuade, you must appeal
to interest rather than intellect.*

BEN FRANKLIN

There are approximately 550,000 words in the English language, almost twice as many than most other languages. And too often the same word means different things to different people. The potential for confusion is endless unless team members make the effort to improve their communication abilities by using the following skills:

- Nonverbal Language
- Imagery
- Mirroring
- Metaphors
- Listening
- Paraphrasing
- Describing

- Repeating
- "I" Statements
- Feedback
- Proactive Language
- Dialogue

NONVERBAL LANGUAGE

Communication is more than just words. Practically everything we do is part of the communication process. Even silence can speak volumes. As much as 85 percent of the information exchanged in face-to-face communication is estimated to be nonverbal nuances. These nuances have emotional as well as factual content that are often below the threshold of awareness. If you do not pay attention to *how* things are said as well as *what* is said you could be missing a lot as the following pie chart indicates.[1]

While there are differences between cultures, nonverbal cues represent a nearly universal language. The signs of basic emotions

Components of Communication

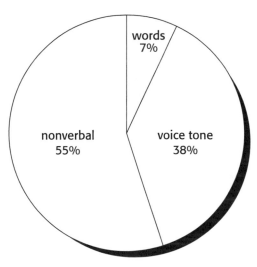

such as joy, fear, anger and sadness are often the same no matter
where you are in the world. Nonverbal cues include gestures, eye
movements, inflection and tone of voice, facial expression, posture and alignment, and use of physical space. By being conscious
of the cues you are sending or receiving you can adjust your message and enhance mutual understanding.[2]

Gestures

- Rigidity or lack of gestures indicates fear or depression.
- Stroking, holding, rocking oneself provides reassurance.
- A hand in front of the mouth indicates fear or embarrassment.
- Wild gestures show strong emotion or need for attention.
- A bouncing leg or tapping fingers shows impatience.

Eye Movements

- Looking someone in the eye indicates interest and trust.
- Staring in someone's eyes indicates dominance or aggression.
- Avoiding eye contact could show a lack of interest or sincerity.
- Dilated pupils indicate attraction or interest.
- Raised eyebrows express surprise or delight.
- One eyebrow higher than the other shows doubt.
- Looking down indicates being in one's feelings.
- Looking up to the left or right indicates trying to remember.

Inflection and Tone of Voice

- Soft tones might mean a lack of confidence.
- High or hard tones are signs of stress or anger.
- Rising tone turns a statement into a question.
- Harshly accented pronouns show disapproval or anger.
- Monotones reveal boredom, low energy, or depression.
- Rapid speech implies nervousness.
- Shakiness of voice indicates strong emotions.

Facial Expression

- A fixed smile may mean anxiety or fear.
- Continued chewing can be an expression of hostility.
- Narrowed eyes and lowered head indicate distrust.
- Smiling signals approval and acceptance.
- Licking lips reveals desire.
- Color in the face or the lack of it shows a strong emotional reaction.

While the similarities across cultures are striking the differences can cause significant confusion. Eye contact and use of physical space can mean very different things even between people with the same culture. Good communicators are aware of the impact their communication style has on other people.

Posture and Alignment

- Leaning towards a person expresses interest.
- Sitting on the hands implies hiding something or holding back.
- Slouching portrays relaxation or rebellion.
- Avoiding eye contact, crossed legs and arms show caution or distrust.
- Eye contact, open arms and legs communicate acceptance.
- Hands grasped behind the head shows dominance or well being.
- Hands held behind back or in front of waist may show submissiveness.
- Hands on hips indicate a sense of control or confidence.

Use of Physical Space

- Placement of objects shows degree of involvement.
- Sitting or standing above another can show dominance.

- Positioning at the same height can indicate acceptance.
- Less than eighteen inches of space expresses intimacy.
- Maintaining five feet or more of space reveals low trust.
- Two or three feet of space are a sign of acceptance.
- Sitting at the head of the table indicates leadership.

Trust is built when your words match the rest of the message expressed by your body and voice. People are quick to sense any incongruence between what you say and the way you say it. A classic example: a man loudly proclaims, "I am not angry," as he slams his fist on the table. The ability to read body language is a useful team skill. People do not always say in so many words what they are really feeling or thinking. The body, however, speaks in a language that always tells the truth.

IMAGERY

The use of language reflects the different ways the mind works in processing information.[5] If you communicate with someone using her preferred imagery you will have a better chance of developing rapport. People are more comfortable with others whom they perceive think like themselves. This imagery has three possible modes:

- *Visual.* I see what you mean: "It looks good to me."
- *Auditory.* I hear you: "It sounds okay."
- *Kinesthetic.* It feels like the right choice: "You're right on target."

Listen to the words other team members use to describe their experiences. Notice which type of imagery—seeing, hearing, or feeling—they use most frequently. Try speaking to them in their preferred mode and observe if this helps you get your point across. When others hear you using imagery similar to what they use, they are more likely to respond to what you have said. In effect, you are speaking their language.

If someone speaks to you using visual imagery and you normally processes information kinesthetically, consciously switch into his mode and try to visualize what he is saying. You might reach a deeper level of mutual understanding.

MIRRORING

Behavior is a form of communication.[4] To make someone feel comfortable with you, do what he does. Chances are, you have already done this if you feel at ease with him. Metaphors, belief systems, body language, feelings, and voice tones are often copied by those seeking more acceptance from a person or group. As teenagers, we started "mirroring" our peers without even thinking about it. The ancient social injunction, "When in Rome do as the Romans do," was given as a necessary expedient to get a message across. However, do not forget that integrity is the natural congruence between what you actually believe and feel and what you do to express those beliefs and feelings. People sense when there is any inconsistency between the two. Examples of mirroring include:

- With a fast talker, talk fast.
- With a slow talker, talk slow.
- Speak with the same tone and volume.
- Hold your body in a similar position or manner.
- Use similar gestures.

METAPHORS

Depending on how they are used, metaphors can cause confusion or help build rapport. The English language, as it is spoken in North America, is highly metaphorical. A metaphor conjures up a mental picture in the listener's mind that communicates a lot of information with few words. Phrases that relate to sports or military terminology like: "Let's hit this one out of the park" or "We need to out-flank our competitors" illustrate the jargon used in the business world. A workplace filled with a multitude of subgroups, each with their own ethnic and cultural orientation, requires that the metaphors used be suitable to the intended audience.

The new director of a large medical research organization emphasized there would be no "sacred cows" during his tenure. The large group of Hindus who worked there were deeply offended. A useful metaphor provides a shared understanding that includes instead of excludes. In this sense metaphors are used as a "bona fides" by affirming to the person spoken to that "You're one of us."

One team created its own metaphor during an outdoor training course. Instruction was given on "spotting". The term "spotting" refers to the ways the participants work with each other to maintain safety. After the training was over the term was used back in office. Asking someone to "spot" you was the new way of requesting help. Coining the new phrase also had another benefit. The ordinary interpretation of the word "spotting" was altered because it was used in a different context.

In order to understand what the word meant, the listener had to supply the intended meaning by searching through past experiences as they related to the life of the team. The listener had to identity with the speaker and his shared experience to understand what the speaker said. This identification created a sense of rapport.

Consider doing the following to increase team rapport:

- Determine which metaphors have the potential to create confusion in your office? Start explaining them or drop them from use.
- Look at your common history and shared experiences as a team. Did you learn anything in that shared experience that you would like to see applied in other situations?
- Give those shared experiences a name and turn them into metaphors the rest of the team can understand and use.

LISTENING

The importance of good listening, like motherhood and apple pie, has wide social acceptance. Still, very few of us listen to someone with our full attention. What Constantine Stanislavski, the proponent of method acting, says in his book, *An Actor Prepares*, is instructive:[5]

> *Average people have no conception of how to observe the facial expression, the look of the eye, the tone of the voice, in order to comprehend the state of mind of the person with whom they talk. If they could do this (listen in a way to understand what they hear), life, for them, would be better and easier, and their creative work immeasurably richer, finer and deeper. . .*

Really listening with your full attention is one of the most sincere compliments you can pay a person. Just the sense of being truly heard can bring about a physiological change in the speaker. Good listeners listen with a concern for the higher purpose driving the conversation. The traits of a good listener include:

- Listening with an open mind without judging
- Taking no offense when none is intended
- Paying full attention to the speaker (few people can or do)
- Asking questions for greater clarity.

It is as simple as it is difficult to listen empathetically, especially if the topic is emotionally charged. A person's mind, however, is like a parachute, it only works when it is open. An empathic listener does everything a good listener does, as well as:

- Listens with no agenda
- Knows and accepts the emotional state of the speaker
- Does not offer advice unless asked
- Cares about the speaker as a person
- Desires to really understand the speaker's point-of-view.

Some of the best sales people are those who can listen with no agenda to their clients; building trust and rapport. This requires a high level of emotional intelligence more than a high IQ. Most medical doctors listen an average of 22 seconds to a patient before interrupting. Listening to understand instead of listening to respond is especially difficult when the speaker is intent on blaming you. You are more likely to understand why a person feels the way he does (and be less defensive) if you can remember that he is responsible for his own feelings just as you are responsible for yours.

Inner Monologue

Our listening ability is affected by the extent to which we are engaged in an inner monologue. Because the mind can think much faster than it can listen, an inner conversation can easily outpace the outer one. Good listeners are able to stop the inner monologue and focus attention on the other person. For some, shifting attention from themselves to another person requires considerable practice. People sense when they have a person's full attention and instinctively become more emotionally engaged in the conversation. Suspending judgement is another trait of an effective listener, since this also requires stopping or slowing down the inner monologue.

> The ability to listen is a function of a clear awareness. Practice by sitting down in a quiet room and listening to your own thoughts for twenty minutes. Listen for the silence that is the source of those thoughts. If you don't fall asleep the experience might be profound.

Hearing Is Not Necessarily Believing

The content of a message can have both an intended and perceived meaning. Listeners assign the perceived meaning to what they hear by drawing upon the body language and past behaviors of the speaker and their own prejudices, beliefs, and state of mind. The perceived meaning of a message is in the impact it has. You may have said, "Good morning," but if someone responds as if you implied, "Get lost," that is what your message meant to them whether you intended it or not.

Plain-spoken people who mean what they say and say what they mean are refreshing to work with. However, even with a frank and direct communication, it is easy to assign a meaning that was not intended. Good listening clarifies a message by verifying its intent. Frequently, subordinates get caught up trying to respond to what they think is an implicit command from their boss when there was none. The results can be as humorous as they were in the following incident:

> Walt Disney was screening clips of a film in production. "That sky is really blue," he noted to several of his deputies in an offhand manner. After Disney left the screening room the executives rushed over to the artist who had colored that part of the film. "What are you going to do about the sky?" they demanded. "Nothing," he replied. "Walt only said it was blue." The executives mulled over their dilemma for a few minutes until they came up with a solution. "Well, change it without really changing it enough to be noticeable," they instructed the artist, "just in case Walt wanted it changed."

PARAPHRASING

A common communication breakdown between two people is the difference between what one person said and the other heard. They both assume they understand each other and fail to verify their interpretation of what was actually said. Rephrasing is the act of stating in your own words what you heard. In other words, you, the listener, offer your understanding of what the speaker said. This is also known as active listening.

Confirm your understanding with statements or questions that start with:

- "I'm hearing that you want to . . ."
- "What I'm getting is . . ."
- "In other words . . ."
- "My understanding is . . ."

Paraphrasing summarizes the key points of a conversation as a way to reach mutual understanding and avoid faulty assumptions. By summarizing two conflicting points of view in a group a participant can open up the dialogue so others can participate or test for agreement and move the discussion toward closure. Paraphrasing can also turn a negative statement into a call for positive action. For example, "If what I hear you saying is that morale is bad and productivity low, then what can we do to improve them?"

Skilled paraphrasing helps the conversation to go beyond the initial concern stated by the speaker and allows deeper issues and feelings to be aired. This is more likely to happen if the listener is sensitive to the tone and context of what the speaker is saying as well as the words. One way to build rapport with the speaker is to actively identify with her experience. Statements that show your sincere empathy indicate you grasp both the factual content and emotional implication of what the other person has said.

No one feels truly heard unless the listener's response reveals both an emotional and an intellectual understanding. Responses that show an emotional or sympathetic understanding often start with:

- It must be frustrating when that happens . . .
- That would be hard to deal with . . .
- You sound excited about the new project . . .

It is wise not to try to build empathy by telling people what they are feeling. That approach can seem patronizing. Sincerity requires we speak from the feelings the speaker has aroused in us. Try stating the other person's feelings in the form of a question.

For example, "It sounds like you are upset about your transfer. Are you?"

DESCRIBING

One way to give feedback in a conversation is to simply describe the nonverbal behavior of the other person, as it occurs, without judgement or interpretation. Instead of jumping to a conclusion about the meaning of the message, the observer simply states what she observes. The other person will usually respond by explaining the behavior once it is pointed out. For example, a yawn could mean a late night or it might indicate boredom. If the observation, "You're yawning," does not prompt an explanation, it will at least make that person aware of the nonverbal message she is sending.

REPEATING

Repeating is a simple, yet subtle, way to raise the level of communication. Listen for and repeat the key words or phrases that someone uses to make a point. Repeating their exact words back to them shows that you are listening and want to understand. Adding a slight inflection to the phrase is one way to indicate either a desire for more information or a question about what was said.

"I" STATEMENTS

Many people preface their remarks with the pronoun "you" even when they are speaking about themselves. You can put more power in your speech by saying "I" when you are talking about your beliefs. An "I" statement is also an effective way to get a point across without blame. Instead of saying, "You don't make any sense," a person using "I" statements would say, "I can't make any sense out of what you are saying."

The latter is more truthful and elicits less defensive behaviors in response. "You" statements can be used to label a person, discounting either how others might see that person or the person's own point-of-view. "Royal We" statements tend to do the same, claiming the validation of group consensus when there really may not be any. When the speaker says, "I feel confused," (or any other emotional state), the speaker is taking responsibility for his or her own feelings or opinions. This gives the listener more opportunity to find common ground with the speaker.

Asking people to use this type of address is to ask them to be accountable for the statements they make. The speaker shows his respect for the points-of-view of others. There is no implicit claim of absolute truth, only what is true for the speaker from his perspective.

When "I" statements are the norm the following are often used as prefixes:

- In my opinion . . .
- I believe that . . .
- The way I see it is . . .
- Based on my experience . . .
- What I believe, feel, or think is . . .
- What I hear you saying is . . .

Establish the norm of using "I" statements in your team. Gently point out to those who use "you" or "we" that they do not have the authority to speak for others.

The Truth That Can't Be Argued

What happens when someone makes an absolute statement like:

- You never . . .
- They always act that way . . .
- That person is a &*6$%!!

When confronted with a judgement masquerading as a fact or opinion most people get defensive, especially if that judgment is directed towards them. The most effective "I" statements, those that open a space for real dialogue, offer information from the speaker's point-of-view. If a statement is unarguably true it could lead to a breakthrough. Voicing words with this level of impact does not take long; maybe ten seconds or less according to Gay Hendricks.[6] But to communicate at this level of integrity the speaker has to be able to describe his viewpoint authentically— the way things really are for him and not as they are supposed to be. If you take responsibility for everything in your life (the way it is and your feelings about it) you are probably already a superb communicator.

An authentic communication might start with the following:

- I feel really sad about this . . .
- I am afraid that we won't be able to . . .
- I am excited that we can talk about . . .

FEEDBACK

Feedback is a technical term first used in the science of cybernetics to describe the process of self-correction. In a group setting, feedback is the sharing of information and feelings and making a request. Feedback is most useful when it simply informs a person what impact his or her behaviors had without trying to criticize or judge. Most people become defensive when they feel they are being attacked. Nonjudgmental information that includes specific requests is more likely to prompt a change in behavior.

Feedback is modeled as:

. . . I think or feel "X" is happening . . .

. . . I believe that creates the problem "Y" . . .

. . . Will you do "Z" instead?

Admonishments like, "You don't listen to me," often fail to elicit much empathy or cooperation. A better way to address the problem is through a statement that makes a specific request instead of blaming. Without a request for action the desired action is not likely to happen.

An example of asking instead of blaming:
. . . When I feel like I am being interrupted . . .
. . . I get frustrated when I don't get to finish . . .
. . . Will you hear me out?"

Effective feedback focuses on the *desired* behaviors instead of personalities or the past. Inherent in this approach is respect for the other person's feelings. This respect would have been missing if the person had said to his co-worker, "You talk too much." Few people can be on the receiving end of sincere feedback from their primary work group without going through some degree of self-assessment.

The process needs to be done in a manner that maintains the psychological safety of the recipient. Otherwise, the person might feel too threatened to assess the effect of his or her actions on others. The best situation is when a person seeks feedback or indicates he is willing to receive it. When in doubt check for that willingness. Ask.

Another model for feedback is:
. . . The "Z" behavior is helpful.
. . . The "X" behavior is not helpful.
. . . Please do more of "Z" and less of "X."

For example:
. . . I believe it perks everyone up when you praise his or her efforts.
. . . I observe it discourages others when you belittle their work.
. . . Please give more praise and make fewer cynical comments.

What is Your Intention?

You may have heard the maxim, "people don't know how much you know, but they do know how much you care." In giving feedback your intention is everything. If your intention is to help the person succeed because you care about him as a person you are much more likely to be effective. If your intention is to discharge your pent-up emotion at a convienent target, do everyone a favor and postpone the session.

Specific and Timely

The more specific and timely the feedback the more likely it is to be useful. The phrase, "You showed good teamwork," means more if it is followed by a description of identifiable and repeatable behaviors such as, "The team spent ten minutes planning their activities and everyone got to speak." The act of giving feedback reveals as much or more about the giver than the recipient. It is not easy when you are reacting to what someone did or said to take responsibility for your own feelings. Remember the adage, "when you point a finger at someone you are pointing three fingers back at yourself."

PROACTIVE LANGUAGE

Listening to someone talk about her job or his relationship you can soon tell if she is a proactive or reactive person. Stephen Covey, states[7] that proactive people act and speak from the belief that the locus of control for their lives is within themselves. They are in charge of and responsible for their actions and emotions. Words invoke action. Salespeople have long known the response received from a message is largely determined by the words used.

Reactive persons believe others have power over them. They speak of themselves as victims and blame others or circumstances for their feelings and actions. The reactive worldview complains that the cup is always half empty. The proactive worldview focuses on filling the cup. The attitude inherent in each worldview and the language used to describe them defines a person's day-to-day experience. Because the proactive person takes responsibility, he or she is also ready to take action to fill the cup to the brim.

Proactive language says:	*Reactive language says:*
A mistake was made.	You did this to me.
I choose to feel upset.	She makes me so mad.
I set my priorities.	I never have any time.
What do you think?	This is the way it is.
How can we fix it?	Who is to blame?
You got 60% right.	Your error rate is 40%
Let's clean this up.	This place is a mess.
Your report needs editing.	Your report is lousy.
Will you do this?	You better do this.

DIALOGUE

A meaningful dialogue is one that results in some kind of move-ment; action is taken, understanding increased or feelings resolved. A dialogue is not possible unless the participants are really listen-ing to each other, emotionally and intellectually.

Typical listening uses "closed" responses that acknowledge the speaker has spoken without exploring what has been said or why. This kind of conversation can become a set of competing mono-logues, lurching from one unrelated topic to another. There is limited intellectual or emotional exchange. Statements are made, but nothing has changed in the speaker or listener. Both are left where they started.

A dialogue uses "open" responses that take the conversation to the next level of understanding. The participants help each other reach that level by building upon each other's ideas. The message of the speaker is reframed by the listener with an observation or comment that validates the speaker's opinion. The ability to en-gage in a dialogue, especially on sensitive subjects, shows maturity.

Indicators of Dialogue

Some signs that a dialogue is taking place are comments and ques-tions like:

- How does *x* factor impact *y* outcome?
- This is why I think that way . . .
- Have you considered the implications of . . . ?
- Why do you think or feel that way?
- Have we reviewed all the factors?

Problem solving, brainstorming, or conflict resolution in a group setting is more effective if the members know how to engage each other in a dialogue. Groups get bogged down and frustrated with each other when the members engage in unrelated monologues. Staying with one topic, building on each other's ideas, seeking to understand each other's viewpoints and creating a new level of shared understanding until there is agreement or closure indicates a highly developed team.

5
Facilitation Skills

The Learning Company

The important thing is not to stop asking questions.

ALBERT EINSTEIN

As a team develops, the capable leader will become more of a facilitator than a director. Instead of having the right answers the leader will strive to ask the right questions. In an age of cross-functional teams and ever changing technologies just asking the right questions is a highly demanding job.

THE MIDWIVES

Facilitators are like midwives. They assist with the process but someone else is producing the results. The facilitator's job is to help people discover what they already know, asking the questions that bring this information out. The facilitator helps the group decide what needs to be discussed (content) and how it will be discussed (process). Part of the groundwork for a productive group discussion is defining what the problems or issues really are and how they will be addressed. Once the groundwork has been laid, the facilitator maintains the direction of the discussion so the ideas expressed can piggyback on each other.[1]

LEVELS OF FACILITATION

There are three basic levels for group facilitation. The level selected determines how involved the facilitator will be in directing the process of the group and building a team. In actual practice, the distinctions between the three types can and do blur. What is important is that the facilitator has a clearly defined agreement with the team or client on the degree of facilitation she is to provide. The levels are:

- Process
- Meeting
- Leader

Process Facilitator

Someone who is not a group member performs the role of process facilitator. The process facilitator offers observations on what the group is doing in order to do its task, that is, how it conducts itself. The facilitator's comments address how the group is working together. The facilitator maintains her role as an outsider by using language that reinforces an objective attitude. The group is addressed as "you" or "the group," but seldom as "we." The observations offered by the facilitator are neither critical nor laudatory, but simply point out the behaviors being displayed, such as, "The group seems to have lost interest in this topic." When the group needs some direction the facilitator will help it find its way by asking a question like, "The group looks excited about Dan's proposal, does this mean everyone is in agreement with what he proposed?"

Meeting Facilitator

The meeting facilitator can be a member of the group or an out-sider who has been asked to take this role for a limited period of time. The meeting facilitator asks questions or makes comments that set the tone and direction of the meeting. She also calls on people to speak and assigns certain roles like timekeeper or scribe. Unlike the process facilitator she is more likely to sit at the table with the other team members or stand up in front of the group—positioning herself so she can direct the group. Her focus is on helping the group to define and utilize the processes it will use to share information, solve problems, or make decisions.

The meeting facilitator ensures that everyone gets a chance to speak and no one dominates the discussion. If the facilitator is a group member her comments to the group will more often be stated in terms of "we" instead of the "you" used by the process facilita-tor. However, she will usually maintain some degree of impartial-ity and avoid taking sides by expressing an opinion about the con-tent of the issues being discussed.

Leader Facilitator

The leader facilitator is the de facto group leader although he or she could also be a consultant conducting a team building ses-sion. At this level of facilitation the agenda and group process are determined or highly influenced by the facilitator. The leader fa-cilitator poses questions and seeks answers from the group; how-ever, she is also likely to provide information, instruction or guid-ance that will influence the group discussion. Normally, the leader facilitator sits at the head of the group or stands up in front when giving instruction or focusing the group on the task at hand. She contributes to the content of a program or decision after everyone else has given his or her input, so as not to unduly influence any-one. If team building is the primary purpose of the meeting, the leader facilitator is likely to invite the group to explore various process issues as they surface. For example, the group might discuss how certain behaviors in the group (like everyone talking at once) affect performance and what behaviors might better serve the group effort.

WHO SHOULD FACILITATE?

In a team meeting, the team leader is expected to both run the meeting and contribute to the content of what is being discussed. However, it is usually sensible to assign the function of running the meeting to another member. By participating as an equal the team leader reduces the extent his or her opinions will skew the opinions of others. The team members are more likely to support a decision they have helped make through an open and fair discussion. New teams especially have a need for someone (either the leader or a designated facilitator) to set the agenda and facilitate the interactions between team members. As the members learn how to work with each other they usually get better at managing their own interactions and discussions during a meeting.

An outside consultant may be needed if the team is dealing with highly charged issues where confidentiality is considered crucial. An outsider is likely to be less attached to any particular outcome and team members are often more willing to trust an outsider to maintain confidentiality.

THE ART OF QUESTIONING

Helping a person develop his understanding through a series of questions is known as the Socratic method, a tribute to the Greek philosopher, Socrates, who taught his students and won arguments through the questions he asked. Developing good questioning skills is a subtle art that takes practice. One way to start is to do less telling, lecturing, or complaining and more observing, asking, and listening. Good questions move the discussion in the right direction.

Four types of questions used by a facilitator are:

- *Open-ended* elicits discussion.
- *Closed* elicits yes or no answer.
- *Leading* directs toward desired response.
- *Probing* seeks specific insight or information.

Facilitators, for the most part, tend to use the "open-ended" approach to questioning. As a group gains more experience managing its meetings the participants will ask each other the questions needed to keep the process going.

FACILITATIVE ACTIONS

Facilitation starts with the attitude that the group has all the knowledge and skills it needs to solve its problems and do an outstanding job. The challenge is in finding the means or process that will allow the group to make full use of all its resources. Facilitative actions define or deal with the processes used by the group to build a team and get its work done.

These actions do the following:

- Help the group select and focus on a topic
- Help define the problem or issue
- Manage the flow of ideas and interactions
- Create a collaborative, win/win environment
- Clarify team member roles and responsibilities
- Encourage participation; keep the energy up
- Manage conflict and feedback between team members
- Enforce the group ground rules and norms
- Maintain psychological safety in the group
- Ask the questions instead of tell the answers
- Stay neutral and guide the group discussion
- Manage "air time"—no one dominates the discussion
- Clarify and summarize proposals

Facilitation is helping to "operationalize" a variety of facts, ideas, stories, and problems into some organizing concept that the team can implement. The team effort falls apart when the members assume they are in agreement or that everyone else understands what is going on when that is not the case. The facilitator draws upon the following skills to help a team organize itself and do its work:[2]

- *Summarizing.* The main points of a discussion are summed up to create a transition point where decisions can be made.
- *Testing.* Similar to summarizing, this includes clarifying what has been said and testing for understanding, agreement, or consensus.
- *Generalizing.* Lessons that seem to apply to isolated incidents are turned into principles that can be used in other situations. "Where else does this point apply?"
- *Synthesizing.* Different viewpoints and proposals are modified and combined so that something new is created.
- *Observing.* Observations are offered on how the group is working together and the behaviors being displayed. Often the group may not be of aware what it is doing nor be able to articulate what is happening.
- *Assessing.* Guiding a discussion while staying neutral, objective, and nonjudgmental. The team assesses its own performance by answering the questions: "What is working?" and "What is not working?" Properly done, frequent informal assessments can build rather than deplete a team's self-esteem.
- *Exploring.* Guiding a group through a discussion about the behaviors and issues that affect how its members work and relate to each other. This requires a high degree of interpersonal and group facilitation skills.
- *Redirecting.* Bringing the group back to the topic or moving to the next topic when the group gets off track. When a significant point is raised and no one responds, an alert observer will raise the point again by asking if anyone heard what was just said.

- *Reframing*. Meaning is determined by context. What appears to be a failure or a struggle can also be seen as a worthwhile learning experience.
- *Harmonizing*. Resolving conflict by focusing on common goals, shared beliefs, or the points of agreement.
- *Contracting*. Helping the group clarify and agree to the ground rules that define how the members will work with each other. When needed, the facilitator reminds individuals or the group of their agreements, especially when psychological safety is at risk.
- *Disclosing*. Saying what everyone knows but no one will talk about requires courage and the willingness to take a risk and speak what is true for oneself.

In a high-performance team most of the members will perform one or more of these functions during a team meeting. When a team is learning how to be a team it is helpful to have a professional facilitator model some of these skills. Most teams catch on quite quickly and soon start facilitating themselves.

LISTENING FOR THE GROUP

When a team ponders a significant question a dramatically new level of insight or understanding is possible. The facilitator's job is to define the topic and then shepherd the conversation so that the time devoted to it is well spent. Some members of a group will be predisposed to take up more than their fair share of "air time." But some participants will abdicate or withdraw if one person does most of the talking. Others will hesitate to contribute their questions and ideas even though they may have some good ones. A skillful facilitator gives everyone a chance to speak by staying alert to the full range of nonverbal cues in the room. Listening as a facilitator includes listening for the group. Questions a facilitator silently asks while observing the group include:

- How are others responding to the speaker?
- Is their body language showing agreement or discomfort?

- What is needed to draw out the different points-of-view that are still unexpressed?
- Is this method or process working for the group?
- Are the goals of the meeting being met?
- What needs to happen here but isn't?

The facilitator knows when to interrupt so someone else can have their turn, when to bring the discussion back to the original topic when it strays, and when to change the direction of the conversation so the ideas expressed can build on each other. He gets this knowledge by constantly scanning the faces and body language of the participants. As Yogi Berra put it, "You can observe a lot by looking."

CHALLENGES

Facilitation skills have to be built on a foundation of emotional and intellectual maturity that can handle the consequences if things don't go as planned. In fact, you are almost assured that they won't, which is part of the fun and most of the challenge in working with any group. Most facilitators find themselves floundering when they try to force their own agenda. Winning that kind of contest is not easy. There are too many other minds to contend with. Facilitators need to be careful about monitoring their own individual "air time" as much as they do for the rest of the group. An effective facilitator will remain quiet until her contribution is needed.

SAFETY FIRST

The lack of participation in a group discussion, silences that are more awkward than they are long, could indicate a low level of safety. Express an unpopular opinion and you get criticized or ridiculed by the other members. By encouraging the group to define and maintain a set of ground rules the facilitator can help establish a safe atmosphere. Modeling a nonjudgmental attitude and manner is essential.

GROUND RULES

One of the most important ground rules is to respect the ideas and views of the other members. A team member does not have to agree with someone to give them a fair hearing. A comment like, "Your idea, Bill, is the dumbest I ever heard," is more of a personal attack than an objective criticism. Ideas dry up when the likelihood of personal attack is high. At first, when this kind of attack occurs, other team members may pile on with their own comments or laugh to hide their embarrassment. The timely intervention of a facilitator can limit the damage that occurs when this happens.

For example, if Gail made the above comment to Bill, the facilitator would immediately ask the leading question, "Gail, are you honoring the agreement we had not to put-down anyone?" If Gail gives a sincere, "yes," than that agreement needs to be redefined so it is clearly understood. After this type of intervention has been modeled once or twice by a facilitator, a team should start policing itself.

DIRECTING TRAFFIC

The facilitator directs the traffic flow of conversation. In a team that meets frequently the roles of directing the flow of conversation and maintaining the ground rules can be shared by all the members. For example, anyone in the group might tell a member, who just abruptly cut someone else off, "Wait a minute, Jim. We need to let Sally finish explaining her idea before we comment on it." That member's intervention reaffirms one of the ground rules that the group agreed to honor: everyone gets a chance to express their views.

BOGGED DOWN

Occasionally a group will get stuck. A sure sign that not much effective listening is taking place is when certain members keep making the same point to each other over and over again. Usually, everyone but the repetitious members begin to lose interest and make signs of dissatisfaction or withdrawal. Effective groups focus their energy. A lack of focus is evident when the participants start going off in a wide variety of topical directions. The facilitator should rein in the divergent members and keep the discussion moving coherently.

Some facilitative actions are:

- Call on someone else to give his opinion.
- Bring the discussion back to the topic.
- Move the discussion on to the next topic on the agenda.
- Suggest a short break.
- Point out that the group appears to be stuck and ask for suggestions how to get unstuck.
- Encourage the group: "We're almost there; let's not give up now."
- Use some humor. A pithy statement at the right moment will energize the group.
- Coach the members in active listening—so people on both sides of an issue really do understand each other.
- Summarize the key points, orally or on a flip chart.
- Test for consensus on the key points.

The energy level of the team is the sum of everyone's participation. Facilitators monitor the group energy level and adjust the group process if the level gets too low. When a member checks out mentally, the collective energy drops. When a member gets excited the collective energy increases even if the person is not directly expressing the excitement.

REALITY CHECK

Occasionally, the mood of a group is not congruent with the issues being discussed. If you pay attention to how your body feels when this occurs you may notice more tightness than usual. You might also find that the productivity of the group discussion is quite low. This kind of inertia is common before the advent of a major breakthrough or breakdown. What is denied and avoided affects us the most. If the issue can be identified and discussed, its power over the group will be dissipated.

It may not be a good idea to immediately proclaim to the group your diagnosis of what is going on. As the facilitator you are concerned with the group process instead of content. Whatever the issue the facilitator remains nonpartisan and neutral. The facilitator's job is to ask the questions that help the group, through self-reflection, understand and master its own process.

When something is not being expressed that needs expression, the facilitator might ask the group:

- Is there something else we need to talk about?
- Does anyone have an opinion about what is going on?
- Does anyone have a reaction (feeling, idea) they are willing to share with the group?

The most direct way to tackle the issue is to report to the group what you are sensing, emotionally and physically, and/or what you are observing (low energy, checking out) and ask for a reality check:

- I'm feeling that we are missing something here. Does anyone else feel that too?
- Do others have similar reactions or observations?
- If so, what do they think is going-on?
- What should the team do?

As the mood and energy change in a group the facilitator may want to point this out, even if it is obvious. A quick reality check comments on observable behaviors, for example, "I've noticed people are looking at their watches. Has anyone else noticed that?" If others agree you can ask what that behavior means: "Do we need to take a break?" Keep using your emotional radar to track where the energy in the group is going. Find out and go with it.[3] Allow the energy to get to where it is going by helping different viewpoints to emerge. Help the group stay focused on the topic so they can make an informed decision after considering all the relevant facts and feelings.

SUCCESS

One highly skilled facilitator attributed his success to his absolute commitment to making whatever needed to happen, happen. Of course, with this commitment was the ability to see the bigger picture of interrelationships that was driving the group process. Not every one is gifted with an exceptional level of insight but you, the facilitator, can still do good work when you remember to put your focus (and focus all your efforts) on the group's success. Worrying about your own success or winning the approval of the group diverts your attention from the group and its needs. Checking with what you are thinking and feeling is essential but do not stay there. To do high quality work the question is not just: How am I doing? Instead, the skilled facilitator makes the frequent mental inquiry:

- How is the group doing? and,
- What else needs to happen right now?

6
Conflict & Negotiation

Stream

*The old law about "an eye for an eye"
leaves everybody blind.*

Dr. Martin Luther King Jr.

The word, conflict, has unpleasant connotations. Hardly anyone likes to think about a conflict much less deal with one. Yet in any group setting there is going to be conflict. It may be inevitable, but conflict is neither good nor bad. It is the choices people make about how to handle conflict that determines whether the outcome is positive or negative.

SOURCES OF CONFLICT

Conflict is often the result of faulty assumptions and unspoken expectations. The conflict itself becomes the reason for continuing the conflict because the real issues have been obscured or never clarified. When two sides actually discuss what the issues are, it can turn out that the reasons for the conflict were not what they thought they were. Information that was skewed, misinterpreted, or just plain wrong is usually the culprit. The sources of conflict can be structural, personal, or both.[1]

Structural Conflict

Structural conflict is based on systems, processes, and procedures that create competition for control over resources and rewards. It may also be based on objective or situational differences that have an intellectual rational.

Some issues are inherent in the structure of an organization. Different departments compete with each other for funds, personnel, or bureaucratic turf. Sales gets upset with Finance over credit restrictions. Production dislikes the promises made by Sales to close a deal. Management wants Staff to be more productive and do less complaining. Staff thinks Management demands too much work for too little pay. Yet, when a person transfers from one group to the other, perceptions and loyalties also change sides. Mysteriously, the situation alters and it is now the previous group that is being unreasonable.

Personal Conflict

Personal conflict is based on different values, belief systems, personal preferences or cross-cultural behaviors that generate an intellectual and an emotional reaction. The source of personal conflict can frequently be traced to different personal styles that dictate how we relate to the world around us. These different styles and how they impact the workplace are described in Chapter 11, "Different Work Styles". We tend to assume other people think and act just like ourselves. When these assumptions are not met it is natural to attribute negative reasons as to why.

Personal conflicts have a certain predictability according to psychological inventories. For example, individuals with a high value on flexibility and relationships judge those who value structure and order as insensitive and controlling. In return, they are seen by the other group as disorganized and overly sensitive. The second group is frustrated by the lack of regard for details and specifics. The first group is impatient with what they regard as nit picking and not enough focus on the "big picture." Neither side is wrong in the approach they use. They just have different preferences. When the preferences are acknowledged it puts them into context where the potential for conflict can be turned into an opportunity to draw upon different strengths. More understanding means less conflict because it is helpful to know "where the other person is coming from."

Going Ballistic

There is a tendency for structural disputes to become personal just as personal disputes will find structural reasons to justify their existence. Either way, conflicts that degenerate into rigid posturing obscure the real reason for their existence.

An emotional "hook" can quickly transform a structural conflict into a personal one. This hook can have little to do with the real issue. The passions generated by a statement that hit a psychological sore point can demolish any chance for a rational dis-

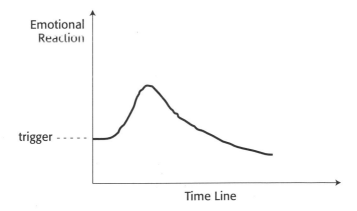

cussion. The sensitivity of a potential "hot button" increases when a person is stressed or fatigued. Intense emotions prevent a dialogue from taking place since anger or fear can block rational thinking. The physiological response of "flight or fight" actually shuts down the part of the brain responsible for cognitive reasoning.

CONFLICT AND NEGOTIATION

According to the Thomas-Kilman Conflict Matrix[2] there are five ways to respond to conflict. Each response is also a negotiating style. Depending on the situation, one style may be more effective than the others. Five conflict negotiating styles are:

- *Avoidance.* No one wins; no one loses.
- *Accommodation.* You win; I lose.
- *Competition.* I win; you lose.
- *Compromise.* We both win and lose some.
- *Collaboration.* We both win.

RESPONSES TO CONFLICT

Few people consciously choose the style they use to deal with conflict. Especially, when we are under stress (and when is conflict not stressful?) we use the style we are most used to even though it may not be the best one for the situation.

The relationship of the five conflict management styles to each other and teamwork are diagrammed below:

Avoidance

Ask someone to describe conflict and you'll hear words like . . . *scary, painful, yucky, hard, stressful,* and so on. Most people—practically all people—would rather avoid something with those attributes. Avoiding conflict seems to save energy and egos at first, but in the long run it drains the energy out of working relation-

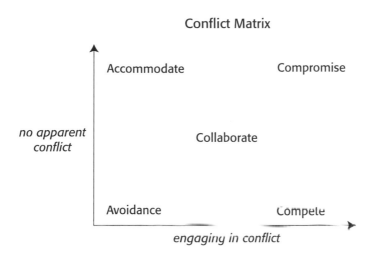

ships. Both sides lose as the tension of unresolved issues continues to build up. Problems long denied become more difficult and expensive to fix. Some questions to ask are:

- Is this really that important to me?
- If so, why?
- What will I lose by avoiding this issue?
- What will I gain by confronting this issue?
- Will the potential benefits compensate for the risks involved?

Avoidance is a useful approach when the issue is too trivial to bother with, too difficult to resolve, or other issues are more pressing. Some issues are not important enough to expend the time and energy it would take to resolve them. It could be a mistake to engage in a conflict without a clear understanding of why you are doing it. Excessive pride or the desire for revenge are emotional reactions that led to behaviors in which both sides lose.

No Conflict Rule: In new groups an extra effort is made by everyone to be polite. Gradually, as people get to know one another the facade of excessive politeness will fade. In on-going groups excessive politeness could mean there is a conflict that no one is willing to talk about. Some groups have an unspoken rule that there will be no disagreements.

Maintaining that facade can be exhausting. However, any relationship is as strong as the topics that can be discussed. A team needs a forum for airing disagreements in order to achieve real agreement. Without that forum the team can fall into the trap of "group think" and lose the benefit of different points-of-view.

Accommodation

Accommodation is letting the other side win. This approach is cooperative, but unassertive since the concerns and needs of others are treated as more important than your own. Agreeing with someone's criticism is a form of accommodation that can be disarming. At times, a good team player will accommodate others for the sake of the collective effort. This is a sign of character, but it is wise to set some limits. A person who always accommodates in order to win friends may end up losing respect, especially his own. The level of motivation to resolve a situation in one's favor can differ greatly between two people. Because one side experiences a conflict does not mean the other side does to the same extent. Accommodation may be the rational response when there is little to be lost.

Competition

Competition is the *heads I win, tails you lose* approach that defines much of Western culture. Cutthroat competitors give competition a bad name when they put winning ahead of any principle or moral value. True competition lets the best idea, product, or argument win to serve the highest good of the team. Competing or opposing interests can keep team members from developing the synergy that will help them compete in the marketplace. Instead they expend enormous amounts of energy competing against each other.

Since divergent interests can fragment a team, a common cause is needed that will enlist every member's commitment. The question that can help uncover this cause is, "What is in the best interest of our entire team or organization?" For public service organizations or any company with a customer service approach the question would be, "What is in the best interest of all our clients?" The commitment to a shared purpose as opposed to competing, individual interests encourages a working consensus to emerge that all the team members can support.

Compromise

Compromise requires give and take by both sides. Splitting the difference is the traditional way of mediating disputes. Neither side completely wins or loses.

According to a study conducted by the management consultant Rosabeth Kanter, the element for dealing with conflict in successful companies was the shared belief that, ". . .a working compromise is better than an optimal solution poorly implemented. . ."[3]

Finding a compromise to a personal or structural conflict is more likely if there is a "let's talk" norm that encourages people to discuss the issues as they arise. The conversation will at least keep the process moving. Somewhere in the dialogue is a compromise both sides can live with to their mutual benefit. Finding a compromise solution requires asking the pertinent questions:

- What can I give up?
- What must I have?

The story about two men who wanted the same orange illustrates the limitations of compromise:

Two men both claimed ownership to the last orange in the store. They compromised by cutting it in half and returning home. One ate the pulp and threw away the peel. The other grated the peel for a cake and threw away the pulp.

Had the two men discussed what they really wanted (the pulp by one; the peel by the other) the outcome could have been more to their mutual advantage.

Collaboration

Collaboration is the problem-solving approach. It enables both sides to win by separating the real interests from stated positions. As in the example with the last available orange above, the key to collaboration is finding out what each side really wants as opposed to what they say they want. The two sides acknowledge their concerns and search for the innovative option or alternative that will satisfy their separate interests. The best solution is one where both sides are satisfied with the outcome.

Professional mediators often use the principle of separating "position" from "interests" when they negotiate a dispute.[4] The following story, illustrates how this works:

> Two women were in a meeting. One wanted the door closed. The noise from another room down the hall was making it difficult to hear. The other wanted the door open because the room would be too stuffy otherwise. The room had windows that were sealed shut. The meeting was disrupted while the two women argued. Finally, someone thought to go out and close the door down the hallway where the noise was coming from so the door to the meeting room could be left open.

Both women were satisfied by the outcome because each obtained her real objective or interest. Stated positions are usually presented on a "win-lose" basis. Actual interests are less likely to be mutually exclusive. With some brainstorming a good problem-solving session can dream up solutions that both sides are happy with.

SELF AWARENESS

Everyone's response to conflict is reasonable from his own point-of-view. People do the best they can based on what they know.

However, the way people respond to conflict is usually unconscious and automatic. You can choose a different response when you become aware of your habitual pattern and the fact that there are at least four other options.

Chapter Two, "What is Teamwork?", discusses how the participants in a team are interdependent. Everyone influences and is influenced by everyone else. If a member of your team changes, you may have to change because you are affected by his new behaviors. It is also true that when you change others are likely to change as well. By consciously choosing your response to conflict you can increase your power to achieve a desirable outcome. Real freedom is the freedom to choose your behavior and the way you respond to a set of circumstances. Eleanor Roosevelt, who in her day dodged more barbed brickbats than even Hillary Rodham Clinton, said, "No one can make you feel bad about yourself without your permission."

WHO OWNS THE PROBLEM?

The typical picture of conflict is usually two people facing each other in some kind of show down or stand off. Each sees the other as the source of the difficulty they are experiencing. They become identified with their positions; resolution is possible only if one side wins and the other side concedes defeat.

Who Owns the Problem

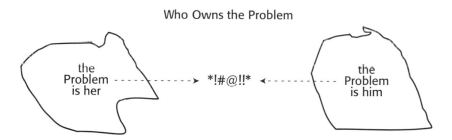

Win/win become a viable option when the two antagonists turn and face the problem instead of each other. This objectifies the problem by giving it a name that separates it from the person.

Objectifying and depersonalizing the conflict allows both sides to "own" the problem without conceding too much. Together, they can identify shared interests and search for solutions that are mutually acceptable instead of mutually exclusive.

For example, the conflict between the management and staff of a unionized company degenerated into the usual finger pointing. Neither side trusted the other and they both expended a lot of energy defending their positions. Relationships didn't have the opportunity to improve until the common issue, "You are not trustworthy," was redefined into, "We have a problem with trust."

MINIMIZING CONFLICT

Conflict may be inevitable, however, that does not mean you have to deal with it all the time. Ways to reduce the level of conflict include fine-tuning your team in the following four areas:

- *Information*
  - ✓ Develop a data collection/sharing process.
  - ✓ Define the criteria for validating data.
  - ✓ Share information freely.
  - ✓ Keep each other informed.
- *Systems*
  - ✓ Develop and clarify team processes and procedures.
  - ✓ Mutually define team ground rules.
  - ✓ Encourage communication.
  - ✓ Establish a conflict resolution process.
  - ✓ Develop social relationships.
- *Control*
  - ✓ Equitably distribute resources/rewards.
  - ✓ Clarify roles, responsibilities, and standards.

✓ Give feedback and encouragement.
✓ Define measures and standards of success.
✓ Encourage input and participation.
✓ Reward collective effort and results.
- *Values*
  ✓ Develop superordinate goals that unite.
  ✓ Define common values.
  ✓ Foster respect for differences.

THE BENEFITS OF CONFLICT

The ability to deal with conflict is a necessary component of a strong team. Groups that cannot or will not deal with conflict, set themselves up for failure. Teams that tolerate and even encourage divergent viewpoints are more creative and productive. Disagreements discussed openly with mutual respect result in better problem solving and decision making. The lack of conflict could indicate a team has become mired in the illusion of harmony. The supposedly unanimous decisions made by such a team, where unity is favored over honesty, often results in costly mistakes.

If the president of General Motors, Roger Smith, had utilized or even just tolerated the conflict created by one of his board members by the name of Ross Perot, the company might not have been forced to lay off thousands of workers several years later. Instead, Smith spent hundreds of millions dollars to buy Perot out and force him off GM's board. As they say, the rest is history. It took huge losses before GM attempted to change a corporate culture where meetings, ". . .were judged a success if everyone got along, even if nothing was accomplished."[5]

EL MATADOR

The heat of an intense encounter with a difficult person does not allow space for an insightful, well-reasoned discussion. Days later you find yourself wishing you had said this or done that instead of what you did say and do. When a difficult person charges at you use the matador approach. If he is the least bit bullheaded it's likely he will continue to do what he has been doing until you take control by redirecting the conversation. The first rush or two from a difficult person may surprise and confuse you. It seems to come out of nowhere when you least expect it. Respond like a matador, who faces the energy coming at him and then redirects it so that it passes by.

- Immediately raise the issue about *how* the conflict is being discussed (reframing the issue).
- Insist the *how* be addressed before the *what.*
- Call for or take a timeout if needed.
- Define the ground rules for resolving the conflict. For example: "We each have five minutes to state our case clearly and respectfully. No swearing, putdowns, or shouting. We have to restate the other person's case to show we understand."
- Start active listening and problem solving.

NAME THE GAME

Difficult people often act out their hostility in a set pattern. That pattern, and the way it gets acted out, does not really change. You may not have been able to deal effectively the first time the pattern showed up but by the second or third time you can anticipate what is going to happen. Once you know the "game" the difficult person is trying to play and the way he is playing it you can name it. Just the act of naming it is enough to bring the "game" to a dead stop.

- Use focused feedback to name the behavior you object to: "I hear a lot of hostility in your voice."
- State how you feel about the behavior and what you want instead: "I get angry when I think someone is trying to intimidate me. I want to be treated with respect."

Naming an objectionable behavior takes the attention off its object (you) and puts it on the subject (the difficult person). When you break your patterns your opponent has no choice but to break his. He might even become your friend if you close with a gesture of goodwill like a handshake.

WHAT ARE YOUR INTENTIONS

Another approach that is just as direct as Naming the Game is to question the motive behind a person's behavior.

- What do you mean by that comment?
- What is your intention in making that remark?
- How is your behavior helpful or relevant?

Instead of "acting out" resentments, bad feelings, insecurities, blame, or anger in an unprofessional, if not adolescent, manner you are asking for an adult-to-adult discussion about the underlying issues. Point out the overall goal and ask how what the person is doing or saying is relevant to achieving that goal. The response, "just kidding" is not acceptable because it is too often an excuse for a wide range of abusive or dysfunctional behaviors.

COVERT ISSUES

According to the *Course in Miracles*, we are never upset for the reason we think we are. One reason dealing with an upset person (or with your own anger) is so difficult is that the overt rationale for the conflict may be secondary to the covert issue. The problem-solving approach does not work because you are trying to solve the wrong problem. Often the covert issue driving the entire interaction does not have much to do with the topic being discussed so there is little you could do or change that would make any difference until you find and address the real issue.

One way to establish understanding is to listen and observe so deeply that you can respond from more than one level. Often behind the expression of a conflict is an unexpressed request.[6] Mindell suggests you:

Find the hidden Ki (energy)—notice when people are not just angry but needy—feed the need, not just the anger. When someone is criticizing you, notice if she is shy about it and address the shyness, if your opponent is belligerent and also correct, compliment the correctness.

It could be that someone's protest over what you said in a meeting is really a request to acknowledge his contribution. When you make that acknowledgement the shift from confrontation to collaboration could be immediate.

TAKING RESPONSIBILITY

If the act of taking responsibility was placed on a continuum you would find at one end the type of person who looks for someone to blame when things go wrong. At the other end of the continuum is the person who thinks everything is his fault. When these two types work together they seldom have an open conflict. But if two persons work together who are addicted to being "right" inevitably they will expend a great deal of energy making someone (their boss, a coworker, or each other) wrong.

The dichotomy between "blamer" and "blamee" is self-imposed. The real issue is the inability to take the appropriate amount of responsibility and identify the true source of the emotional upset. Giving away responsibility (either by making yourself totally responsible for how someone else is feeling or by making someone else responsible for how you are feeling) is really giving away personal power. The loss of both is the loss of a part of one's inner self that only you can stick up for. The way to reclaim that part starts with asking a few questions. Some questions to ask are:

- Am I willing to take responsibility for my experience?
- What do I do (consciously and unconsciously) to create these kind of experiences?
- What is my payoff for creating this situation?

PERSONAL ARCHEOLOGY

Taking personal responsibility and making changes is not easy. Many of us have a significant personal and economic investment in the identity of being wronged or victimized that is reinforced by the legal system and social programs. Giving up that identity and the accompanying attitudes and behaviors might reveal a void that is scary to confront. What would some of your coworkers talk about if they no longer gripe or complain? What would they do with all that extra time and energy on their hands?

Frequently, most of the force behind an emotional upset over a petty incident has little to do with the actual conflict that triggered the reaction. Someone cuts a driver off in traffic and he goes ballistic. The real reason for the intensity of the reaction is that some unresolved emotion, usually buried in the past, was triggered by the present incident. If you look deeper within yourself to discover and experience the source of that emotion you can build a sense of personal freedom and self worth that cannot be eclipsed by the actions of others.

Some questions that will help in the digging are:

- How is this like other situations in the past?
- What am I doing to create these situations?
- What changes can I make in my beliefs, behaviors, or communications that will resolve this pattern?

An Eastern yogi once said that, "people are to you as you are to yourself." How are you being to yourself? To a great extent it is true that you will be to others as you are to yourself. Do you practice acceptance, nonjudgment and compassion?

POWER PLACE

Taking responsibility is an act of power. To blame others or the world for the problem is to give that power away. Taking responsibility is not taking the blame—a subtle but important distinction—nor is it abdicating the slightest amount of self-respect. It is simply investigating what is your part in a conflict instead of using your energy in self-defense, self-reproach, or making others wrong.

Shifting from blame to responsibility is not easy. The experience reported by Gay and Kathlyn Hendricks illustrates the challenges:[7]

> . . . it took a great deal of discipline and practice to retrain ourselves to look inside for the source of the problem. It was so tempting to see the problem in the other person! We found, much to our surprise, that it was always when we were most convinced that it was the other person's problem that it turned out to be most clearly our own.

THE RESPONSIBILITY APPROACH

Use the responsibility approach by doing the following:

- Actively listen to restate what you hear.
- Acknowledge the emotions associated with the problem (yours and theirs).
- Make it clear you need some time to think about the situation so you can see what your part (as well as their part) is in it. (You might ask them to do the same.)
- Set a time when you will get back together.

During the break and when you get back together try to:

- Look for the truth in what your opponent is saying.
- Acknowledge that truth no matter how small.
- Ask what he wants.
- Ask for what you want.
- Problem solve for a mutually agreeable solution.

Norman Vincent Peale said words to this effect, "Why be offended by the truth? And if it is not true why worry about?"

COMMUNICATION ROULETTE

There is a simple model that predicts the outcome of any interaction. If you know the level of trust between two people you can make an educated guess as to how they will interpret each other's behavior.

Communication Roulette

PERCEIVED + OBSERVED → PERSONAL
INTENTION   BEHAVIOR   IMPACT

When trust is low the intentions of the other person will be seen as negative. No matter what the other person does his actions are viewed as unfriendly or even hurtful. The justified response is to avoid, act defensive, or attack. This tendency towards mutual reinforcement explains why a personal conflict between two people can be so difficult to resolve. Breaking the cycle means someone has to give the other person the benefit of the doubt by asking what his intentions really were.

Except in moments of anger most people have good intentions. Faith in the goodness of people is the belief that people are basically good even if their behaviors do not match their intentions. When you really trust someone they can do just about anything and you will be okay with it. But, let the guy you don't trust say, "good morning," and you might wonder the rest of the day what he meant.

SEEK FIRST TO UNDERSTAND

How often in an argument have you noticed that the opponents never make the effort to listen and understand each other? Each person ends up talking to the air while the other person ignores what is said. Why send a message if there is no one there to receive it? The fifth habit of highly successful people is to seek first to understand.[8] For a few minutes at least, you need to set aside the need to be right and become sincerely interested in understanding the other person's experience.

- Ask questions that come from a place of genuine concern and desire to understand.
- Test your understanding by restating your opponent's key points and how he feels about the situation. "You're angry that this decision was made without your input."
- Once you have demonstrated your understanding to your opponent's satisfaction—the kind of "you got it" satisfaction that comes from the gut—ask if he will do the same for you.

Mutual understanding does not necessarily mean conceding your point-of-view. It does mean a real resolution of the conflict is more likely. Remember, you cannot judge someone and at the same time try to understand him.

BEING HEARD

A physiological change takes place in a person who feels understood by a listener. That sense of being understood has as much to do with the body language and tone of voice as the degree of intellectual agreement since emotional understanding is conveyed nonverbally. When people feel understood they often feel less threatened. A greater sense of safety enables them to be more open and to begin to listen. They might even find enough closure to let go of the issue and go on with their lives.

FIGHTING FAIR

Since conflict is inevitable it is useful to develop guidelines that govern how conflict will be resolved. Guidelines that are known and accepted by the team will ensure the members fight fairly. Einstein reportedly defined insanity as doing the same thing over and over again even though it does not work. A conflict that continues to drag on and on is a big sign that what the team is doing needs to be changed. You can be sure there will be plenty of opportunities to deal with a lingering conflict until the right change is made. Some guidelines that sum up the ideas presented on resolving conflict include:

- Breathe; it is hard to stay tense when you are consciously breathing.
- If people are standing ask them to sit down.
- Slow things down. "Let's go back to the beginning. . ."
- Focus on the problem, not personalities. Maintain respect.
- Look for and build upon areas of agreement and common purpose.
- Check your intentions: are they to heal or to hurt?
- Seek to understand as well as be understood.
- Verbalize the other person's point-of-view. Use active listening.
- Examine and take responsibility for any emotional reaction you have to the situation.
- Allow no personal attack ("HOW could you be so stupid!").
- Vent strong feelings first by writing a letter you do not mail or in a conversation with a friend.
- Define and communicate the ground rules and personal boundaries.
- Encourage a problem-solving approach instead of blaming or withdrawing.
- Use the responsible feedback model and "I" statements.
- Keep a dialogue going. Speak and listen to create more understanding instead of seeking to score debating points.
- Define the criteria of a solution that will satisfy both parties.
- Let the other side know what you want or will accept. Ask what they want or will accept. Keep checking for acceptance.

- Keep looking for new solutions or options both parties might accept, but have not thought of yet.
- Know your preferred style for handling conflict. Try a different one if the usual approach does not work. Cultivate self-awareness and the willingness to change.

A conflict (between team members) is not really resolved unless both sides are satisfied with the outcome and consider it fair. An acceptable outcome can be as simple as feeling understood both intellectually and emotionally. Often that is enough to bring the issue to closure.

RESPONSIBLE FEEDBACK

Feedback is a powerful tool. Most people hesitate to use it because they are afraid of the reaction they might get. This fear is why many people deal with personal conflict by avoiding it or accommodating the other side. The truth, what you recognize as true for you, is a potent force. If you can hit someone with a pack of truths and name the behavior being acted out you will be able to deal with the situation on your terms—not theirs.

Responsible feedback is a respectful communication that seeks understanding and a workable solution. Responsible feedback builds on the feedback model outlined in Chapter Four, "Communication Skills". It is responsible because it communicates feelings without the baggage of blame or insult.

- Assess your intention. Do you want to get even? Or do you want to repair and improve the relationship? If your intention is payback then it is wise to wait until you calm down.
- Ask permission. If you give feedback without asking, the recipient may not hear a word you say.
      "Will you listen to how your behavior affects me?"
      "Do you want to know my reaction to that?"
- Explain the behavior as you see it. Be objective:
      "When you say. . ."
      "When you come in late. . ."

- Explain the impact, emotionally and materially. Use "I" statements:
    "I feel put-down."
    "Others are overworked."
- Ask for clarification and seek understanding:
    "What is your intention?"
    "What do you really want to tell me?"
- Ask for what you want:
    "Please be here on time."

If possible, frame your requests in a positive way. According to one school of thought, the subconscious misses the "don't" part of a command or a request. You will have better results if you ask for what you want instead of complaining that what you get is what you don't want.

CLEARING RESENTMENTS

Most conflict is personal. People take things personally, especially if the trust level is low. Small resentments can build up over time making it difficult for two people to work together. The clearing of resentments works best with a facilitator who leads the clearing person and the receiving person through the process. The purpose of the exercise, which should always be stated at the beginning, is to heal and repair a relationship.[9] The person doing the clearing takes the following steps:

1) *Data*. State the facts as you see them.
2) *Feeling*. Say at least one word describing your feeling about the facts. Angry, sad, afraid, happy, and ashamed are the basic emotions that can be applied to any situation.
3) *Interpretation*. Describe your beliefs or judgments about what has happened based on your own interpretation of the data.
4) *Request*. State what you want from the other person.
5) *Offer*. Identify what you would be willing to do to repair the relationship and help make it work.

6) *Ownership*. Define any part of the breakdown or problem for which you are willing to take responsibility.

As the clearing person goes through the six steps the facilitator guides the receiving person through active listening to make sure he understands the intellectual and emotional content of the clearing. The facilitator checks with the clearing person to make sure the receiving person has been both accurate and complete in restating the clearing person's point-of-view. Accurate means he got it right. Complete means nothing was left out. The facilitator also checks with the receiving person after steps two or three to make sure he understands the clearing person's point-of-view. This does not mean he agrees with it. It only means the receiving person understands why the clearing person thinks or feels the way he says he does. If the receiving person does not understand then he needs to ask some clarifying questions.

The receiving person responds after all six steps are completed. He does not have to respond to all six steps, but he should answer the request. The receiving person may need to do a clearing in return but in my experience the actual response is usually limited to the receiving person's point-of-view or points of clarification.

Just enabling both participants to better understand each other (steps one and two) is often enough to resolve the problem.

Here is an abbreviated version of a clearing:

1) *Data*. "Last week you told me I was wrong and dismissed how I was trying to deal with an issue at our team meeting."
2) *Feeling*. "Angry and hurt."
3) *Interpretation*. "When you act this way I have the impression you think you are the only person who knows anything and you think I don't."
4) *Request*. " Let me try my approach and see if it actually works before you intervene. I would like an apology for how you treated me last week."

5) *Offer.* "I will accept your apology."
6) *Ownership.* "I could take things less personally and be less quick to take offence."

The clearing session ended in an apology and stronger relationship between the two co-workers.

Section III
Tools for Team Building

7
Ground Rules & Agreements

Team Building Associates

All men like to think they can do it alone,
but a real man knows there's no substitute
for support, encouragement or a pit crew.

TIM ALLEN

Every organization has unwritten and unspoken rules. These rules reflect the culture of the company molded by the precepts of the founding members. These precepts, surviving long after the founders have departed, represent the unwritten part of an employee's contract. Dress, social conduct, or after hours socializing are all aspects of a unilateral agreement that goes beyond the expectations of labor for pay. Conformity to the unwritten and even unspoken rules is a requirement for advancement and even employment.

Some of these requirements can affect the employee's personal life. For example, Electronic Data Services, before it was sold by its founder, Ross Perot, to General Motors, guaranteed its employees in the 1980's immediate termination if they broke any of the unwritten rules. Those rules included living with a member of the opposite sex without the benefit of marriage, consuming an alcoholic drink at lunch during the workweek, growing a beard, or having an extramarital affair. Perot did not put this in writing; it was simply stated verbally by his corporate recruiters to prospective employees.

GROUP AGREEMENTS

In every team there are a number of agreements, unwritten and even unspoken, about how the members will treat each other.[1] New employees learn about these agreements, also known as group norms, by observing their coworkers and supervisors. These norms can vary from one department or team to another. Peer pressure can play a subtle or not so subtle role in enforcing them.

ESTABLISHING FUNCTIONAL AGREEMENTS

Organizations with functional group agreements are usually the kind of places both you and I would like to work. People treat each other as they would like to be treated: with respect, consideration, and good will. Unfortunately, the personal dynamics in many organizations reflect varying degrees of ill will, animosity and a lack of consideration. Some organizations have been that way for so long these behaviors are not even questioned.

The level of emotional safety in an environment where people devalue each other is very low. This kind of behavior adversely impacts work performance and the related factors of physical health and employee turnover.

Concerned team members need to have their eyes and ears open, assessing the quality of the interactions within the team. Perhaps you notice a degree of gossip and backbiting. Maybe certain people are in the habit of making sarcastic comments and jests at the emotional expense of others. If so, it is time for the team to create a social contract between team members that encourages more supportive behaviors.

Building functional norms need not be left to chance. A team can forge its own ground rules and norms to guide how its members interact with each other. These agreements are more likely to be honored if the entire team works together to define them. The team leader and others who influence the group must actively model the new agreements and encourage others to do so.

TEAM CONTRACTING

Most companies have written contracts with their employees that spell out wages, benefits, and working conditions. There is another form of contracting that is a verbal agreement between team members. People know how they want to be treated. Through an open discussion the group defines how the members will work together and what constitutes successful job performance. This verbal form of "contracting" has been used to create trust and define performance expectations with teams that range from clerks to research scientists. "Contracting" works as follows:

> During a team meeting one person writes down on a flip chart suggestions and ideas from the other members about how they want to work together and what behaviors should be encouraged or discouraged. The team develops a list of ground rules or norms that define the standards of behavior and work performance the team members want to maintain. The list is modified as questions, comments, and concerns are addressed. When an acceptable list is produced each team member is asked in turn if he or she agrees to abide by all the items or norms listed. Norms any person cannot live with are discussed and, if necessary, renegotiated. In some companies the team members sign their names to the final flip chart listing what the group developed.

One list produced by a team included items such as:

- Ask for everyone's opinion before making a decision.
- No put-downs or "zingers" between team members.
- Listen respectfully to opposing opinions or ideas.
- Know that it is okay to ask for help.
- Assist someone else after finishing your task.
- Share information; keep each other informed.
- Celebrate individual and team wins.
- Assume nothing; check things out.
- Maintain confidentiality.
- Talk problems out with the people involved.
- Work to solve the problems instead of assigning blame.

WALK THE TALK

During a "trust walk" activity on a retreat, each member of a department had an experience of totally relying on another person. Working in pairs, half of the participants were blindfolded and silently led through the woods by their partners. Each team of two first made agreements and developed a system that enabled them to communicate with and trust their partner in a challenging situation. This brought up the open-ended question: "If we can create this kind of working relationship here, how can we create a similar relationship in our workplace?" The answers provided some of the norms listed above.

MAKING IT STICK

Just agreeing to something does not mean it is going to happen. Unless there is some kind of follow up most groups will drift back to their old habits. Two or three weeks after the initial agreement is made it is beneficial to meet again as a group. During the meeting review the ground rules and ask people to assess how well they are doing, both individually and as a group. It takes time and effort to replace an old habit with a new one so emphasize that you are looking for progress not perfection. Ask for a volunteer to keep tabs on the group's progress. At least once a week that person will report to the group or ask the members to report on themselves at a staff meeting. Modify or explain the old ground rules or add new ones. Get the story out every time one of the ground rules has a positive impact.

TASK CONTRACTING

Team leaders can also create a quick verbal contract at the beginning of a project. Anytime a new task is assigned it is useful to first reach an agreement on standards and procedures. After giving instructions and answering questions ask if everyone agrees to do what has been required or requested. Look for a "yes," or a nod indicating yes, to show a commitment to the agreement. If someone hesitates find out what her concern is and discuss it. Some additional explaining may be needed before everyone understands what you want them to do.

For example, a records manager who just received a large and time-consuming request from a client, contracted within the team for the following standards for this particular task:

- Select the items you know best from the document retrieval list.
- Give other team members a little added encouragement and help during this crunch period.
- Re-file completed documents within 24 hours.

FUNCTIONAL NORMS

Typically, when team members form a "contract" with each other they experience a new sense of confidence in their team. The members begin to appreciate the range of talent, energy, skills, knowledge, and leadership that reside in the team as a whole.

Often the members may feel more at ease knowing they do not have to do it all themselves because now it is acceptable to support others and ask for support.

A primary means of building trust is the understanding that everyone's contribution is valued. Since everyone is a full-fledged member, fewer assumptions are made about who has what to offer. As the level of emotional safety increases more of the members will begin to clearly articulate the issues, concerns, and options facing the group. In this kind of dynamic, the personal power and influence of every member increases. In a group run by nonfunctional norms, power is a zero-sum game. The more one person has the less others must have. The struggle for influence reduces cooperation and trust and drains away any potential for synergy.

AUTHENTIC RELATIONSHIPS

Relationships are as viable as the topics that can be discussed. Issues that cannot be vocalized cannot be resolved. When people feel free to state their opinions or make their case for a particular action they are more likely to support the final decision.

A team "comes together" when the members feel psychologically safe to open up and share concerns, problems, and disagreements with each other. The work environment that allows people to be authentic and say what they think, in a way that respects the feelings of others, fans the sparks of group creativity.

BUILDING TRUST

Teamwork is based on trust. Trust cannot be bolted on to a team by some program or activity. It grows out of the daily interactions that, over time, define how the team members work and relate to each other. A lack of trust creates an atmosphere where people argue endlessly over trivial or irrelevant issues, ascribing negative motives to even positive behaviors. In dysfunctional groups, "team defeating" or "red ink" behaviors are passed around from one member to another, doing a great deal of damage with each exchange. This cycle of distrust will only stop when one or more members refuse to accept or pass on these kinds of behaviors.

The emotional climate of a functional group is one of acceptance. Discounting the personal worth of others with jests and judgments is a strategy used by some to alleviate their own sense of inadequacy. It is important to identify and label damaging behaviors and words for what they are. Naming the dysfunction takes away much of its power. Instead of criticizing, the alternative is to state what is on your mind and deal with the problem by giving and receiving feedback and requesting what you want. If the team has accepted the norms of acceptance and non-judgment, the team itself will enforce its own agreement, when a member slips back into a less useful pattern of behavior.

Teams build a climate of trust when the members adopt or enact the following norms:

- Let go of the past. Holding on to bad feelings is a waste of energy.
- Look for and affirm the good work of others.
- Be a "good-finder" instead of a faultfinder.
- Take a personal interest in each other; you are more than your title and so are your coworkers.
- Talk to people; you have to be knowable to be known.
- Take responsibility for your feelings and actions; no one can make you feel anything without your consent.
- Seek to understand and to be understood.
- Replace judgment with curiosity.
- Ask for what you need or want.
- Don't assume others can read your mind.
- Say what you mean; do what you say.
- Disagree without being disagreeable.
- Misunderstandings will occur; clear as you go.
- When one of us wins we all win; let's help each other win.

AFFIRMATION

Maintaining a car is not maintenance if you wait until the equipment breaks down before changing the oil. In the same manner good teamwork requires an amount of human maintenance that acknowledges the dignity of each person. An important milestone in the development of a team is when the members take a personal interest in each other's success.

People usually hear about it when they make a mistake, but seldom is anything said about the good things they accomplish. Some people are natural "affirmers" who thrive on giving positive feedback and acknowledgement. Every team, no matter now technical the work, needs a few members who have the talent for making people feel good about themselves and other people. Are you willing to be one of those people? If you are try the following:

- Notice people. Look for the good things they do and say.
- Take a minute or two each day to praise or acknowledge someone's contribution.

8
Team Building On-the-Run

Team Building Associates

*The perfect human being is all human beings
put together, it is a collective, it is all of us
together that make perfection.*

SOCRATES

The activities in this chapter can be incorporated into part of the workday at the office. These are the tools, techniques, and actions you can use to build your team. The activities draw upon the skills presented previously, in Chapter 7, "Ground Rules and Agreements," skills you have to use to work effectively with others. Team building on-the-run includes:

- Group exercises that strengthen team cohesion and spirit.
- Problem-solving and planning techniques based on a cooperative and synergistic approach.
- Communication strategies that improve understanding and increase team confidence and participation.

KNOW YOUR CAPABILITIES

Human behavior is anything but predicable. It is a good idea to be aware of your capabilities before attempting to lead any of the activities or exercises described in this book. Ask yourself if your skill level in small group facilitation is equal to the nature of the group or the situation with which you are dealing. Teams in which a lot of emotions have built up over time usually need the assistance of person skilled in group dynamics who can take the role of a neutral, third party.

If you have doubts about your ability to maintain your objectivity, especially if you are the leader of the team, it would be wise to consider the services of a professional team-building consultant or an in-house facilitator. Even doctors and lawyers know better than to be their own clients.

REAL PEOPLE

The people on your team are not bodies that do certain tasks, but real live human beings. In the continuous rush to meet the latest deadline remember to ask about a person's life outside the office—his spouse and children—her sports and hobbies. Any sincere sign of interest shows you know and care about them as real people. This caring is an essential part of group cohesion. It is far too easy to take people, especially support or administrative people, for granted. Showing personal interest, according to Stephen Covey, is one way to put a significant deposit in your "emotional bank account" with an associate.[1]

BUILDING TRUST

Trust is based on what we know about a person socially as well as professionally. Getting to know each other on a personal level is a wise investment of time that pays off in a higher level of group synergy. Team maintenance covers the range of discussions or activities that develop the human side of professional relationships. Opportune times to develop that human dimension are hard to plan for but easy to find if you look for one during the day. When the appropriate moment presents itself try asking a question like one of the following:

- What is your favorite TV show, movie, or sport?
- What kind of books do you like to read?
- Who is your personal hero or heroine and why?
- What was your biggest learning experience?
- What is your biggest satisfaction at work?
- What is your biggest pet peeve?
- What accomplishment are you most proud of that is not in your resume?

Another way to get to know your teammates is to pose the desert island question. If you had to live on a desert island for several years, what three luxury items (books, music, favorite snack, so forth) would you take with you? Another question to ask at lunch while everyone is waiting to be served: What was your most memorable meal?

MORE THAN A RESUME

Do your team members know what you do, what you have done, or where you went to school? It is also not unusual to find people with the same job titles on the same team who hardly know each other even after working together for years. Except for the leader, it is likely no one else has seen your job description or your resume. This lack of knowledge about each other can mean missed opportunities and underutilized resources. Synergy is generated when team members know and appreciate each other's talents, accomplishments, and idiosyncrasies.

Have people spend a few minutes getting to know each other before you get down to business. Ask people to interview each other on one or more of the above questions like: What are you most proud of that is not on your resume? Then ask people to report on what they learned about their partner. You and others may be surprised and impressed by the information that is shared. The more people talk to each other the more they discover things they have in common. Sharing those commonalties builds mutual trust and rapport.

NEW KID ON THE BLOCK

Think way back to when you were a child. Did you ever have the experience of moving into a new neighborhood or enrolling in a new school during the middle of the school year? If so, you may remember that it was a scary experience.

Finding out what was expected, where everything was and who your friends were took time. Starting a new job can be just as scary. When you were a new employee you may remember the anxiety you felt as you strained to learn the professional lay of the land. Hopefully, your questions as a new person were welcomed and not responded to as an intrusion. Paradoxically, the employees leaving a company, instead of those arriving, are the ones who get treated to lunch.

Just as it is important to say goodbye and honor a person's past contributions, giving a new member a warm welcome is a central part of the team-building process. Below are several steps you can take that will help to smooth the transition from the "new kid" to a productive team member.

- Present the new team member to the group and say a few words about his or her background.
- Welcome the new member with introductions, handshakes, and even applause.
- Assign them a mentor or office buddy who can answer questions.
- Give an in-depth briefing about the organization, what is expected, and how things are done.

People can be "new" even when they have been on the team for a long time. During a meeting an industrial team developed a system for performing a certain task. One member was out of the room and did not learn the system. Everyone was absorbed in the task when he rejoined the group and no one thought to brief the "new" member. He was on is own in figuring out what was going on and finding a way to catch up. The team realized later that this oversight reduced their effectiveness.

THE POWER OF BELONGING

Nearly everyone wants to be a valued and accepted member of his or her work group. Until membership is established, verbally or non-verbally, there will usually be some degree of holding back from full participation and commitment.

High-performance teams know how to integrate new members as well as solidify the sense of acceptance among on-going team members. Each member makes a unique contribution.

Set aside time for some "group maintenance." Ask the following question in a context that is relaxed and informal. Have the members answer in turn or discuss with the group the question, "What do you bring to the team?" When people talk about what they bring to the team, such as energy, creativity, humor, and technical expertise they inspire themselves as well as their team members.

BUILDING A TEAM CHARTER

Most effective teams develop unwritten and even unspoken guidelines that fuel their success. The process they use to create their culture is largely accidental, a happy accident, but one still dependent on chance. Consciously creating a "team charter" will improve your chances of building a high-performance team. A team charter covers the following areas:

- Goals
- Roles

- Norms/Values
- Mutual Expectations
- Team Processes/ Procedures

There are no guarantees that you will have a great team if you come up with a charter, but it will certainly be a step or two in the right direction. The first four items in the above list are covered below. Chapter 22, "Process Improvement", discusses how to map team processes and improve them.

GOAL CLARITY

"If you keep going in the direction you are headed you will probably get there." This statement may sound like a father telling his son to shape up. But Dad may have had a point. Many teams are not sure if they are going in the right direction because they are not sure where they are trying to go. The leader's job is to make sure everyone understands the ultimate goals.

If the goals are clear to everyone it is likely the team can self-organize around what need to be done without a lot of supervision. Ask each team member to do the following:

- Define team success.
- Write the definitions down on paper, one idea per piece of paper in large block letters.
- Post the definitions on the wall using masking tape.
- Explain what you wrote.

ROLE AMBIGUITY

The nature of work has shifted. Roles are no longer as rigid as they were even ten years ago. Matrix management, downsizing, and the drive to do more with less means not every base will have an assigned player. A certain level of ambiguity is inherent under these conditions. One way to manage this ambiguity is to call a meeting and have each person explain what they do and whom they do it with and for. After everyone has presented their responsibilities ask the following:

- Did anyone learn anything new?
- Were there any surprises?
- Are there any disconnects or areas that no one is attending to?

ROLE CLARITY

Work teams of just about any configuration can get tripped up over who is supposed to do what. In a fast-paced environment it can be hard to tell if all the bases are covered.

One way to get organized is with a work breakdown structure. The figure below is a simple example. "A" stands for approves (or you could use "L" for leads), "D" for does, and "S" for supports.

Work Breakdown Structure

	Task 52	Task 67	Task 108	
Sally	A	D	S	
Fred	S	D	S	
Sue	D	A	D	
Bill	D	S	A	

NORMS AND VALUES

Chapter Seven, "Ground Rules and Agreements", covers the importance of functional team norms and presents examples developed by teams. It is not enough to assume you have a respectful workplace where people are friendly and professional to each other. "Just kidding" by one person can be harassment to another. Spelling out the Standards of Behavior or SOB's can preempt the development of a hostile workplace. The best standards are the ones the team defines. Call a meeting and ask, "What standards of behavior will we hold ourselves accountable to?"

MUTUAL EXPECTATIONS

People can contribute more of what they can bring to a team when more of their individual needs are met. Those needs are as diverse as the people on the team. Everyone has expectations, yet people seldom state what they expect from others. Even those whom they are closest to and expect the most from, are left to practice mind reading; a habit so commonplace as to be something of a human trait.

Naturally, you are more likely to get what you request than what you passively expect. An open discussion around expectations can produce revelations that resolve small issues before they become big ones. Some questions to ask team members, especially at the start of a new project or during the formation of a new team, are:

- What do we need/expect from each other?
- What do we need/expect from our team leader?
- What does the team leader need/expect from us?

Since most of our expectations remain unstated, even unconscious, it can be extremely helpful in any relationship, personal or professional, to discuss what we want from each other. The things people say they need can range from the general, "I need encouragement," to the specific, "I need my coworkers to occasionally stop by my desk and say hello." or "I would like frequent feedback on how I am doing?"

ASKING FOR HELP

Many people in the workplace find it difficult to ask for the help they need. A competent person, according to our cultural norms, is supposed to go it alone and persevere no matter what the difficulties. This go-it-alone norm is reflected in the melodramas produced by Hollywood. When the hero is in a jam he seldom calls a buddy for help, but if he does, the phone usually goes dead.

You probably have been rebuffed or have seen someone else rebuffed in a request for help with one of the following refrains:

- I'm too busy. Ask someone else.
- That's not my job.
- I'm not going to do your work for you.
- You mean you don't even know how to do your own job?

For some, asking for help is admitting failure or incompetence. Better to fail quietly than to let others know you screwed up.

These same people think and act from scarcity. If someone else does well it means they suffer a loss. High-performance teams have a different set of beliefs. This is because the members have the following agreements:

- It is okay to ask for help.
- Helping you succeed is helping myself succeed.
- Ask for help before the situation becomes helpless.
- The only dumb question is one that isn't asked.
- Helping others succeed is as gratifying as when I succeed.
- When one of us looks good, we all look good.
- There is enough of the good stuff (recognition, rewards, advancement, and opportunities) for everyone.

Even the Lone Ranger didn't ride alone. At your next team meeting do something radical. Ask the following:

- Does anyone need some help?
- Who can provide help?

KILLING FEAR

A big killer of productivity is fear. Some worries are born from a lack of information. When something is not said people assume the worst. There are three simple antidotes: communicate, communicate, and communicate. As the team leader or manager it may be useful to ask your staff what questions or concerns they have. Then ask about any topic such as their work, the status of a project, the financial health of the company, or any unknown. When a question is voiced respond to it and the underlying concern that may be behind the question.

Most concerns or fears can be dealt with either by providing specific information, problem solving, or reaching a mutual agreement. Concerns are often unfounded. But people won't know which ones are unfounded unless they ask. It takes a certain level of trust to get past the fear of repercussions that may result from stirring up a sensitive subject.

Once that trust is there, putting the other fears to bed is comparatively easy. Just being able to give voice to a worry can help a person let go of it. If you do not know the answer to a question be willing to say so. For example, your employees may be worried that a merger will lead to layoffs. It may be too soon to know what the impact of the merger will be. But you can say you will let them know as soon as the information is available.

READY-FIRE-AIM

"Prior planning should be done in advance," is the standard refrain of a military logistician, when faced with a last minute request from some hapless lieutenant. How does your team react when given a new job or a rush assignment? Responding to a tight deadline with fits of frantic hustling is often more impressive than productive. Careful planning is essential because speed does not help, if you are going in the wrong direction. However, when some teams try to plan they run the risk of "analysis paralysis." Getting organized does not have to be a long, tedious undertaking. The right balance between thinking and doing can be the difference between success and failure.

Planning Balance

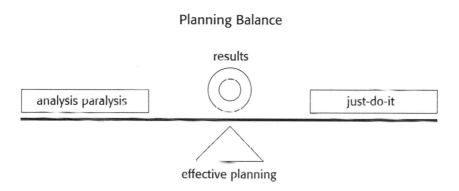

effective planning

"Failing to plan is planning to fail," is another adage of the logistician. Instead of jumping into action when given a new assignment try some fast and focused planning:

- Call the team together for a planning session.
- As a group, consider various approaches, define and consider the pros and cons of each option.
- Reach a decision through a process appropriate to the development of the team and the nature of the task.
- Develop a schedule and assign areas of responsibility.
- "Contract" for the standards that define how the task will be performed and people will work together.

Even in tasks that are considered routine a few minutes spent discussing what to do can prove cost or time effective. These few minutes are essential in the life of any group for creating synergy. Before performing a task successful teams ask themselves one or more of the following questions:

- Are all team members "on-board" with each other and the proposed plan?
- Does everyone understand the requirements and standards for the project?
- Does the team have the guidance and data it needs?
- Has everyone expressed his or her ideas and opinions?
- Does everyone understand the plan and their roles?
- Can everyone "live with" and support the decision that has been reached?
- What are the milestones or standards for success?
- Are there any related issues that need to be resolved before taking action?

SILENCE DOES NOT MEAN CONSENT

The quality of the planning process is a key component in generating team synergy. During a planning meeting some team members naturally express more of their opinions; others are less outspoken. Do not assume that silence means consent. If the team has an appointed leader with high control needs, planning sessions may be little more than opportunities for note taking.

Planning is planning because of the discussion and evaluation of options. When one or two people dominate all the "air time," many important considerations, doubts, and possibilities remain un-addressed. The dominant members of the team rush off thinking they have consent and support of the entire team only to find the execution of their plans marked by confusion, a lack of commitment, or after-the-meeting complaints like, "What a dumb idea." The best way to prevent this: do not assume that silence means consent. The key to building a team is to encourage every member's participation. Try the following:

- Call upon each person in-turn to comment on or ask questions about the proposed course of action.

- If time is short and the responses long, "contract" for limiting the "air time" to two or three minutes per person. Quite a lot can be said in two minutes when everyone is listening.
- If someone has not commented, ask her for her opinion.
- Establish as a ground rule that the team listens to someone's ideas without interruption for a given period of time.
- Evaluate the ideas later after the input from everyone is out on the table.
- When a minority disagrees with a plan the majority wants to adopt ask those who are in disagreement: "Can you support or at least not block the plan even if you disagree with some aspect of it?
- Look for changes everyone can live with.

Encouraging each member to contribute his or her viewpoint increases the overall level of commitment when it is time to implement the chosen plan. Whether a person's viewpoint is adopted is often secondary to the effect of having one's opinion heard.

REMEMBER: Do not assume that people will speak up if they have something to say. Go around the table and ask each person his or her input to the plan. When deciding on the plan again, *ask each person in-turn if he or she agrees to the plan.* Public commitment does not guarantee personal commitment, but it does improve the odds of getting it.

THE POWER OF REFLECTION

In business, taking care of business is the first priority. But in every endeavor, no matter how routine, a period of time should be set aside for conducting an assessment. A group effort is a dynamic and changing process. What works one month may not work the next. In the past it was enough for the workers to do the work and the boss to do the thinking. This approach no longer keeps a company afloat in the global marketplace. As was

discussed in Chapter Three, "Theories and Models", in the as-
sessment/adjustment phase of the Performance Model, successful managers gather their teams together in order to consider as
a group three basic questions:

- *What is working?* When a team knows what it is doing right it
  can do more of the same. Things are working because of the
  way the team approaches tasks. Certain actions and behaviors make the crucial difference between success and failure.
  Determine these actions and behaviors that result in success
  and acknowledge those who did them.
- *What is not working?* Analyze what is not working and why.
  Focus the discussion on fixing problems instead of assigning
  blame. There is always something that can be changed or
  modified for the better. Identify the behaviors and actions
  that reduce productivity so they can be dropped or modified.
  Exchange feedback and seek to resolve misunderstandings.
- *What do we need to do about it?* Based on the results of the
  previous two discussions, develop a list of what the team will
  do differently. Seek consensus on the type of changes needed.
  Brainstorm new ideas, norms, systems, procedures, and solutions. Adjust and modify the processes and procedures used
  to make decisions, solve problems, or carry out tasks.

MAKING ADJUSTMENTS

The ditty "If you always do what you always did you will always
get what you always got," is as true as it is popular. When the
outcome to something is not to your liking it makes sense to look
at the inputs and make some changes. One reason the former coach
of the Washington Redskins football team, Joe Gibbs, was inducted
into football's Hall of Fame was his ability to make adjustments in
his game plan at half time. If you are going to win consistently, or
at least win more than you lose, the ability to stop, evaluate, and
adjust is essential.

TEAM LEARNING

A lot has been said and written by Peter Senge and others about the "learning organization."[2] When organizations are a patchwork of separate, even warring fiefdoms little in the way of organizational learning can take place. Without continuous learning an organization usually continues to make the same mistakes until it blunders its way out of existence or undergoes a painful restructuring.

The dynamic of blind competition can extend to every level of the organization, pitting individual against individual even on the same team. Like the blind men and the elephant each person or each department has a piece of the knowledge that would benefit everyone if it was shared in the context of learning as a team. Learning as a team means empowering the members to use techniques like the Plus/Delta model in Chapter Three, "Theories and Models". The answers to the problems and challenges are there, but first someone has to ask. The process is like putting a puzzle together. You have to bring those parts together and share a lot of information to solve the puzzle.

GETTING THE WORD

Some people expect their coworkers to be mind readers. It is true if you know how someone thinks you can anticipate his actions or decipher his cryptic notes. In large groups it is not unusual to find a small percentage of the workforce "did not get the word" about an important message. That percentage might be reduced by rephrasing the message or communicating through multiple channels.

There is a story that during the Revolutionary War, George Washington would read his communiqués to one of the soldiers guarding his tent, before dispatching it to his generals. If the guard did not understand the gist of the message Washington would rewrite it until he did.

Ask the following questions as an internal communications check:

- How often is someone left out of the loop?
- Are team members afraid to ask a "stupid" question?
- What needs to be done to keep everyone informed?

It is easy to assume people have received and understand the information they need unless they tell you otherwise: an assumption that causes more than a few breakdowns. Several teams working for an international development organization handled this problem by setting up the following structure to get the word out:

- The team meets together for a brief meeting at the beginning of the workweek.
- Every member briefly reports on current activities and upcoming events.
- People who need assistance or information have the opportunity to ask for it.

ASKING FOR COOPERATION

Occasionally, you must implement difficult and unpopular decisions. As the bearer of the bad news you probably had little to do with determining the new policy, yet you definitely feel the heat while implementing it. As a manager, you may need to thicken your skin and forget about personal popularity for awhile. When announcing an unpopular decision three actions will help ease the pain and deal with the fallout the decision generates:

- Explain the decision and its rationale.
- Ask for your team's cooperation and understanding.
- Appeal to higher values and a common purpose.

No matter how the leader asks the affected group for their support most appeals can be summed up as the statement:

I know it's tough. I know it may not seem fair. I've done everything I can. However, with some situations the only choices available are in how you deal with them. As professionals (or union workers or patriotic Americans or whatever) I ask for your understanding and cooperation.

The simple act of asking for their understanding can help bring upset and dissatisfied workers back together as a team. People settle down and get on with their jobs when they have a reason to put a difficult experience behind them. The first step is to acknowledge their feelings about the situation. The second is to ask for their cooperation in a manner that respects their ability to choose.

CONFIDENCE BUILDERS

During the formative stage of a new team or during a slump in an ongoing effort, a small victory can be a major morale booster. Good leaders know the strengths and weaknesses of the people working for them. They prepare the groundwork for future "wins" by setting up their team members for small but obtainable victories. Groups, like any object in motion according to Newtonian physics, develop momentum. In a group, enthusiasm or despair builds on its own momentum. When discouragement gathers force something has to be done.

One antidote: a project or objective that is sure to produce the experience of success.

- Target a project or activity likely to produce a victory even though it may not be significant in terms of sales volume or other measured results.
- Give people tasks that match their range of competence before giving them more challenging assignments that might require some "stretching."
- Acknowledge and celebrate individual and collective "wins." Reframe mistakes as "lessons learned" that will lead to success.

Proactive mistakes show the team is taking the risks needed to build a foundation for future victories. Gaining a few victories, even easy ones, builds the confidence of the team. A reservoir of confidence is essential for dealing with the tougher challenges. Without that confidence some team members will give up when things go badly. As their self-image of being a winner in a winning outfit develops, team members become more willing to take risks and give what it takes to succeed.

DEVELOPING A GROUP IDENTITY

Organizational development consultants have noted that you can tell if you are in a successful company or an efficient government agency by the kind of stories the members relate to each other.[3] Especially important are the stories old employees tell the new ones when they first come on board because they define the organizational culture. These stories could be about the feats of the founders of the company or how a group of workers joined together to help out another employee with a serious illness by donating their sick leave. The stories are concentrated capsules of information about what it means to be a member of that organization. Besides the stories that are shared company wide, each working group usually develops its own set of stories that describes what it means to be member of that team.[3]

The most significant stories are recounted time and time again at company events, award ceremonies, and other less formal occasions. These stories convey something larger than life in their telling. The listeners are invited to share in the glory of the past accomplishments by virtue of their membership in the organization. The stories are modern day tribal myths that impart a sense of belonging. Sharing these myths is a way of affirming, "This is who we are. This is our heritage and we are proud of it."

- Every organization has a few stories of exceptional performance or concern. What are they? Are they being told? Dig them up.

- Analyze the stories that have become part of the office culture. If their tone is too cynical and negative, search for new stories that are more encouraging.
- Take on the role of the team storyteller.
- Tell the positive stories at the beginning of a meeting, during a coffee break, or put them in the company newsletter. Let others know about the inspiring things their coworkers have done.

Negative stories weaken the team effort. Positive stories build confidence and community. Strengthen the bonds of community by referring to the positive stories often. Show how they are vivid examples of the company's vision and values. Putting employees through an outdoor team-building course (Chapters Twelve and Thirteen, "Ropes Course" and "Wilderness Adventure") can be an effective way to create some new stories. Employees leave a well-run course with tales of teamwork and camaraderie they will recount to each other for a long time.

THE NAME GAME

Organizations often have informal names, given by the employees, as a way of defining their own identity. Informal names emerge from significant, work-related experiences. They sum up what the members feel about their team or their parent organization. The name can be a source of pride or a peg to hang your angst on. Behind the name is a story that embodies the group's aspirations or its frustrations.

Sports teams, military units, and social groups encourage the use of informal names as a way to increase group cohesion. IBM, for many years was called, Big Blue; a reference to the color of its mainframes computers before personal computers began to dominate the market.

The best names are those that come from challenging circumstances. One famous example is Yankee Doodle: a derisive term used by British troops during the revolution until the Americans adopted it and made it a patriotic nickname. There will be plenty of energy in any group to come up with a name when morale is high.

- If your team gave itself a name what would it be?
- Float the idea of name without pushing it too hard.
- Let the name emerge from some experience that captures the essence of the group.

PERFORMANCE COUNSELING

It has been said when things go wrong there are two types of people: those that automatically blame others and those that take the blame no matter what the circumstances. Either approach may be missing the point, which is not to avoid or accept blame, but to problem solve in a way that leads to improved performance.

Reprimanding a person links his actions with his self-esteem. A better form of performance counseling deals with the behavior in question rather than the person. Separating the person from the problem makes it easier to think of ways to correct the situation. Some questions that need to be asked:

- What went wrong? (Identify the problem or outcome)
- What did you (or we) learn from this outcome?
- What are you (or we) going to do to improve the situation?
- What help or extra training do you need?

The final question leads to "contracting" for the desired behavior or results. The manager and the employee negotiate an agreement the employee can fulfill to meet the expected standard of performance.

CRISIS MANAGEMENT

A confused situation can become highly charged with emotion unless you step forward and provide a clear sense of direction. High anxiety makes it difficult for people to think clearly. Clear thinking and frantic activity do not coexist. If the team begins to slip into confusion and uncertainty during a crisis, move decisively to restore confidence by asking the following questions:

- What happened?
- How did this happen?
- How do you feel about it?
- How did you react?

The first four questions reduce the level of the confusion. After you have done some emotional "damage control," problem solving will be more productive. Ask the questions:

- What can we do to correct or prevent this situation?
- Do you commit to doing what we need to do?

Incomplete answers are okay. What is important is that people see something being done to stabilize the situation and get things back on track. Discussing concerns and addressing them in a constructive manner dissipates the general anxiety. How things are said is as important as what is said, so speak with firmness and confidence to set the right tone. During a crisis strong leadership is a must. People are reassured when the person in charge has the attitude of calm confidence.

STRUCTURED AIR TIME

In more than one team the members do not listen to each other effectively. Time and information are lost when everyone talks and no one listens. Even when the members are aware of this trait they share, they can still end up trying to out talk each other in an effort to make themselves heard. One team responded to this problem by providing an allotted amount of "air time" for each person to speak and be heard. After setting up the structure the members found it easier to listen while waiting their turn.

Try the following process:

- During a team meeting set aside a specified amount of time for each person to have her say when discussing a topic.
- Determine the amount of airtime for each participant that is proportional to the discussion period.
- Appoint one member to be the timekeeper.
- No interruptions are allowed during the allotted time.
- The timekeeper calls each person to speak in turn.

CHECK OUT TIME

Setbacks, upsets, and other obstacles are inevitable parts of the process in any individual or group undertaking. When the going gets rough some people emotionally and energetically reduce their level of participation. They may still be showing up physically, but they add little or even take away from the group effort. Clear signs of checking out include: apathy, low energy, clock watching, physical distancing, or an underlying manner of discontent and malaise. People tend to act out their feelings instead of talking about them, so you might not know what the problem is until you ask.

Whatever the specific reason for the withdrawal it often has something to do with expectations not being met. Fortunately, a group has its own internal mechanism by which it can refocus itself and renew the sense of collective commitment. This exercise is more than just a gripe session. Properly conducted the process will help team members resolve the emotional reactions that block full participation:

- Hold a brief meeting at the beginning or end of the workday.
- Reaffirm the team's commitment to all of its members by reviewing the agreed upon norms and ground rules.
- Give each person a couple of minutes to talk about what is happening on the job and how he feels about it.

- Encourage "I" statements and taking responsibility for one's comments and emotions.
- No comments are made in response nor is problem solving conducted unless it is requested.
- Emotional "dumping" on any person on the team is not part of the process.

Self-disclosure is the congruence between what our inner experience is and what we tell others. A lot of trust has to be established in a group before the members will talk openly about their experiences as they relate to each other, their organization, and their work. People are more willing to speak their truth when the group acts as a sounding board, affirming the individual by simply listening objectively without comment.

Empathetic listening by a concerned group is a powerful tonic. People tend to isolate themselves when they believe only they have a certain problem, concern, or gripe. Often others share these concerns. What everyone knows but is afraid to talk about becomes a sticking point that drains energy. When people acknowledge the factors causing them to disengage they are more likely to reengage and recommit. Once people start communicating they can also start problem solving.

THE POWER OF SILENCE

A highly trained and articulate intellect is an asset in most endeavors. However, the more educated the team members are, such as academics and scientists, the greater the likelihood they will trip over their own left-brain mentality.

When failure stares a highly educated team in the face often the reaction is usually more of the same kind of intellectualizing that got them into trouble in the first place. As the saying goes, your greatest strength can also be your greatest weakness.

When things are not working, it is a good idea to do something, practically anything, different. The intentional and collective silence of a team, generated when everyone sits quietly for a few minutes, powerfully sets the stage to get unstuck.

The following experience shows the power of silence:

> A team of professionals was not getting anywhere with a certain project. Top notch people with armfuls of degrees kept talking and talking, but nothing seemed to click. Finally, as the frustration turned knuckles white, someone suggested everyone stop talking for a couple of minutes and sit quietly. Almost spontaneously, out of that silence came a suggestion that led to a breakthrough and the successful completion of the task.

COMMUNICATING A SENSE OF URGENCY

A problem for some managers is the gap between the seriousness of a pressing situation and how the team is reacting. You're worried, you know speed is essential, you know how important this particular job is; so why does everyone else seem so relaxed?

A sense of urgency is moving with deliberate haste. When this is lacking, critical opportunities and obligations can fall through the proverbial crack. Communicating this sense of urgency to others is a big part of a leader's job. One way to determine if a communication was understood as it was intended is to check for the desired response. Just remember frantic activity for its own sake accomplishes little. A leader can wake a team up in a number of ways. Start with some personal self-disclosure followed up with specific requests for action:

- Using "I" statements lets the other team members know your feelings about the situation.
- State the problem in non-judgmental terms.
- Words like worried and upset are not a sign of weakness but an indication of the depth of your concern.
- If the signs of focused activity and initiative are lacking find out why.

- Define the specific results that need to be obtained and the behaviors or activities that will help obtain those results.
- "Contract" for the results that need to be achieved.

When the leader has one agenda and set of expectations and the team has another the resulting misunderstanding can ruin everyone's day. A team leader or member can seldom go wrong by asking a few questions to find out what the others think is important, what they are excited about, or what work-related issue is on their minds. This background information could prove crucial to establishing credibility and enlisting support.

CROSS-FERTILIZATION

Cross-fertilization is a process nature uses to maintain a healthy diversity. Companies could also make use of the same process if they would set aside an hour or two for this activity to take place. The key to the accomplishment of any endeavor is support. A group of interested listeners represents a huge reservoir of encouragement, information, and suggestions that can turn practically any goal into a reality or find a potential solution to a pressing problem. There could not be a better way to sum up teamwork. Yet this information never reaches those who could most benefit from it. An inordinate amount of time is wasted "reinventing the wheel." Too many "best practices" are never shared with other departments because no one took the initiative to ask.

This teamwork exercise has four steps.

1) Members from various groups assemble in a meeting room. The participants are paired off and for a few minutes tell each other about their work and the challenges they face.
2) Ask if anyone would like to use the group as a sounding board. Have that person describe the challenges he or she is facing in a project.
3) Brainstorm as a group on ways the person or his department can meet its challenges and achieve its objectives.

4) Close the session by asking members to report on what they learned from the session that will be helpful to them.

Naturally, the focus of the brainstorming session is on exchanging useful ideas, tips, sources of information, procedures, and other constructive suggestions. This format may not be the place to address interpersonal conflicts or leadership problems. This approach does give the entire group the opportunity to utilize the potential benefits of the global team approach. It can provide the added benefit of helping employees learn about the operations of "those-other-guys" down the hall as well as the person sitting two desks over.

TEAMWORKING

This and the previous exercise are based on the excellent work Barbara Sher is doing with the process she describes in her book, *Teamworks*.[4] Everyone has some personal or professional goals that lie outside the domain of what they believe is possible or practical. There never seems to be enough time or money or faith to pursue those goals. Sher recommends assembling a team with the specific purpose of providing each member the mutual support needed to turn dreams into reality. Here is how it works:

> During the networking session a member of the group voices a long cherished desire, like building her own home, but the obstacles seem insurmountable. In a group it frequently happens that somebody will know somebody who knows somebody who wanted to do the same thing under similar circumstances and did. Phone numbers are offered, book titles given, expert builders recommended, special financing suggested and so forth. Within a few minutes the person with the dream has enough leads and resources to turn the dream into a reality.

Even if some of the goals expressed in the session are not related to work the exercise will still benefit the organization as a team-building tool. Employees who get to know and help each other will take that same spirit of comradeship back to their jobs.

TRUST YOUR INSTINCTS

One piece of advice often repeated by successful executives is to, "trust your instincts." There is a level of knowing we can feel in our bodies but not really articulate. Subjective knowledge is not limited like the intellect. It is connected to the subconscious, which has a much broader base of knowledge. According to those who follow the intuitive approach: if you don't have a good feeling about something then don't do it or think twice about it. If you do have a good feeling about it, it could be a signal of approval from your subconscious.

Before you try any of the activities or programs in this book or from any other source, check them out with your subconscious. Deep inside do you have a good feeling about them? If not then wait a few days before asking again. They may not be for you, the timing may not be right, or you may need to implement them in a different way. This procedure can apply to other business decisions as well.

A favorite saying of Joseph Campbell, the master of mythology, was "follow your bliss." What Campbell did not say was that it would be easy. Part of the price for your "bliss" is wading through a self-imposed thicket of doubts and reservations. Fulfilling Campbell's injunction may be one of the hardest and most courageous things a person can do.

Friends with the best of intentions will attempt to overwhelm your resolve with their considerations. Not that you should ignore advice, but do not forget to listen to the inner prompting of what Gandhi called, ". . .the small, still voice within." Some successful people claim if they had listened to the counsel given by well-meaning associates they never would have made the changes or taken the risks they needed to achieve their goals.

HIGH NOTES

You hear about your mistakes right away. A goof, like bad news, is a speedy traveler. Yet, the good news about who you are and the work that you do is less often commented on. One way to get the news out is through the following activity:

- Pass out index cards so that each team member has one card for each team member.
- Write on the back of the card the name of a fellow team member.
- Write on the front what you appreciate about that person. Include some specific comments about the things the person does well.
- Sign the card (or leave them all unsigned).
- Write one card for each team member.

Pass the cards out to those they are written for. Let the members read the cards and share any reactions they may have. How does it feel to be appreciated? How does it feel to appreciate others?

ARE WE HAVING FUN?

Are we having fun? The question may seem irrelevant (and irreverent) to anyone with his or her eyes on the bottom line. Yet teams that are highly productive and creative often seem to be having more fun than their less productive counterparts. In an uptight and self-conscious environment no one is willing to let down his or her hair and look the least bit silly.

Maintaining appearances in this kind of atmosphere takes a lot of energy. Many people have a business persona that they put on and take off with their business suit. But if people limit themselves to one rigid persona they may not be drawing upon the full range of their inner resources. A profound shift takes place when team members let down their guard and take the risk of looking silly in front of each other. The energy tied up in maintaining appearances becomes available for creative instead of protective purposes.

Employees begin to ask questions and take actions that they used to refrain from because of the fear of embarrassment. Getting a group to "lighten up" and do something for the fun of it just for a few minutes helps a team access new levels of creativity.

SILLY DILLIES

When a new product team begins a brainstorming session some facilitators will lead the members through loosening up exercises known as "silly dillies." Drawn from method acting, the dillies are exercises that encourage people to do just what name implies, act silly. The purpose of the activities is help people lighten up and get the creative juices flowing. Other teams find different ways to stop taking themselves too seriously.

A division of du Pont Corporation, one of the oldest companies in the United States, at one time, set aside a few minutes every Friday morning for a session to get the energy moving. Upbeat music played while employees danced a form of the Texas two-step in the halls. Now it may seem unbelievable that employees from such a staid and established industry did this, but they did. What made this possible was an extensive team-building program attended by every employee in the division.

What does your team do for fun? Does your team take the kind of breaks where it is okay to laugh? In some structured team-building programs your team may go through a few exercises that help a group to loosen up and have fun. An exercise called "Knots," described in Chapter 16, "Business Games" is good for warming up a group in preparation for some creative problem solving.

CELEBRATIONS

Celebrations build community. The occasion itself is less important than the opportunity it provides for the affirmation, and renewal of a group. A reason to celebrate can always be found if you look for one. An office party, company picnic, or catered lunch are some of the ways to celebrate a birthday, a contract win, employee of the year or a good year of sales. It only takes a few minutes to bring out a cake and say a few words about the accomplishments of the team. If the occasion is someone's birthday it only takes a few more minutes to acknowledge the birthday person with several anecdotes about her history at the company and some of the good things she does at her job. The team leader gives these compliments, everyone applauds and then they eat the cake. People go back to their desks feeling better about each other and their team.

During the annual parties at some companies, competitions are held to see who can tell the best story about office events. The stories, the laughter, the sharing of food and drink make the celebration a community building event. Newer workers learn the values and culture that define what it means to be a member of the organization. When the employees return to work the next day their ties with each other have been renewed or strengthened. Lending someone a hand or asking for help seem more matter of course and less of an intrusion. Celebrations do not have to be boring as this resourceful team proved:[5]

A department in a professional services firm reportedly made a deal with their manager. If they finished an urgent project on time they could have a beach party in the office. Their somewhat staid boss was astonished when the project was completed on time. The following Friday, beach umbrellas, coolers, watermelons, and even a plastic wading pool and sand were lugged in. Everyone put on bathing suits or cutoffs and schmoozed to the music of the Beach Boys. The manager tried to get away with wearing a tee shirt and shorts, but his staff refused any leniency. A bathing suit was procured and after he changed every woman posed with her portly taskmaster for a picture. Years later, people were still talking about the party.

9
Decisions & Problem Solving

Team Building Associates

*Problems can not be solved at
the same level of awareness
that created them.*

ALBERT EINSTEIN

Everyone has heard the expression; "two heads are better than one." Decisions made by a group are usually better than those made by a single individual. Yet getting a group to the point where it can make a good decision is not a given. Often there is more frustration over the decision making process and its speed than the quality of the decision. The first and often the toughest decision for many groups is to decide how they are going to decide. Before a new group begins the problem-solving process it can save itself a lot of time and confusion by taking this first step. And like a lot of first steps it is the one to watch out for.

POWER DISTRIBUTION

Proposing and deciding are both expressions of power within a group. How the power is distributed, either centralized within one person or shared among the team, determines which set of unspoken messages gets communicated. These messages include:

- *Leader proposes.*
    - ✓ I have an idea.
    - ✓ I want your input.
- *Team proposes.*
    - ✓ We have ideas about what to do.
    - ✓ We want your approval.
- *Leader decides.*
    - ✓ Because it is my decision.
    - ✓ I know best.
- *Team decides.*
    - ✓ All of us are smarter than one of us.
    - ✓ The best decision is one everyone supports.

Using the team approach for every decision may not be realistic or efficient. It is best reserved for the bigger decisions that require everyone's active support to implement. Four decision-making methods used by groups include consensus, majority-vote, minority-consent, and consent voting; they are discussed in the following sections.

CONSENSUS

Consensus decision making is best used when:

- The decision affects all the team members.
- The decision is considered important.
- Time is available for a group discussion.
- The team members are knowledgeable and skilled.
- The team is cohesive and the trust level is high.

During the meeting:

- Appoint a facilitator to keep the process moving.
- Ask everyone, in turn, to state his or her opinion.
- Acknowledge and answer objections.
- Test or check for consensus.
- Agree in advance how to resolve gridlock and conflict (for example: go to minority-consent).

The Supreme Court has nine judges. Unlike a jury, it does not have to achieve consensus to reach a decision. Margaret Thatcher derided decisions reached through consensus as "something no one agrees with but everyone can live with." However, consensus usually produces better decisions as long as the group has the time, motivation, and facilitation skills to make the process work.

MAJORITY-VOTE

The potential quality of, or commitment to, the decision reached through majority-vote is not as great as consensus, but gridlock is easier to avoid.

Unlike the Supreme Court, majority vote is more likely to be used when the decisions are not as important, time is limited, or when the group has not yet become a cohesive team.

Majority-vote in a team works as:

- The majority decides.
- Each person has one vote.
- Minority interests are considered.
- Team leader's vote breaks a tie.

In the event of a tie ask each person to briefly explain the rationale for his vote. Take another vote to see if anyone changed his mind based on what he heard. If the tie continues the team leader's vote determines the decision.

MINORITY-CONSENT

Minority-consent is between majority-vote and total consensus in how the decision is made. If anyone objects to the proposed decision to the extent that they will withhold their participation or block its implementation then another option must be selected. However, if the dissenting person or persons state they can live with the decision even though they may not like it or want it, the rest of group is free to adopt the decision.

In minority-consent decision making:

- Majority decides if minority (can live with the decision and) consents.
- Majority listens to and understands minority objections.
- Majority gives rationale for decision and asks for minority support.
- Minority does not block the implementation and agrees to support the final decision.

Reaching minority-consent is not as democratic as consensus, but it is more democratic than majority vote. The theory is that people know their limits even if they do not understand or support a decision reached by the majority. For example, a horse will pretty much do what you tell him to do within certain limits. However, if you try to jump over a wall that is too high the horse is going to withdraw his consent. You may not be aware of his limits, but the horse is. When the question of the wall is presented he will let you know what his limits are. If a team decision is truly unacceptable to one or more members, they have the power to block it or negotiate a modification to the decision.

CONSENT-VOTING

The concepts about consent-voting were developed by the Dutch management consultant, Gerald Endenburg, based on his experiences with the Society of Friends. Endenburg believed majority-voting inevitably creates winners and losers. The winning majority celebrates their victory while the losers leave the room grumbling; a phenomena that does little to build a sense of community. Consent voting is most effective in groups of up to fourteen people. Larger groups will take more time if everyone is heard from. Here is how it works:

> The voters write on a ballot the option or name they want and sign their names. The facilitator reads the ballots to the voters and asks everyone in turn why they voted as they did. After hearing from each voter and thanking them the facilitator asks the group, "Based on what you have heard do you want to change your vote?" The facilitator takes another tally, and announces which option has a majority. The facilitator then asks each voter in the minority, "Can you live with this decision?" or "Do you object to this decision?" If no objections are raised the majority vote is adopted. If there are objections those who have them state why. The group does some creative thinking about the objections and searches for ways to resolve them. The final result is a decision which the majority wants and the minority does not object to enough to block.

THE FOUR D'S

In any working group, a major source of confusion relates to who has the authority to decide what. There are decisions that only the manager should make. There are others that the manager wants the team to handle. Which are which? A useful shorthand is the four "D" method. The four D's stand for:

- *D-1* Decisions made by the leader. (authoritarian style)

- *D-2* Decisions made by the leader with input from staff. (consultative style)

- *D-3* Decisions made by staff with the approval or review by management. (partial delegation)

- *D-4* Decisions made in a non-hierarchical manner. The decision is made by staff without input or approval from management (delegated decisions) or it is made by management and staff together (participatory decision making) as equals.

Newer and less experienced teams will naturally make fewer D-3 or D-4 decisions. As a team develops it will shift away from D-1 and D-2 decision making towards D-3 and D-4. Except for the most self-managed of teams, certain decisions like pay raises, layoffs, disciplinary actions, or a response to a crisis, will remain D-1's. For some reason when people hear they are going to work as a team they expect that starting tomorrow all decisions will be made at the D-4 level. It is true that successful teams tend to make more decisions. However, learning to make team decisions is a skill that takes time to master.

PROBLEM TO SOLUTION

The most difficult problems are the ones where a team stays stuck and nothing changes. If problem solving does occur the effort is weak and tepid, or it is cut short by gridlock or denial. Teams get stuck for emotional reasons. The feelings may be so raw there is little chance they will talk about the problem. If the team members can talk about the issues, especially the sensitive ones, it is likely they can solve them. Many times at a team-building session I have been amazed how quickly a team shifts from being stuck in a problem to finding a solution once they express and let go of their resentments. See Chapter Six, "Conflict and Negotiation", for some ways to get past the stuck space.

Three Spaces

stuck space   problem space   solution space

TEAM PROBLEM SOLVING

A team's effectiveness in solving problems is determined by the level of synergy between the members. Groups with a high level of synergy solve more problems than they create, while the reverse is true for those with a deficit of synergy. Here is a four-step process that can produce innovative ideas and solutions:

1) Problem
   - ✓ Gather information.
   - ✓ Define the problem. (What is the core problem?)
   - ✓ Define the goal or desired outcome. (What are we really trying to do here? What do we really want? What is success?)
   - ✓ Agree on the approach or process (Ground rules, 4 D's).
   - ✓ Inventory resources and skills. (What have we got to work with?)

2) Solution
   - ✓ Brainstorm solutions.
   - ✓ Get input from everyone.
   - ✓ Select the best option.

3) Plan
   - ✓ Get organized.
   - ✓ Do action planning (Define what needs to be done).
   - ✓ Assign responsibilities, clarify roles (Who is doing what).
   - ✓ Define procedures (How it gets done).
   - ✓ Schedule time line (When things get done).
   - ✓ Define measures of success.
   - ✓ Check for understanding and agreement.
   - ✓ If possible, test and adjust the plan.

4) Implement
   - ✓ Do it. . . . !
   - ✓ Evaluate (Plus/delta model). Make adjustments. (What are we going to do differently?)

✓ Complete the project.
✓ Celebrate (Way-to-go-team!).
✓ Acknowledge and recognize team members.
✓ Reflect on the learning.
✓ Transfer lessons learned to the next project.

GATHERING DATA

The more usable information you have the better job you can do. Part of the job of gathering information is to organize it so it can be processed by the team. When collecting data ask:

- What are the essential elements of information? (What do we need to know)
- How should we collect and organize data? (Who keeps track of what)
- Are any trends or patterns anticipated?
- What does all this information mean?
- What is the big picture?
- What are we really trying to achieve?
- Does everyone have the same understanding of what is going on?

Organizing and assimilating information, drawing inspired conclusions, and then "operationalizing" those conclusions takes good analytical and communication skills. Without these skills no team can take full advantage of the data that have been collected. The challenge is not about gathering more information. It is how to best sort through, organize, analyze, and use the information we have.

DEFINING THE PROBLEM

A problem has to be acknowledged and identified before it can be solved. What appears to be the problem could be just the symptom. A brainstorming session on identifying and defining the real problem is a necessary first step. Ask the following questions to help identify the problem:

- What are the parameters or issues?
- Who owns the problem or who is affected?
- What would success/failure look like?
- What happens if the problem is bigger or smaller?
- Why is this a problem?

The theory behind the "dart board" approach is that if you ask enough questions at some point you will hit the bulls-eye. Keep asking why the problem is a problem and see where the answers lead to. If you keep asking, "Why?" you might get beyond the symptoms and uncover the root cause of the problem.

AGREEING ON THE PROCESS

Defining the problem-solving process is the next step after a problem is acknowledged. Part of defining the process includes asking:

- What resources do we have?
- How will we generate ideas and solutions?
- How will we reach a decision?
- Who is responsible for implementation?
- What concerns and interests do we have?
- What ground rules/procedures do we need?
- Are we all motivated to solve it?

BRAINSTORMING SOLUTIONS

Developing a solution to a business problem is frequently a group effort. Creativity in a group is a function of how much the members can forget about judgement and maintaining appearances. Brainstorming is about coming up with solutions using the energy of the group. A light-hearted tone that avoids critical remarks works best. Keep in mind the old French saying, "All blanket statements are false including this one." For productive brainstorming all you need is a flipchart and these guidelines:[1]

- Warm people up with a few icebreakers or "silly dillies."
- Encourage outrageous, even silly ideas.
- Focus on quantity not quality.
- Have fun: keep it light-hearted and fast paced.
- Build on each other's ideas.
- Postpone criticism and evaluation.
- Break the problem down into smaller units.
- Mind map your ideas.

Keep track of the ideas by having one person write them down on the flip chart. After all the ideas are on the board select the most useful and try to improve them.

REINVENTING THE WHEEL

There is a wealth of talent and knowledge tucked away in every organization. Getting to that talent and drawing upon the experience and expertise is the challenge. Frequently, the problems that beset one person or team have been worked through by another although the solutions were never documented. Any group large enough to be called an organization usually has at least one individual who has been around long enough to have seen it all.

That person is a sort of "corporate historian." If he does not know the answer to your question he can name someone who might. The advice of the corporate historian can save the relative newcomer many hours of effort that might have otherwise gone into "reinventing the wheel." However, some corporate historians owe their longevity to a certain reserve so you may have to seek them out.

To avoid reinventing the wheel:

- Locate the company historian(s).
- Ask for the historian's advice or where to get it.
- Create a forum to share ideas and experiences.
- Take the initiative to learn from others.
- Start trading useful tips in the team.

People enjoy teaching or advising others. Being asked is a compliment. Just use some discretion when you ask, since timing is critical. Pick a more opportune time than when your potential advisor is facing Monday morning and a pile of deadlines.

MIND MAPPING

Part of the creativity of the human mind is its ability to take a concept and make various connections to other related or even seemingly unrelated concepts. Mind mapping is a way to capture ideas on paper in the sequence that you think of them.[1]

Mind mapping will help you organize your thoughts. It might even lead to an insight that generates a breakthrough. To get started:

> Take a blank piece of paper and put a topic in the middle. The topic could be a question or provocative possibility that you are exploring. The question being mind mapped below deals with building a team. Others could be about any desirable goal, such as, increasing sales, developing a performance appraisal system, or improving quality. Each idea or concept leads to several more. Use lines to show the connections. You may be surprised how quickly the page starts to fill up with circles. After completing the mind map put the ideas in some sequence of merit, priority, or implementation depending on the subject you are working with. After culling the concepts, list what you want to do and ask the related questions of how, when, and who.

Mind mapping ways to increase teamwork:

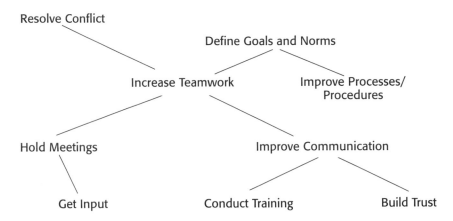

BEGINNER'S MIND

Creative problem solving breaks the boundaries that enclose your thinking so you can play with an expanded range of possibilities. During that play there is an openness to look at the problem from every side and angle. Creative solutions often come when we empty out everything including all our preconceptions and assumptions and start with what Zen masters call a "beginner's mind." This type of mind lets go of what it thinks it knows and, admitting no preconceptions, considers all possibilities. In the beginner's mind the only outlandish question is the one you fail to ask.

The more of those questions you ask the more likely you are to think of one that goes to the heart of the matter. That kind of question and the assertions that accompany it could lead to what futurists call a "paradigm shift." When this shift occurs in an industry it creates a new starting line; a line that puts all the players on a more equal footing. Thomas Edison, Alexander Bell, Henry Ford, and the Wright brothers asked the kinds of questions that led to a number of paradigm shifts. So did the people who invented the digital watch, the video tape player, and the personal computer.

Using the beginner's mind approach you need to:

- Set aside your bias and preconceptions.
- Consider factors that may seem unrelated.
- Look for new or different relationships and patterns.
- Ask, "What if. . ." Consider "Why not. . ."
- Ask for different points-of-view.
- Ask outlandish, even foolish questions.
- Make assertions that challenge accepted beliefs.
- Question your own and others' assumptions.

Our "mental map" of our world is based on our own unique perspective. The more we can allow for and include other perspectives the more complete will be the map we are dealing with. This kind of "map making" requires us to define for each other the underlying assumptions that drive our point-of-view. A conversation of this depth is a group journey of discovery. There are three prerequisites for the trip: an open mind, curiosity, and the ability to listen.

MBTI PROBLEM-SOLVING MODEL

The power of a group effort is unleashed when all the potential resources of the members are utilized. To help a group make a good decision, Isabel Briggs, one of the developers of the Myers-Briggs Type Indicator (MBTI), designed an elegant problem-solving model that draws upon the innate strengths of the different MBTI types. Any decision will be more valid if it is examined from four complementary viewpoints. It is also more likely to be supported by the entire team since all the different styles in making a decision were utilized. Take a look at Chapter Eleven, "Different Work Styles," for more information on using the MBTI. The MBTI model examines a problem from four different viewpoints:

MBTI Problem Solving Model

SENSING: Determine the exact nature of the problem. Data are gathered and evaluated impartially. Just the facts, Ma'am.

INTUITION: Let go of the facts and dream up new possibilities. There may be a number of alternatives that no one has thought of yet. Look for connections and relationships that have gone unnoticed.

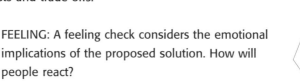

THINKING: Analyze the pros and cons of all the options. Pick the best one based on potential costs and trade-offs.

FEELING: A feeling check considers the emotional implications of the proposed solution. How will people react?

PROVOCATIVE POSSIBILITIES

During a brainstorming session there are no absolutes. Everything is up for grabs or open to questioning. There are no limitations because the possibilities are endless. The more provocative the possibilities suggested by the group, the more likely a valuable nugget or two will be extracted from the pile of suggestions. Ideas that challenge the status quo, that represent a breakthrough, are inherently provocative. Naturally, they are often dismissed as far-fetched and impractical.

For example, even as late as 1980, the idea of personal computers in the home or at work seemed ridiculous. What would people do with them even if they could afford one? Fortunately, visionaries like Steve Jobs, who founded Apple Computers, were not afraid of such a provocative possibility.

APPRECIATIVE INQUIRY

Traditional approaches to problem solving sometimes get stuck in the problem because they focus on what is not working. Appreciative inquiry is a radically different approach that looks at what is working.[2] The inquiry starts with a review of what worked so well that it created a peak experience. The participants take a common topic, pool their peak experiences, and then define the essence of that experience to each other. From that collective pool, certain themes emerge. Have the group identify and explore the most compelling theme for information and insights. Review peak experiences related to the theme and the factors that created them. From this discussion dream up "provocative propositions" that explain the reasons for these experiences. The provocative propositions are the behaviors, actions, and attitudes that have a beneficial impact in the organization.

On a scale of one to seven (seven being the most valid) have the group rate the propositions in terms of two contrasting questions on a chart like the one below:

1) To what extent do I believe this proposition would be beneficial?
2) To what extent do I believe this proposition is currently true in our organization?

For example, the proposition that, "we want each other to win" could be diagrammed below as:

Appreciative Inquiry

Rating		1	2	3	5	6	7
Ideal	We want each other to win						✓
Real	We want each other to win		✓				

In a group, examine the difference between the real and the ideal impact of each proposition. Use the difference between the two as the starting point for a cognitive leap. The mind is naturally motivated to find or develop measures that will close the gap between the real and the ideal. The appreciative inquiry process offers a unique way to unleash the excitement and energy of a group. This energy and information is used to take the group to the next level of optimal functioning available to it.

AFFINITY DIAGRAM

Some problems are so big and complex it is difficult to know where to start. An issue like how to get a new factory up to full production can involve a myriad of overlapping issues and related facts. The Affinity Diagram was developed by a Japanese anthropologist in the 1960's as a way to increase understanding of a complex system. Creating an affinity diagram works best with a small team of six to ten people. Here is how to get started:

> The team defines the issue or problem that needs attending to. The defining statement should be brief and open-ended. For example, in terms of a new factory, the issue might be achieving optimal production. Each team member has a pad of sticky notes. As they write down ideas, facts or whatever else comes to mind (one per note) concerning the issue the facilitator sticks the completed sticky notes on the wall. When the group is finished writing they get up and silently arrange the notes by categories. If a note keeps being moved between categories a duplicate is made. Each category is given a name. The facilitator leads a discussion about what the team produced. Examining the relationships within and between categories can be revealing. Depending on the outcome of the exercise, action items are assigned before the session is adjourned.

"LET'S FIND A CHAIR"

It has been said that the human mind is like a parachute; it works best when it's open. Creativity and innovation are most always the result of an open mind that has let go of preconceptions. Going outside that mental box of preconceptions is known as "divergent thinking." Encouraging that type of thinking takes some degree of alertness. Here's how one team found a way to encourage each other.

> During a team building program the phrase, "Let's find a chair," became a touchstone for a team doing the "lap sit." The task required that the members physically support each other by sitting on each other's laps, without using chairs. Back at the office this phrase reminded the team to use divergent thinking. They realized it was acceptable to look for solutions outside the traditional paradigm of how things had been done in the past. And they didn't necessarily have to limit themselves and their productivity to what they initially were given to do the job.

Your team can look for its own "chair" by asking:

- Is there another way to do this?
- How have others done it?
- What might happen if we do it differently?
- What resources would help?
- What do we have to lose or gain by trying?

DECIDE AND IMPLEMENT

It takes work to make a serious decision that everyone can agree to or at least live with. If a major decision is reached quickly, unanimously, and with little debate, chances are, it was a product of "group-think." Group-think occurs when people are not willing to voice their doubts or when they are caught up in a strong emotion that is affecting the entire group.

A viable option holds up under the following questions:

- Would an outsider say the decision makes sense?
- Has everyone given his or her input?
- Are there elements we have not considered?
- Are the benefits worth the risks/costs?
- Can we sell the decision to the rest of our organization?

TESTING FOR CONSENSUS—FIVE FINGERS

The five-finger model is a handy tool to test for consensus on a proposed decision. There are five possible responses to a proposal that team members can make to show their approval or disapproval.

The responses that show the level of consensus are:

- *One finger.* Enthusiastic, let's do it!
- *Two fingers.* The pros outweigh the cons.
- *Three fingers.* Neutral, I accept the group's decision.
- *Four fingers.* Objections, I am not comfortable with this decision.
- *Five fingers.* No way, I will block this decision unless changes are made.

Have the team members write the number on a piece of paper or hold up the number of fingers that indicates what they think about the proposed decision. The decision reached is the one with the most ones and twos and no fours or fives.

ACTION ITEMS

After the hard work of making a decision is over people are eager to leave the room. But before they go out the door and have a chance to change their minds, it is good idea to assign "action items" that include due dates. Otherwise, the decision may never translate into action. Responsibilities are clear when all the blanks below are filled in:

ACTION PLAN			
ASSIGNED TO	TASK	DONE BY	NOTES
Sally	Call contacts	3/7	
Bob	Buy and install new software	3/9	
Jim	Draft new brochure	3/4	
Mary	Provide last year's sales data	3/6	
Sam	Procurement orders new equipment	4/2	
Sue	Organize next meeting	4/3	

EVALUATE & ADJUST

"Plan your work and work your plan," is a well-known adage. However, no plan is perfect. Adjustments need to be made in order to get the results you want. The questions to ask at this stage include:

- What are the performance standards and milestones?
- How are we doing compared to those standards?
- What part of our plan is not working?
- What should we do differently?
- What additional resources are needed?
- Are we making the most of this decision?

Harry Truman reportedly said, "doing the right thing is easy; the hard part is deciding the right thing to do." When we don't know, deciding not to decide is a legitimate choice. A lot of energy is wasted in agonizing about a decision that's been made, especially if it is too late to change it. Before we make a major decision, we ask ourselves if this is a choice we can live with. Whether the decision is personal or professional, after we decide, the question becomes: "Are we making the most of the choice we made?"

BENCHMARKING

Benchmarking, a term familiar to programmers and systems analysts, is how the performance standards of computer systems are measured. The benchmark is the set of standards that the system has to meet to be certified as fully operational. The highest benchmark naturally comes from the systems with the best performance. Not surprisingly, given the all-pervasive influence of computers, professionals in other fields borrowed the term.

Benchmarking now also means the process of drawing upon the best programs and techniques, validated by objective standards of performance, when designing any new system or program. Benchmarking can be applied to training, manufacturing, social services, or any field with measurable goals or standards. Programs or products that have the greatest level of success are used as yardsticks to measure your own performance. Organizations use both internal and external sources to collect this information. The process of sharing information allows divergent or even competing groups to learn from each other's successes and failures. Benchmarking requires an organization to do the following:

- Clearly define performance goals and standards.
- Develop objective performance measures.
- Develop and maintain collaborative networks that cross organizational or corporate boundaries.
- Conduct research, front-end and cost-benefit analyses.
- Share information with potential or actual competitors.
- Systematically evaluate progress towards the stated goals.

Section IV
Team-Building Programs

10
Organizational Interventions

Broderbund

If we don't hang together we will hang separately.

COMMON SAYING

Organizational problems that affect performance and morale take on a life of their own. The source of the problems and what to do about them can seem frustratingly obscure. Most managers want to know what their people are really thinking so they can do something to address their concerns. However, fear, distrust, or excessive politeness can hinder the flow of essential information between staff and management. When this occurs a third party is needed that both sides trust enough to confide in.

ORGANIZATIONAL DEVELOPMENT

Doing something different in an organization that can bring about an improvement is called an "intervention." Management consultants in the field of Organizational Development (OD) base their interventions on the action/research model. Any action taken is based on facts uncovered through research. An effective intervention requires collecting enough information to determine the nature of the problem before attempting to do something about it. An objective observer can look at a situation with a fresh pair of eyes and see what others have missed because they are too caught up in the dynamics of the group.

Kurt Lewin, commonly cited as the father of OD, escaped Hitler's Germany in the 1930's and immigrated to the United States. Lewin brought with him a keen interest in studying the dynamics of autocratic and democratic management styles. Lewin was especially interested in the impact these different styles have on an organization. He researched organizational change by drawing upon concepts found in the behavioral and political sciences.

ACTION/RESEARCH

Lewin's theories influenced John Collier, the United States Commissioner of Indian Affairs from 1933 to 1945. In Collier's efforts to reform his agency and improve relations between Native American tribes and the Federal government he conducted studies to determine the "central areas of needed action."[1]

He coined the phrase, Action/Research, based on his belief that there is, "no action without research and no research without action." The field of Organizational Development has evolved a great deal since Collier's day, but the concept of "finding out what is going on before you do anything" is still with us. One of the more popular approaches to Action/Research has seven stages:

1) Contracting for Partnership
2) Data Collection
3) Data Analysis
4) Management Feedback
5) Team Feedback

6) Implementation of Changes
7) Evaluation.

CONTRACTING FOR PARTNERSHIP

Organizational development interventions are most successful when the consultant and the client form a collaborative partnership dedicated to finding the answers to the challenges faced by the client. An intervention is likely to flounder when the consultant thinks he or she has all of the answers instead of some of the questions. Recommendations, unilaterally developed by a consultant and deposited on the client's desk in the form of a nicely bound report, will do little more than gather dust. Most teams have the knowledge concerning their best course of action. What they need is help in identifying and articulating that knowledge and then translating it into action.

As part of building a partnership it is wise to set realistic expectations. The client and consultant need to reach a clear understanding about each other's role. Human behavior is too unpredictable for any consultant to guarantee that a group of people who have been fighting with each other will suddenly get along like a big happy family. Managing expectations is especially important when the boss wants you to "fix" his staff. His employees, not surprisingly, think it is the boss who needs to be fixed. Actually, both sides need to let go of blame and consider how they can change.

The perennial question is: "How long will it take?" or "Can we get this done in a half day?" The consultant's response is: "There are no short-term solutions to long-term problems." A quick, one-time, fix is not likely to resolve organizational problems once and for all. In reality, building a team is an on-going process that is part of the daily routine of work. What a consultant can promise is to do the things that are within his control, such as, research the issues affecting the team, facilitate the problem-solving discussions about those issues and, as needed, train the client personnel in the skills required to work together.

DATA COLLECTION

An outside consultant has more latitude to gather data than management because he is less bound by office politics, conflicting roles, and fear of hidden agendas. Collecting data is done objectively, through interviews and the gathering of statistics, and subjectively, by walking around to get a feel for what is going on in the workplace.[2]

How information is gathered includes: private interviews, focus groups, written surveys, and review of office procedures and pertinent statistics. Each method has it advantages and disadvantages. Private interviews provide more data but are time consuming. Focus groups are not as time consuming, but may be limited by a lack of anonymity. Questionnaires provide privacy, but can miss the real issues affecting the organization. Performance statistics and written procedures are informative, yet provide only part of the picture.

Personal interviews that solicit opinions and criticisms are conducted on the basis of complete anonymity. When anonymity is assured most employees will talk more directly and honestly with a trusted outsider than they will to their coworkers or boss. The interviews last anywhere from 30 minutes to several hours. The consultant does not reveal the individual source of the information offered in response to his questions. However, he makes it clear to that source that the information provided will not be held in confidence, but will be reported so something can be done about it. The questions are generally asked in the same manner and sequence to each person. Typical questions include:

- How does management help you in your work?
- How does management hinder you in your work?
- If you had a magic wand and could make any changes you wanted to make in the organization what would they be?
- If your boss was an old friend you wanted to help succeed, what would you tell her?

- What causes you the most stress at work?
- What do you like most about your job?
- Why do you think I was brought in to conduct these interviews?

DATA ANALYSIS

As the data are collected the consultant sifts through it with an eye for general trends. Specific facts are useful to the extent they can be extrapolated back to general causes. What is the most common and recurring complaint? Does it point to a general issue or pattern that affects everyone in the organization? The list of potential issues includes leadership, collective goals, communication skills, equipment, personal and structural conflict, technical knowledge, general procedures, relationships, and roles. The consultant's task is to identify the issues that others have felt but were unable to articulate.

However, before he can discover the right answer the right question must be asked. The consultant tries to ask the questions that define what the problem really is, instead of what it appears to be. If you can name it you can tame it. What seems at first to be the source of the problem, either an organizational, personal or technical issue, may be a symptom of some more central and harder-to-define issue. With good coaching, the team members themselves can best clarify and answer the questions that will lead to a breakthrough. Chances are, no one ever asked them about their point-of-view, an omission that increased the odds they would be part of the problem instead of part of the solution.

MANAGEMENT FEEDBACK

Consultants who unilaterally develop a set of recommendations run the risk of being caught between an angry staff resisting any "answer" imposed from above and an impatient manager who demands an "answer" that will bring instant relief. A better approach is to use the collected information as a starting point for problem solving with the client. After all the interviews are conducted, the responses are grouped by topics and analyzed for trends and patterns. The findings are discussed first with management and then, presented in a meeting with the work group. Giving the feedback first to the team manager helps him or her prepare for any unanticipated bad news. The manager needs time to process the findings before convening the entire team, otherwise, presenting the findings in an open meeting could result in an unpleasant surprise for both the manager and the consultant.

In certain cases the staff may be ready to conduct problem solving as a group but management is not. This reluctance is very understandable. Dealing with a room full of angry people is not for the faint of heart. However, when crossing a mountain stream it is best to keep going until you get to the other side. If people can talk about the problems they can solve them. Undisclosed problems are the proverbial elephants in the room. Everyone knows they are there. It takes a lot of effort to step around them. But no one says anything about them. So nothing changes for the better.

TEAM FEEDBACK SESSION

The function of the feedback session with the entire team is three-fold: to discuss the findings, open channels of communication, and develop strategies that help management and staff work together to deal with the challenges they face. When tensions are extremely high, facilitating a group meeting in a productive manner takes a high degree of skill. If employees are angry and cynical about the past, any effort to plan positive actions for the future will be resisted. In a manner that fits the situation the bitter feelings of cynicism and despair have to be acknowledged before an agenda of realistic problem solving can be introduced.

Team feedback sessions are best held at a conference center located far enough away from the office to discourage running back to "check on things." The sessions can last from one to several days. Two days are considered minimal for most teams.

Using flip charts the findings from the personal interviews are grouped under different topics and posted on the walls. At the beginning of the session the data are presented either by the manager or by the facilitator, depending on the needs of the group. Some facilitators quote the interviews verbatim. Others abstract what was said. Before the findings are discussed the team develops a list of ground-rules to guide the discussion. During the session useful information is shared and feedback is given and received.

This exchange of information creates more mutual understanding and insight, thereby helping to resolve old misunderstandings. It is important that the mutual understanding be both emotional and intellectual. The discussion of these issues also helps create a psychological release, a process started in the private interviews, that leads to healing of team relationships. Once the information has been shared, explained and understood by everyone, problem solving is conducted. Instead of seeing each other as the problem, the problems are objectified so that the team discusses, as a team, what is not working and what to do about it.

LEARNING HOW TO FISH

Throughout the feedback session the consultant helps the team focus on how it does things—especially the ways and means used to make decisions, solve problems, and resolve conflict.

Certain processes and behaviors are brought to awareness, discussed and dropped or modified so as to remove blocks to team productivity. In the spirit of teaching a person how to fish instead of giving him a fish, the consultant helps the team learn how to conduct its own process. Brief, just-in-time classes can help the team develop its skills in meeting management, communication, conflict resolution, and other pertinent areas.

IMPLEMENTATION

Excitement and creative energies are unleashed as the team members gain a better understanding of how to work with each other.

The next step is to figure out how to take what was learned and experienced and apply it back in the office. Part of taking it back is in developing a list of agreements and actions everyone can support or at least live with. Names are assigned and time lines agreed upon for any action items. Follow-up meetings are scheduled to assess the progress towards accomplishing the action items and implementing the agreements. Obtaining input from everyone is vital. Measures proposed and adopted by other teams who have gone through this process include:

- Team vision, mission and values statement.
- Team goals and measures of success.
- Team norms or guidelines.
- Revised procedures and systems.
- Interpersonal and team agreements.
- Redefined roles and responsibilities.
- Action items on specific issues.
- Training in interpersonal/teamwork skills.
- Introduction of new technology or processes.

TAKE-AWAYS

The most important "take-away" from an off-site may be intangible. Just being able to have an open and honest discussion about the issues within the group can have a profound impact. People are usually reluctant to let go of their judgments and perceptions about something that happened to them until they feel emotionally understood.

The spoken truth (acknowledged as one's own perspective) is a powerful tonic. When a group finds it can discuss sensitive and difficult subjects and not fall apart, a sense of trust begins to develop. That trust enhances communication between all the group members. It might be hard to pinpoint when or how the shift occurs but it does. And that shift in attitude enables the group to focus on the present instead of grouse about the past or worry about the future.

EVALUATION

A program is more likely to be successful if it has clear objectives and a means to evaluate progress towards those objectives. The success of most interventions is seldom measured in a scientifically controlled manner; that measurement takes more money and time than most companies are willing to spend. It is useful and fairly inexpensive to use assessments such as written evaluations and to collect anecdotal stories. More objective measures such as measuring task performance, absenteeism, and turnover are usually not applied to management teams. With any evaluation of a program it is important to keep in mind that successful interventions are more than a one-shot effort. A team-building retreat represents a beginning, not a completed, process of change.

PACKAGED PROGRAMS

In contrast to the team-building intervention based on internal research and assessment, a number of national training companies offer packaged team-building programs that are generic in nature. The programs combine written materials, videotapes, and lectures with interactive exercises between the participants. The advantage of the off-the-shelf approach is the relative ease of involving large numbers of participants, compared to an OD intervention.

Another advantage, like eating at McDonald's, is that no matter where you are geographically, you pretty much know what you are getting in terms of the training design and the basic skill level of the trainer. A significant disadvantage of a packaged program is that the design may not actually address the real issues you are trying to deal with or even uncover. The better programs give the instructor/consultant a high degree of latitude in these areas.

But even with the best programs you may not get the chance to interview a number of potential trainers and pick the one most suited to your needs. As with any team-building intervention, the skillfulness of the facilitator is a crucial factor in determining its eventual success.

You might expect that the more customized the design of a program, the more you have to pay for it. However, that is not always the case. Independent consultants and small training companies do not usually spend a great deal of money on advertising and other overhead. They specialize in developing programs and often design and deliver them for less than the off-the-shelf variety from a large company. The number of generic training programs offered on the market changes frequently. The best way to find what is available is to peruse the advertisements in a recent copy of "TRAINING" or the "Training and Development Journal."

11
Different Work Styles

Broderbund

Treat others as they want to be treated.

Have you ever noticed how some individuals regard other people as imperfect versions of themselves? Most of us find it frustrating that the people we live and work with are not more like us. You may have seen this happen at work. Bill wonders why Joe wants to talk all the time. Joe, however, thinks Bill doesn't like him. He always acts like he is too busy to take time for a chat. Bill believes Joe is too disorganized. He gets things done but without a schedule or a usable filing system. Joe cannot understand why Bill is so uptight. He always wants a decision right away and hates it when Joe tries to make any changes. Do these complaints sound familiar? If they are it is because the people involved do not realize that their interpersonal friction is due to different styles of working and not from some deliberate lack of consideration or competence.

STYLES AS TYPES

An effective team is one that can make use of all its human resources without letting judgments or misunderstandings get in the
way. It is easier to accept different perspectives when they are
seen as "typological" instead of toxic. Knowing why a colleague's
point-of-view or way of doing things always tends to be organi-
cally different than your own can turn a potential liability into a
permanent asset. The Myers-Briggs Type Inventory (MBTI) helps
a team appreciate the personal differences that define the way the
members relate to the world and each other.

FOUR PAIRS OF STYLES

The differences and similarities between us run deeper than race,
culture, or gender. According to MBTI there are four pairs of contrasting psychological traits that define our personal style:

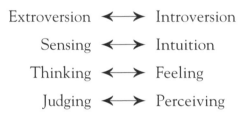

The preferences of one style over another are preferences in
the same way you prefer to use your right hand over your left. You
can use your left hand for the same tasks as your right, but it feels
awkward if you are right-handed. The sixteen psychological types
defined by MBTI are based on the responses to four types of questions about how we live our lives. The answers to these questions
indicate our preference for one style over another. The four pairs
of preferences are explained as:

1) *Extroversion (E) versus Introversion (I).* Where do you like
   to focus your attention; inside yourself in the world of ideas
   or outside yourself with relationships?

2) *Sensing (S) versus Intuition (N)*. How do you prefer to acquire information; with your senses or with your intuition?

3) *Thinking (T) versus Feeling (F)*. How do you make decisions or form opinions; by logical thinking or by how you or others feel?

4) *Judgement (J) versus Perception (P)*. How do you organize your life; in an orderly and structured fashion or with spontaneity and openness?

All MBTI preferences are just preferences. None of them are more correct or valid than any of the others. They do not measure competence or intelligence.

The degree to which one preference is dominant over its opposite varies from person to person. Few people completely favor one preference over another. Each preference has particular advantages, as well as, potential shortcomings. However, these preferences are "hard-wired" in our personality. For most of us they change very little over our lifetimes.

EXTROVERSION VERSUS INTROVERSION

What is your idea of a good weekend? If reading a book always seems more appealing than going to a party, it is likely you are more of an introvert than an extrovert. These two contrasting traits are really about how you are energized, internally or externally. Extroverts gain energy when they are interacting with others; introverts do not. After socializing awhile, introverts want to go off and be alone so they can recharge themselves. Extroverts are attracted by the outer world. Introverts are more interested in the inner world of ideas and imagination. Extroverts discover what they are thinking as they speak. Introverts are "fore-thinkers"—preferring to think a few seconds before talking. Extroverts are uncomfortable with long pauses. Introverts welcome some silence so they can think about what they are going to say next. The general population has slightly more extroverts than introverts. A few guidelines can smooth the process when these two different types work together.

Extroverts working with introverts should:

- Put it in writing.
- Be patient—allow time for reflection.
- Interact one-on-one.
- Ask—Wait—Listen.
- Don't assume silence is consent.
- Respect private time and space.

Introverts working with extroverts should:

- Show energy and interest.
- Speak out—especially at meeting.
- Express their thoughts, feelings, and ideas.
- Don't assume it's obvious.
- Learn to interrupt the extroverts.

Teams are most effective when they get input from everyone. The introverts have great ideas, maybe even the best ideas. However, those ideas do not get used because they do not get expressed. The productivity of team meetings will make a quantum leap when the extroverts do three things in succession: 1) Stop talking. 2) Ask the introverts what they think. 3) Listen carefully, without interrupting, to the responses.

SENSING VERSUS INTUITION

A common type in the United States are the extroverted sensors who are outward, doing and pragmatic. These traits are reflected in the general culture of North American society. Sensors take data and live in the present moment. They are practical, realistic and focused on the here and now. Sgt. Friday on the television show, Dragnet, was famous for the line, "Just the facts, Ma'am." People like Friday who focus on the details are known as sensors. Sensors make great witnesses and reporters because of their awareness of details. They pride themselves on the results they achieve as practical and action orientated people. Their "typological" counterparts, intuitives, are more interested in the theoretical meaning of facts, than the facts per se.

Intuitives like to think about the "big picture." Their personal style is similar to the one portrayed by the television detective, Colombo, a man who loved to conceptualize about the hidden relationships implied by a set of possibilities and reach inspired conclusions. His favorite line. "Just one more thing. . ." was often the precursor to a cognitive leap that solved the crime.

Sensors' strong points include the ability to:

- Go step-by-step.
- Read the fine print.
- Pay attention to details and schedules.
- Control expenditures and other resources
- Follow directions.

Intuitives bring to a team:

- New ideas and new possibilities.
- A grasp of the big picture.
- Anticipation of future trends and implications.
- A flair for the dramatic.

A team of intuitives would do well to bring a sensor on board to keep things focused on reality when they start dreaming about building the next space station. A team of sensors needs an intuitive or two to keep the team from trapping itself in limited thinking.

Sensors working with intuitives should:

- Start with the big picture before the details.
- Entertain possibilities/options before facts.
- Delay any negative response to a lack of facts.
- Encourage inspiration and thinking big.
- Go easy on the details.

Intuitives working with sensors should:
- Consider the details and the facts.
- Reconsider the details you may have missed.
- Be definite, precise, and explicit.
- Explain your conclusions step-by-step.
- Focus on the practical here and now.

A pair of professionals managing an R&D program were always in contention with each other. The one who was an intuitive liked to focus on the implications of the different aspects of the program and how that affected the overall scope of the work. The other, a sensor, preferred to focus on the statistics used in managing the program. Whenever they produced a report, the discussions often became heated before they could reach mutually acceptable conclusions. Despite their differences or because they found a way to use them, the program was accomplished under budget and on time.

THINKING VERSUS FEELING

The distinction between thinkers and feelers has a lot to do with how each type makes a decision. Thinkers collect data in a systematic way, analyze the data, and then decide. Feelers are more likely to decide first based on a "gut feeling" and then go out and look for the facts to support that decision. In the television show Star Trek, Spock's classic line, "That's not logical, Captain," is that of a thinker who objectively analyzes every situation. Thinkers value task performance, fairness, and clear standards. They might not even notice if someone has had their feelings hurt by one of their blunt critiques. Feelers consider how others will be affected by their decisions or actions. Instead of criticizing, they are ready to show their appreciation. Feelers will be the first to notice when the atmosphere in the group tenses up. Harmony is more important to them than clarity. The natural strengths of thinkers include the ability to:

- Discipline, confront, or fire others if needed.
- State and analyze the facts objectively.
- Make the hard decisions.
- Organize activities.
- Be firm, consistent, and stay the course.

Feeling types play important roles in a team for:

- Harmonizing and bringing people together.
- Persuading, encouraging, and selling.
- Concern for individual well being.
- Appreciating and motivating others.
- Understanding office politics.

Thinkers are naturally good at handling things and ideas, but need the assistance of the feeler when it comes to handling people. Feelers can help develop the social relationships that bind the team together, but may lose sight of the task that was the reason for the team in the first place. Feelers tend to put people before the task, while thinkers do the opposite. Optimal teamwork requires a balanced consideration of both factors.

Thinkers working with feelers should:

- Get to know the person.
- Make people feel important.
- Appeal to the human impact.
- Ask questions concerning the feelings of others.
- Show appreciation and approval.

Feelers working with thinkers should:

- Deal with task performance issues first.
- Use structure, logic, and sequencing.
- Define pros and cons.
- Avoid appealing to sentiments.
- Appeal to logic and fairness.

In the corporate or government world the thinkers seem to out-number the feelers by ten to one. It can be lonely for the strong feeler who knows he feels out of place but is not sure why. At a training session for one company the participants were divided into two groups, thinkers (30 people) and feelers (two people). The two groups were asked what they needed from each other. With total sincerity one of the feelers, a male manager, looked at the other group and said, "Please love me!"

JUDGEMENT VERSUS PERCEPTION

The difference between judgers and perceivers is in the way they evaluate the world around them. Judgers will clearly define their opinions, positive or negative, about something, be it a movie, a current event, or a person. Perceivers are more likely to acknowl-edge the facts without making a personal assessment. They like to consider all sides of an issue and may have trouble reaching any final conclusion. Judgers will push to bring closure to a process and reach a decision; if not now, at least by the close of business.

Judgers get upset with perceivers for never deciding and chang-ing things at the last minute. Perceivers can tolerate a lot of am-biguity. They are flexible, curious, adaptable, and like to keep their options open. Judgers prefer the order and structure that helps them control events. Perceivers are more content to respond to events as they unfold.

A classic example of judgers in action was the young couple who planned a trip around the world for a year. They sent a six-page, typed schedule to all their friends that specified what city they would be in for each day of the 365 days of their trip. In contrast, a "perceiving" couple, taking off to see the world, might not know the next country they would go to after their first stop.

Judgers bring to a team the ability to:

- Organize and plan.
- Manage schedules and time.

- Follow through to completion.
- Provide clear opinions.
- Decide and commit to a course of action.

Perceivers contribute to a group with their:

- Flexibility in responding to new requirements.
- Adaptability to conflicting demands.
- Ability to work under pressure and deadlines.
- Curiosity and sense of fun.
- Openness to new opportunities.

A team comprised of judgers could suffer from tunnel vision and might cling to plans and procedures that need to be changed. A team of perceivers has the flexibility to make changes, but might try to keep their options open past the point when a decision should be made.

Judgers working with Perceivers should:

- Maintain flexibility.
- Be patient with a lack of structure.
- Accept ambiguity.
- Consider other sides of an issue (shades of gray).
- Discuss options.
- Be patient with decision making process.
- Allow for spontaneity and fun.

Perceivers working with Judgers should:

- Focus on the plan.
- Be mindful of time.
- Make a decision. Be decisive.
- Stay focused on the task.
- Take a stand.
- No surprises.
- Discuss qualifications.
- Respect the need for structure and closure.

A perceiving manager could not figure out why his judging staff was so upset by even minor changes. "Why can't they be more flexible?" he asked his peers. Changes, even last minute ones, had to be expected as part of doing business. However, to his staff, any change seemed capricious and unwarranted. By agreeing to give more warning he was able to reduce some of the angst about the ambiguity inherent in their environment.

"TYPOLOGICAL" CONFLICTS

Personal conflicts have a certain predictability according to Myers-Briggs. When differences are seen as "typological" instead of personal, the damaging effects of conflict are easier to avoid. To understand someone "typologically" as well as idiomatically is to know "where he or she are coming from." Some typical conflicts that spring up between the four pairs of different preferences include:

Extroverts Versus Introverts

Extroverts are likely to feel rejected when an introverted friend withdraws seeking the tonic of solitude. Introverts can feel imposed upon by the desire of the extrovert for interaction. This classic conflict happens throughout the world when the introverted spouse comes home to the extroverted spouse at the end of the day. If the introverted spouse has been "extroverting" at work all day, she may want to be alone at the end of the day. If the extroverted spouse works at home he may have been alone all day—fueling his already strong desire to spend some time extroverting. Since people tend to resent differences instead of understand them, these dueling preferences often result in confusion and hurt feelings.

Sensors Versus Intuitives

Intuitive types are sometimes considered "flaky" in a society of pragmatic sensors. Sensors believe their intuitive counterparts are impractical and unconcerned with the facts. Intuitives feel that sensors are overly concerned with details and miss the big picture. From their side, sensors feel frustrated by the lack of specificity from an intuitive when they need directions. For example, a sensing daughter with an intuitive mother was often mystified by the instructions her mother gave for cooking. Mom's style of throwing things together with a bit of this or that made no sense to the daughter who needed the step-by-step instructions that a cookbook would offer.

Thinkers Versus Feelers

People with a strong preference for thinking can perceive feeling types as irrational and overly sensitive. Those with a strong preference for feeling sometimes regard thinkers as cold and inconsiderate.

Judgers Versus Perceivers

Perceivers can see judgers as uptight, with strong needs for control. Judgers think the perceivers' free wheeling style is unorganized or even irresponsible.

PROFESSIONAL MISUNDERSTANDING

The potential for misunderstanding extends to the related professions the various MBTI types will be attracted to. The engineers (introverts, sensors, judgers) need for precision will strike the marketers (extroverts, intuitives, perceivers) as overly restrictive in what they can promise a customer. The accountants' need for order (introverts, thinkers and judgers) will run counter to the tendency of sales (extroverts, feelers and perceivers) to estimate and extrapolate. Neither side is wrong in the approach it uses; each just has different approaches. Acknowledging and appreciating these differences puts the predictable conflicts in a new context.

GROWTH POTENTIAL

Our dominant functions represent the areas we prefer to use the most. And the more we practice a preference the more proficient we become at it. The behaviors that are not so easy for us are termed inferior functions. When under stress, our ability to function in these areas takes a nosedive. For example, a person whose inferior function is "sensing" will have more difficulty keeping track of things or details when the pressures of meeting a deadline begin to build up. Developing our inferior function is where the greatest growth lies. According to Carl Jung, ecstatic experiences take place through your inferior function because it holds the most potential within you that has been accessed the least.

However, too much of anything, especially a growth opportunity, can be just too much. A lack of clarity about your own preferences is an invitation for stress. For instance, a person with a strong preference for introverted activities who takes an extroverted job, such as sales, is likely to experience a higher degree of job-related stress. This is not unlike a right-handed person being forced to write with his left hand. A person can do it but the added effort may be exhausting. The "falsification of type" means a person is thinking and acting in ways that fail to reflect who he really is. A person has to who know who he is before he can seek opportunities that make full use of his real strengths.

INSTRUMENT RELIABILITY

The MBTI inventory is considered to be more than 90 percent accurate, which is a high degree of validity considering 65 percent is the norm in social science research. However, the MBTI should not be blindly relied upon. Like any instrument, it is only as good as the information it is given. That information can be skewed by what a person is going through on the day the inventory was taken or by other environmental factors. Cultural considerations can influence the outcome as well. The changes in our society in regard to gender roles have also shown up in the Myers-Briggs. Until a few years ago, 65% to 70% of women were "feelers" while men were predominantly "thinkers." Now the percentages are almost evenly distributed between the genders.

IMPLEMENTATION

The first step in utilizing the MBTI for team building is to have the members of your team take the inventory. You can contact the author of this book who is a certified MBTI trainer to conduct a program for your organization. You can also contact the Center for Applications of Psychological Type or the Association for Psychological Type for the name of a certified Myers-Briggs consultant in your area. The inventory can be administered in less than an hour. Just knowing your Myers-Briggs Type Indicator and a general idea of what that means is not likely to do much for your team. Schedule a training session so a trainer can interpret the indicators and explain how they predict the dynamics between the different types in your office.

The organizational chart takes on an expanded meaning when people begin to understand how their preferences affect the interactions between team members. Some people have even been inspired to have their MBTI type engraved on a nameplate so they can display it on their desk.

USING DIFFERENT STYLES

In any workplace dealing with different styles is unavoidable. The challenge is to deal with them as something to be utilized instead of ignored or argued about. Using differences wisely gives a team a competitive advantage. A team made up of people with different work styles is likely to out perform one that does not have or does not make use of its diversity of type. A team with all the same type is more prone to fall into the trap of "group think" and either overlook new possibilities or fail to adhere to budgets and schedules.

THE DISC SYSTEM

A number of personality inventory systems are being offered that are easy to learn and use. Carlson Learning Systems markets a personality profile known as DISC. The instrument measures four traits or styles people use to interact with others. The four traits are:

- Dominance .... *Extrovert/Task Focused*
- Influence .... *Extrovert/People Focused*
- Steadiness .... *Introvert/People Focused*
- Conscientiousness .... *Introvert/Task Focused*

Each person will score higher in one of these traits than the others. As you might suspect, the person who scores highest in the dominance trait is likely to be someone who seeks a leadership position. Influencers are more persuasive in their style of relating to others and are often attracted to careers like sales where they can use their people skills. Steady persons are team players who prefer structure and routine and are consistent and predictable in their work habits. Conscientiousness persons like to focus on the details and seek to maintain quality and accuracy in their work.

Depending on the degree to which one trait is greater than the other, the DISC system describes different roles where an individual's natural inclinations could best be fulfilled. One feature of the DISC system is its simplicity. A team can gain a number of useful insights after working with the instrument for a couple of hours. Sales groups in particular find DISC useful in understanding different buying styles.

12
Ropes Course

Team Building Associates

Being challenged in life is inevitable,
being defeated is optional.

ROGER CRAWFORD

Do just once what others say you can't do and you
will never pay attention to their limitations again.

JAMES COOK

A ropes course is a series of individual challenges and group prob-lem-solving activities that develop individual confidence and teamwork skills. There are three possible components to a course. They are:

1) *High Ropes.* In these events you are up in the trees, riding a "Zip Line" or traversing two parallel cables dubbed the "Postman's Walk" or as the photo above shows, taking the leap of faith off the "Pamper Pole." The events are any-where from 15 to 40 feet above the ground. Most high ropes

events focus on individual challenge and fostering self-esteem. In the "Climbing Wall" or the "Quad Wobble" you can practice teamwork under challenging conditions with two or three other teammates.

2) *Low Ropes.* Low ropes challenge the team to negotiate a common obstacle. The action could take place less than a foot off the ground or as much as 14 feet as the team tries to scale "The Wall" relying only on each other.

3) *Team Problem-Solving Activities.* The props for team problem-solving activities are portable. Most of the activities can be conducted indoors as well as outside. In a typical activity, such as "Bridge It," the team is on the ground, working together with several planks of wood and cinder blocks to construct a bridge across an area considered contaminated by "poisonous peanut butter." Teams learn a lot about themselves and teamwork as they strive to complete their task within the allotted time.

Icebreakers and warm-up games are conducted at the start of and during a course to help prepare the team for learning. A course might have aspects of all three components or just one. Which components are selected and how much one is emphasized over another depends on what the client wants to take away from the program.

TYPES OF PROGRAMS

There are three approaches towards team building that use one or more of the three components of a ropes course. These approaches are:

1) *Team Spirit.* These courses offer a shared experience to foster trust and better communication between the participants. The participants could be from the same organization but not necessarily from the same team or office. The emphasis

is on the activities for their own sake. The activities, especially the high ropes activities are conducted in a "rah rah" manner that generate a lot of emotion and excitement. The support and applause of the team for each member as he or she tackles a high ropes event creates a strong sense of camaraderie in a surprisingly short amount of time.

2) *Intact Team Development.* The purpose of the course is to strengthen the interpersonal dynamics of the team. Group problem-solving activities, such as the "Bridge It" mentioned above, are used to create metaphorical experiences that reveal how the team members work together back at the office. After each activity there is a discussion about what occurred and what changes should be made to achieve a higher level of performance. The learning comes not only from doing the activities, but from the insights shared in the discussions after each activity.

3) *Learning Laboratory.* This approach is for groups that are not intact teams, but have come together for the purpose of learning more about teamwork, leadership, and the related skills of feedback, listening, conflict management, and problem solving. Working in a team of eight to twelve members, each participant has a chance to practice his leadership and interpersonal skills and receive the feedback of the group in a supportive environment.

TIME OUT

Intact work teams go through the ropes course to identify and develop behaviors and attitudes that optimize the collective force of the team. This requires some degree of risk taking. It is not always easy, or comfortable, to surface and discuss issues that adversely affect you or your team. The events on the course offer a team experiential metaphors that replicate the dynamics of the workplace. Whatever happens at the office or home is usually faithfully recapitulated during the event, but at the rate of high-speed photography. Like a coach during a football game, the facilitator calls a "time out" so the team can make the changes needed to win the game. The point of the discussions held after each event is to understand and improve the process the team uses to make decisions and solve problems. Ideally, the entire course provides a context where significant interpersonal learning takes place. As the sequence of the training unfolds each learning builds upon the other, forming a staircase to greater competency and success.

KURT HAHN

The first ropes course was built by the British Commandos during WWII to develop small unit leadership and teamwork skills. Kurt Hahn, an exiled German aristocrat, included the ropes course as part of a survival training he designed for British sailors. After the war, he founded a program to develop the character of young people through outdoor experiences. Hahn called his new program, Outward Bound, an expression used by British sailors when they were leaving the relative safety of the harbor to face the hazards of submarine infested seas. Although most of the ropes have been replaced with aircraft cables, the name stuck when Hahn brought Outward Bound to the United States.[1]

CHALLENGE BY CHOICE

A new range of growth and healing is possible when a person decides to stretch beyond self-imposed limits. It is empowering to do something you did not think you could do. No one on a ropes course is pressured to do an event. Each activity, especially on the high ropes, is "challenge by choice." Participants are asked to take responsibility for their own level of participation. They learn they can ask for and receive the support and encouragement of their peers. Action, followed by celebration of that action by others, makes a deep impression on the self concept.

DEFINING SUCCESS

The sweetest success comes from achieving the goals you set for yourself; not those someone else has set for you. Participants in the course are asked to define success for themselves and for their team. It is essential that the participants take responsibility for the learning they want to achieve. Any goal that is a "stretch" is valid. Comparing your capabilities to those of another is not relevant. Based on the old principle that if you know where you are going you are more likely to get there—defining your own success will help motivate you to achieve it.

PRACTICE WITH A NET

In any group, when people spend time together, concerns about trust, control, and communication inevitably surface. The way you experience your life in the workplace or at home will also be played out on the ropes course. The difference is the atmosphere of emotional safety established by the facilitator and maintained by the group. New behaviors and attitudes can be tested and practiced in this kind of social atmosphere. Effective teamwork is established upon the bedrock of trust. When relevant thoughts and feelings are shared honestly and respectfully within the group the impact is far-reaching and beneficial. As trust and confidence increase a team becomes ready to tackle the more challenging events and intractable issues.

ACTION/REFLECTION

Ropes course facilitators work with their groups using the action/ reflection model. At least one facilitator is assigned to a small group of participants. The ideal size is about eight to twelve people. The participants work together on an event and then talk about what they did. Group and individual issues triggered or surfaced during the activity are addressed during a discussion or "debriefing" led by the facilitator. Insights are shared and feedback exchanged. The facilitator's job is not to provide answers, but to ask insightful questions, or at least the kind of questions that lead to insightful answers. Teams have the answers; they just need some help in bringing this information out so everyone can benefit from it.

THE POWER OF METAPHOR

One reason for debriefing each event is to generalize a lesson from a specific experience. Generalization means connecting experiences previously thought to be unrelated by identifying the underlying concepts and principles. Connecting seemingly unrelated experiences is done through the use of metaphor. One of the best moments in a ropes course is when that metaphoric "Ah ha" of understanding and inspiration occurs. Some of these insights can be life changing as one woman reported following her experience on an event known as the "Grapevine."

The Grapevine is an activity where a person traverses a cable strung from one tree or pole to another, thirty feet in the air. Along the treetop route are the "vines," pieces of rope, strung at intervals of eight feet or more from another cable overhead. The woman was certain there was no way she could reach the first vine without falling. Her teammates on the ground reminded her that she was attached securely to a separate rope that ensured her safety and encouraged her to try. As she described it:[2]

> *Reaching that next vine meant letting go with my left hand and lunging sideways across several feet of empty space. I was convinced I could not do it. I went for the vine anyway and completely surprised myself. This happened all the way across. Each time I was absolutely sure I couldn't make it and was going to fall. But I tried and made it. This taught me something. Now, I really question myself when I think I can't do something.*

Making the connection from a specific incident to other parts of your life is the conscious use of metaphor. The woman, a mental health practitioner, changed her working environment after the ropes course so that she could enjoy more independence. This was an arrangement she used to think was not one of her options.

BANDURA'S THEORY OF SELF EFFICACY

Alfred Bandura, a social psychologist from Stanford University, developed a learning model that has been used to explain why a ropes course has the impact that it does. The corner stone of Bandura's theory is the concept of efficacy. Self efficacy is the amount of confidence we have in our own competence to deal with unknown and ambiguous conditions. People often withhold their participation in a new activity because of their unwillingness to accept the risk of failure. Efficacy is having the ability, matched by belief, that you can perform the activity in question.

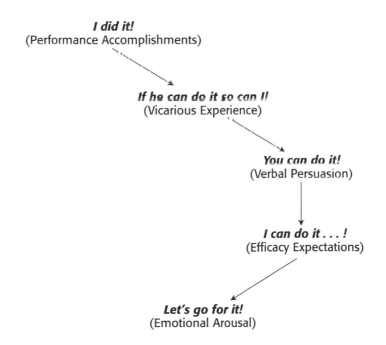

Expectations of efficacy come from:

I did it!
(Performance Accomplishments)

If he can do it so can I!
(Vicarious Experience)

You can do it!
(Verbal Persuasion)

I can do it . . . !
(Efficacy Expectations)

Let's go for it!
(Emotional Arousal)

Expectations of efficacy are influenced by several factors including previous failures or accomplishments. Bandura believes that the level of this expectation, . . .*determines how much effort people will expand and how long they will persist in the face of obstacles and adverse experiences.* Efficacy expectations are raised by four possible means: performance accomplishment, vicarious experience, verbal persuasion, and emotional arousal.[3]

Successfully completing a task or activity can have a significant impact in developing a person's sense of self efficacy. The more the challenge is perceived as difficult the more psychological benefit there is from its accomplishment. The sense of achievement gained from climbing the "Pamper Pole" or riding a "Zip Line" is internalized, it affects the attitudes and actions in other areas of a person's life.

ASKING FOR HELP

An issue for some people is the difficulty they have in asking for help. Many adults grew up in families or worked in companies where it was not acceptable to ask for assistance. Learning to ask for and receive support, as well as give it, can be a significant personal or team achievement. Unfortunately, many of us respond to a challenging problem or painful emotion by denying it or withdrawing in some fashion. Using what you have gained and practiced on the ropes course you can stop and make the conscious choice as to how you will respond to a given situation. When you are aware of, and able to express, your true feelings and desires, you can better articulate to others what you want or need. An event called "The Wall," a wooden edifice as high as 30 feet , is a perfect metaphor for this challenge of asking for help. No one can get over on his own. The wall is high enough so that everyone in the group needs to trust and communicate with each other if the entire team is going to make it to the other side. Some people have the attitude, "I don't need anyone's help. I can do it all on my own and you should too." They quickly learn on "The Wall" that full participation requires both giving and receiving assistance.

On the Climbing Wall (and up against it)

Team Building Associates

COMMUNITY BUILDING

"The Wall" has also been used a metaphor for the emotional walls that people erect between themselves and others. The cost of maintaining those emotional walls can be quite high. As a group goes through the challenges on the course together, the trust and cooperation between the members deepens. For some people the feeling of camaraderie is something they never experienced before or even thought possible. This kind of community is no accident; but someone has to risk the first step. On high ropes events participants find themselves thirty feet in the air doing things they thought they could never do. The simple acts of ensuring physical safety for and encouraging each other, creates a bond between the team members that will last long after the course is over. As one trainer put it:

We're helping them become a tribe. They may not, at first, even want to be bonded to each other, but that is human nature when people share these kinds of experiences together.

TRANSFER OF LEARNING

Because of the emotional impact of outdoor team building, it is easy to assume that the benefits of doing a ropes course are automatic. Just get everyone over "The Wall" or down the "Zip Line" and the employees will return to work feeling empowered and full of team spirit. In actuality, a company is short changing itself if that is all it gets out of the training. Group energy and good feelings are valuable, but they tend to wear off within a few days or weeks. The real benefits of the course are in learning new behaviors and strategies that optimize both individual and group productivity. Each event on the ropes course provides a team opportunities to identify and practice teamwork skills. Some facilitators encourage the participants to make notes after the debriefing of an event so nothing significant is forgotten.

In the final large group debriefing, the teams report on what they learned on the course. New policies, both formal and informal, are proposed so that the advantages of what has been learned will be enjoyed by other members of the organization. Some groups post what they have learned and the agreements they have made on a flip chart and sign their names around the margins to show their commitment.

Most progress towards change is incremental; small steps alternating between insight and action accumulate over time into significant progress. But once in awhile the changes can be dramatic. One group that went through a ropes course experienced a near epiphany on an event known as "Bridge It." According to one of the participants:

We were all talking at once and no one was listening. So the bridge collapsed when we tried to cross it because not everyone knew what was expected of them. It hit us during the debrief that's ex-

A team on the Bridge-It activity:

Maxcomm Associates

*actly the way we always operate. There was no escaping we had
to do things differently.*

APPLICATION

Most ropes course providers understand how to generate a powerful learning experience. What is not well understood by most providers is how to take the energy, trust, and insight that were gained
from a course and apply it to some bottom line business issues.
Ideally, the application process should start before the participants
get on the bus to go home. Along with a day or two of team building at least a half day or more should be set aside to address business issues. The application session could cover one or more areas
that are vital to the success of an organization, such as: strategic
planning, new product development, reducing costs, improving
productivity, or identifying concerns and problem areas and developing action plans. Whatever issues are addressed, it would be

a waste not to take a team that has honed its problem-solving skills on the course and turn it loose on a real business challenge.

FOLLOW-UP

It is a very satisfying sight to watch a team develop a high degree of enthusiasm and commitment during the ropes course, but sustaining that commitment requires some form of follow-up. The Fibers Division of du Pont, for example, conducted a series of two-hour training modules each month for more than a year after the initial ropes course. The modules built on the understandings and insights employees gained while working together outdoors while covering skills such as communication and problem solving.

CHOOSING A PROVIDER

The few studies that have been done on ropes courses generally agree that the skill of the facilitator is as important as any other factor in determining the overall success of a program. The training firm providing the course is as good as the trainers it hires to design and conduct the training. The ideal trainer has excellent facilitation skills. It is also helpful if he has management experience and possesses a familiarity with the kind of issues the organization may be grappling with. Running a safe, productive course demands technical as well psychological skills. A capable provider will conduct a needs assessment before designing a training program for an intact work team. A good design modifies the events to reflect the capabilities of the team and bring out the issues the members are dealing with. Professional programs require extensive preparation before the participants arrive at the training site. But program designs, like some rules, are made to be changed. The facilitator has to be flexible and deal with what comes up even if the new issues or concerns bear little resemblance to the original training objectives.

SAFETY

What keeps a ropes course safe is the judgement exercised by the facilitator and the commitments made by the participants to take care of each other and themselves. When high ropes activities are going to be used this process begins back at the office. The course facilitators review the medical forms filled out by each participant for the high ropes program. Based on this information, events and activities are selected and tailored so that they challenge but do not overwhelm team members. Team members are requested to take responsibility for their safety and not do anything which might reactivate old injuries. Anyone with heart trouble or high blood pressure should consult with their physician before attempting a high ropes event. During the more strenuous events team members with physical limitations can still participate in other ways such as planning or problem solving during an activity.

PROMISES VERSUS REALITY

There is an abundance of anecdotal and some scientific evidence that ropes courses help develop teamwork. In the research that has been conducted, significant improvement was found in the individual variable of problem solving and the variables of group awareness and group effectiveness.[4] Other evaluations have shown positive changes in factors such as interpersonal trust, feedback, time management, goal setting and communication. Researchers have noted that the outcomes of a course have "as much to do with the facilitator and the composition of the participating group as it does with the program itself."

Despite the statistical evidence, the fact that the training takes place outdoors has led some journalists to draw negative conclusions without gaining any firsthand experience. One writer from the *Wall Street Journal* charged that an organization could get just as much team building mileage out of a company picnic.[5] Part of the confusion about the efficacy of outdoor programs is that courses run by highly skilled facilitators with years of management experience get lumped together with those led by those with little or no experience. These differences are reflected in the results as well as the initial costs of a program. Course expenditures per participant vary widely. The average cost for the corporate client who employs professional facilitators ranges from 1500 to 3000 dollars per small group (8 to 12 participants) for a one-day program.

TRAINING PROVIDERS

The annual sales for outdoor training programs is estimated to be around $100 million. One study published in the magazine "TRAINING" (May, 1991) estimates that 13.8 percent of American companies have sent employees to an outdoor program.[6] That percentage gets higher every year since several hundred providers of experience-based and outdoor adventure programs are serving this market

Mobile initiatives allow a course to be conducted at any location with sufficient outdoor or indoor space. The course need not be physical or emotionally challenging and can be integrated with other activities such as business planning or classroom instruction. For information on a mobile program you can contact the author of this book at Team Building Associates.

13
Wilderness Adventure

Maxcomm Associates

We are a product of the choices we make, not the circumstances that we face.

ROGER CRAWFORD

*You tell me and I forget.
You teach me and I remember.
You involve me and I learn.*

BEN FRANKLIN

Wilderness adventure used to be the purview of the Boy Scouts and other pursuits in adolescent character building. In the past few years, corporate team building in the wilderness has become common enough to warm the heart of any scoutmaster. Outward Bound puts over 5000 executives through multi-day expeditions every year. A number of other firms scattered throughout the United States also conduct wilderness programs for corporate groups.

WILDERNESS BONDING

There is hardly a quicker way to forge strong bonds of camaraderie and cooperation than living and working together under challenging conditions. The modality of this experience can take many

187

forms; rock climbing, whitewater rafting, cross-country skiing, orienteering, backpacking, or sailing. Much of the program centers around teaching the participants how to use the equipment. Some observers look upon the experience as an extended picnic in an exotic location. A weekend of golf would do just as well. But playing golf does not come close to the team-building impact of living together in the outdoors, twenty-four hours a day.

The wilderness or the sea teaches with total impartiality the lessons of leadership and teamwork. A team must work in a cooperative fashion if they are going to stay relatively comfortable, get where they need to go, (there's warm bed and bath waiting at the end of the trail) and keep each other safe. Contrary to popular expectations, a wilderness adventure is not about "roughing it" since little or no skill is required to make yourself uncomfortable. The Adirondack guide, George Sears, said it best in the 1920's:[1]

We do not go to the green woods and crystal waters to rough it. We go to smooth it. We get it rough enough at home; in towns and cities; in shops, offices, stores, banks. . . Don't rough it; make it smooth, as restful and pleasurable as you can.

SHARED MEANING

Something happens in the wilderness that our language does not have words for. The beauty of nature can renew your spirit, awakening some higher nature within that is not accessible in the crush of city traffic. Just being in the mountains or out on the ocean is significant. The boundaries of common, everyday life are extended in ways that cannot be anticipated. A group undergoing this shared experience, the challenges and discomforts as well as the beauty and excitement, cannot help but be profoundly affected.

COMMUNITY BUILDING

The wilderness environment is extremely democratic. The weather and terrain treat everyone exactly the same. The status gained from expertise or position in the office may not transfer to the woods, a fact of that life that forces an examination of old assumptions and patterns of relating. Each member partakes of the same tribulations and triumphs of the journey. People find new strengths and capabilities that they (and others) did not know they had. Small acts of thoughtfulness help build a foundation of trust where open and honest communication can take place. The team shares in experiences that will be told and retold when they return to office. The telling and retelling of these stories gives each member a common identity to take pride in. The stories create a shared perspective; bonding the team members to each other in a way that can seem almost tribal.

PULLING TOGETHER

The wilderness is an ideal learning laboratory where leadership and interpersonal skills can be tested, practiced, and mastered. Teams are often tested to their limits when faced with a crisis. During a difficult situation, people have the opportunity to put aside their differences and work for the common good. The vicissitudes inflicted by the weather or terrain heightens the level of stress. The team responds to this stress by pulling together or falling apart. The wilderness has a ready supply of metaphors that change an abstract idea into a concrete experience. For example, rafting through a class four or five rapid takes leadership and communication skills. The team either works together or ends up capsizing on a rock. Learning to read the rapids and forge a route under rapidly changing circumstances develops collective decision-making skills. Individual behaviors that help or hinder this effort are hard to hide or hide from.

ENGINEERED ADVERSITY

A team composed of software and hardware engineers had the mission to troubleshoot and repair system failures on short notice. When the computers failed to do what they were supposed to do, it was their job to repair them fast. A wilderness adventure was conducted to test their problem-solving skills under high stress.

The team skied cross-country all day to what was supposed to be a cabin nestled between two mountains. It was the middle of winter and the temperature was in the teen's. Only the team leader and the trainer knew the "cabin" was actually a pile of tarps and string. It was beginning to turn dark when the team skied into the site that was their "home" for the night. After a brief look at the pile of tarps on the ground, one member offered the trainer $2,000 to get him out of there by eight o'clock that night. The trainer laughed. "Three thousand" the man responded, without changing his expression. The team groaned and growled over the situation but finally begin to deal with it. Realizing they had only a few minutes of daylight left they quickly organized themselves and used what they could find to set up a make-shift camp for the night. Jokes and wisecracks made by some team members helped relieve the tension.

Stream

A few in the group shared with the others some extra supplies they had. It was a long night, but not unbearable. The
team skied back to civilization the next morning. In the warm
conference room of a comfortable hotel they discussed how
they had worked together to make the best of a bad situation. Parallels were drawn to the unpleasant surprises the team
might have to deal with in troubleshooting a computer system. The team identified behaviors that helped them handle
unexpected problems.

TEACHABLE MOMENTS

A team in the woods is together day and night for the duration of
the program. Under these circumstances it is difficult not to get
to know each other extremely well. When personal conflicts occur they have to be worked out or at least endured. The group
must stay together until the trip is over. Although the wilderness
is a big place, the radiant warmth of the campfire or the size of the
raft constrains the physical distance group members put between
each other. As you might expect, issues that have plagued the
team back at the office reassert themselves in some form during
the outing. The facilitator's job is to assist in processing and resolving these issues as they are played out.

The facilitator stays alert to any "teachable moment" that pre
sents itself and starts a discussion so the learning can be captured
while the experience is still fresh in everyone's mind. Working
with what is occurring in the moment captures the opportunity
for meaningful change.

FINDING HUMOR

Philosophers have argued since the ancient Greeks that events
have no real intrinsic meaning except the meaning we ascribe to
them. We can celebrate because the glass is half full or despair
because it is half empty. Groups in the wilderness are frequently
faced with similar choices. A sudden downpour could leave ev-

eryone wet, cold, and miserable. Some groups will respond to the situation by focusing on the misery of their physical condition. Others will respond to the same conditions by focusing on what they can do or say about it. The team that learns to finds the humor in their circumstances, when there seems little to laugh about, is a team that can stay cohesive under pressure.

SHARING THE LIGHT

As a part of a management training program a group of executives went on a camping trip. One of their campsites was near the entrance to a large cave. After pitching their tents the executives were led deep inside the cave to a point where the way out was no longer obvious. The facilitator, David Cady, collected their flashlights and let the total darkness settle around the group before he broke the silence by saying:

> *How often in your organization have you felt like a mushroom inside some cave; kept in the dark and living off dirt? How did it feel being kept in the dark! Did the person with the information ever share it or were you left in the dark a long, long time?*

David handed just one flashlight to one of the executives and then withdrew to another part of the cave. Sharing the light source the executives groped around until they found their way out. The adventure sparked a discussion among the executives about how they sometimes failed to keep their subordinates informed or when they themselves were kept in the dark by their associates. Suggestions were exchanged about how they could do a better job "sharing the light."

BENEFITS OF OUTDOOR EDUCATION

The skills exercised in dealing with the wilderness, such as cooperative decision making, group problem solving, planning, risk management and leadership, are the skills essential for success in the business world. According to Alan Ewert in his book, *Outdoor Adventure Pursuits: Foundations, Models and Theories*, the potential benefits of an outdoor program range from psychological and sociological to educational and physical. Ewert catalogued these benefits based on his review of several hundred studies on outdoor education. The chart below (based on Ewert's model) lists some of these potential benefits.[2]

Benefits of Outdoor Adventure

PSYCHOLOGICAL	SOCIOLOGICAL	EDUCATIONAL	PHYSICAL
Self-concept	Compassion	Outdoor Education	Fitness
Confidence	Cooperation	Nature Awareness	Skills
Self-Efficacy	Respect	Conservation	Strength
Sensation Seeking	Communication	Problem Solving	Coordination
Actualization	Feedback	Value Clarification	Flexibility
Well-Being	Friendship	Outdoor Skills	Exercise
Challenge	Belonging	Learning Skills	Balance

Ewert and other researchers concede that the current body of research is no where near definitive. Most of the findings were based on self-reporting measures. The benefits are not acquired just by taking a group of people into the woods. The program design, the facilitation skills of the leaders, and the motivations of the participants, all have a great deal to do with the results obtained.

LEARNING THEORY AND MODELS

A number of models attempt to explain why outdoor education and training has the impact it does on an individual or a group. One model, "Expectancy Theory," states that the participants in these activities have a predetermined set of expectations about psychological and sociological benefits they will gain from the activity. The individual signs up for a course looking to enjoy excitement and challenge with a like-minded group of peers. The shared expectations reinforce each other to help create a self-fulfilling prophecy.[3]

The personal investment of time and money can also be a powerful motivator to ensure that the return in lessons justifies the expenditures. The manager who contracts for an outdoor training is usually seeking specific benefits. However, the primary focus of some of the manager's employees may be avoiding physical and psychological discomfort. The inherent skepticism of these employees is often alleviated as they see others in their team take advantage of the learning opportunities offered by the training.

THE CALL OF AROUSAL

So why *do* people climb mountains or raft rivers? The question is an old one. Working with people in an endeavor that engages their full attention offers a degree of satisfaction the casual bystander seldom appreciates. After enjoying the camaraderie of a wilderness adventure, passive pursuits like watching television seem empty. According to some researchers there is a strong correlation between a person's performance, the satisfaction over that performance, and the level of arousal the individual goes through to achieve that satisfaction.

The diagram below shows a correlation in the relationship between the uncertainty or risk over the outcome of an endeavor and the sense of achievement in its accomplishment.

The more skill a task demands relative to the ability of the performer, the more potential satisfaction there is in its accomplishment. For example, paddling a class one, flat-water river for an expert paddler is not as exciting and gratifying as successfully running a class four, torrent of white water. However, for someone who has never been on a river before, the class one river might be just as exciting for them as the class four would be to the expert.

Performance as a Function of Arousal

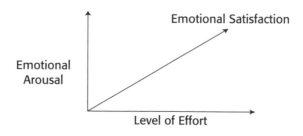

just as exciting for them as the class four would be to the expert.

MANAGING CHALLENGE

The ideal learning environment presents a problem that is challenging, but not overwhelming. A lot of learning can take place when the outcome is uncertain. An event that is too easy for the team may limit the potential for learnings, but an activity that is perceived as too difficult will keep some team members from even trying. If the fear of failure is overwhelming, the team might be tempted to excuse itself with a shrug that says, "What's the use?" Properly organized and conducted, the actual risk is much less than the perceived risk. Trainers refer to this differential when they speak about the illusion of danger since these activities have a way of looking riskier than they really are. Even so, this does not take away from the sense of achievement a participant can gain in completing a wilderness challenge program.

GO WITH THE FLOW

A researcher in outdoor activities, Mihaly Csikszentmihalyi, believes that maintaining the proper balance between the skill level of the individual and the perceived difficulty of the activity creates a sense of inner congruency or "flow." As confidence and competence grow an individual will seek greater challenges. According to the chart below, the ideal learning curve avoids too little

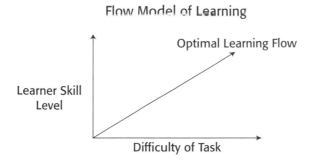

Flow Model of Learning

Optimal Learning Flow

Learner Skill Level

Difficulty of Task

MAINTAINING BALANCE

Between the parameters of boredom and fear is the optimal level of arousal and the greatest degree of learning. In the outdoor setting, whether on a ropes course or a wilderness expedition, more challenging activities are conducted as the skill level of the team increases. Too much challenge too soon can be demoralizing. Too little challenge is boring. At either extreme, little in the way of learning will take place.

ESSENTIAL SKILLS

A well-rounded outdoor trainer leading a corporate program possesses technical mastery, mature judgement, and training and facilitation skills. The technical mastery of reading a map or a river comes from doing those activities over an extended period of time. Participants need instruction in how to use their equipment, set up camp, find a route, and other intricacies of wilderness travel. Good facilitation is essential if the team is going to derive the maximum benefit from the program by applying what they learned about teamwork back at the office.

WILDERNESS SAFETY

Providers of wilderness expeditions like Outward Bound require participants to take a physical and gain the approval of their physician. Even so, older adults engaging in high impact activities need to be aware of the difference between stretching beyond self-imposed limits or breaking those limits in a way that might result in an injury. Alan Hale, the Director of the National Safety Network, made the following observations about outdoor activities:[5]

> Persons under fifteen years get injured trying to do things that are impossible, people over twenty-one get injured trying to stretch to their limits, and those over thirty get injured trying to do things their body has forgotten how to do.

Hale defines an injury as a trauma that requires medical attention by a physician and results in the injured person being unable to participate for at least a half day. The average rate of injuries based on available data has been about three injuries for every 100,000 days of participant training.

JUDGEMENT

It has been said that good judgement is something you develop after gaining the experience that comes from exercising bad judgement. Like maturity, judgement is not an innate trait; it develops over time and a few hard knocks. No rulebook can cover every contingency. Occasionally, it is wiser to break the rules. Good judgement is knowing when. Outdoor activities have varying levels of physical risk that are inherent in the activity itself. Situational risk is the risk that varies with changing conditions. These conditions include environmental factors such as weather, time of day and terrain, as well as human factors such as fatigue and morale. The physical capabilities and technical skills of a group, along with the other factors mentioned above, determines the kind of outdoor activity they can safely engage in.

Maintaining the maximum degree of safety requires a constant assessment of the inherent and situational risks vis-a-vis the physical and emotional state of the team. In a routine field training exercise a patrol of U.S. Army Rangers is expected to deal successfully with higher situational risk than a group of campers, even though the inherent risk of the activity they are both engaged in (rock climbing) is the same. The trainer designs and conducts the outdoor program based on the capabilities of the group and its learning objectives.

WILDERNESS PROVIDERS

The major outfits in the United States that run wilderness programs for corporate groups are Natahala Outdoor Center and

Outward Bound. Both of these organizations belong to the Association of Experiential Education based in Boulder, Colorado.

- *Outward Bound* is the granddaddy of all outdoor adventure programs. Kurt Hahn founded Outward Bound in England just after WWII. Fifty years later there are now 38 Outward Bound schools on five continents. Over 200,000 Americans of all ages have tramped through the outdoors led by Outward Bound instructors. In America, the main Outward Bound schools are located in Portland (Oregon), Boulder (Colorado), Los Angeles, Atlanta, Baltimore, Morganton (North Carolina) and Portland (Maine.) A number of smaller "bases" are scattered about the country.

  A nine-day expeditionary course is offered to individual managers. Customized courses for intact work teams are also offered. The courses are structured according to the needs of the individual corporation. The professional programs include any combination of outdoor activities desired by the client, such as: backpacking, rock climbing, canoeing, sea kayaking, sailing, and a ropes course.

- *Natahala Outdoor Center (NOC)* is located in the mountains of northwest North Carolina near the town of Bryson City. The NOC facility is near several major mountain rivers, the Natahala, the Chattoga, and the French Broad. With such an abundance of white water the team-building activities naturally include rafting, kayaking, and canoeing.

14
Cross-Cultural Teamwork

Broderbund

Think differently.

APPLE COMPUTERS LOGO

The two words, business and international, are increasingly linked. If you are a professional in the business world at some point in your career you are likely to find yourself working with people who consider you the foreigner. As the world shrinks and the global economy expands, the requirement to build a cross-cultural team is becoming more commonplace.

To capture the competitive advantages of economies of scale, major corporations have to go global. 3M, for example, has dozens of plants scattered around the world. To enhance their effectiveness global companies train their managers in cross-cultural communications before sending them abroad. But you do not have to leave home to work with people from a different culture. The continuous wave of immigrants from all over the world is changing the makeup of the workforce in North America, Europe and even cities in Asia like Singapore and Hong Kong.

SOCIAL GEOGRAPHY

What distinguishes one culture from another are the unique values and characteristics of a particular group of people. There are hundreds of national and regional subgroups that display distinct and consistent differences between each other. For the sake of simplicity these groups can be classified by geography representing the cultures of Africa, North America, Europe, Asia, Middle East, and Latin America. The following chart (drawn from a variety of sources including Casse, 1983) diagrams the social orientation of these major cultures:[1]

Social Orientation of the Six Cultures			
Culture	Status/Identity	Relate to Authority	Competition
North American	Profession	Need to know why	Individualistic
European	Title/class	Need to know who	Cooperate by class
Asian	Age/role	Respect authority	Cooperate by work
Middle Eastern	Family connections	Central authority	Cooperate by faith
Latin American	Family wealth	Loyalty to family	Cooperate by social connections
African	Kinship/tribe	Loyalty to tribe	Cooperate with kin

The diversity and complexity of human behavior limits the validity of any generalization about cultures, but generalities can be useful as long as we recognize their limitations. When we understand the predominant traits of a culture we have a better chance of accurately communicating with its members.

CULTURAL ORIENTATION

The culture of a society defines the collective traits of a group of people. Geert Hofstede's pioneering research produced a new model of cross-cultural sociology. Hofstede compared the culture of 53 different countries or regions, measuring four dimensions that define different cultures.[2]

The dimensions are on a continuum between two extremes:

- High Power . . .versus . . .Low Power Distance.
- High Uncertainty . . . versus . . . Low Uncertainty Avoidance.
- Individualism . . . versus . . . Collectivism.
- Masculinity . . . versus . . . Femininity.

HIGH POWER . . . VERSUS . . . LOW POWER DISTANCE

Some societies reinforce the differences in status between members while others try to minimize any differences. High power cultures are elitist. The inequities between individuals are reinforced by various social mechanisms that affirm these differences. Low power societies are more egalitarian, seeking to minimize the apparent differences that position; class, education, or wealth bestow. Those with low status in a high power culture are expected to treat higher status persons with a deference that maintains the social distance.

Some South American and Asian cultures, maintain a high degree of social distance between professions and classes. Questioning the authority of an elder or a boss is not socially acceptable behavior. High power distance cultures limit the delegation of authority. Approval is sought from the leader before any action is taken, even trivial ones. Personal loyalty is more to the leader than the organization. Disagreeing with a superior is considered disrespectful. A superior from a low power culture who asks for suggestions and input from his high power culture employees could be regarded with confusion if not distrust. The superior from a high power distance culture would be surprised by the amount of unexpected suggestions his employees from a low power culture might insist on offering. He could find it disturbing that his foreign subordinates address him by his first name and initiate casual conversations about topics not related to work.

HIGH UNCERTAINTY . . . VERSUS . . . LOW UNCERTAINTY AVOIDANCE

Risk taking is extolled in some cultures. In others caution is the accepted norm. The heroes in Hong Kong are the entrepreneurs who took big risks to achieve profitable results. In countries like Japan, the accepted norm is the salary man who stays with the same company his entire career. Changing companies is an action that goes against the norms of loyalty, job security, and social harmony. Cultures with a lower need to avoid uncertainty are more interested in individual advancement than security. The rate of personal saving is low. The motivating desire is to have it all now. Personal initiative and individual accomplishment are encouraged even if it means risking failure.

INDIVIDUALISM . . . VERSUS . . . COLLECTIVISM

In collectivist cultures social equity is more important than the individual. The rewards are for those who are part of the crowd. Nonconformists are subjected to treatment calculated to instill feelings of shame and guilt. One corporate rehabilitation program for errant salary men in Japan requires them to go to a public area and confess their faults in a manner that everyone can see and hear. A popular saying is "the nail that sticks up gets hammered." At the other extreme, an individualist culture like that of American glorifies the person who differentiates himself from the crowd. The winner takes all. The fear of failure is in part the fear of being average.

Social networks play a central role in collectivist cultures. In India, when wealthy couples marry, not only are their families joined together but the companies owned by these families form new alliances as well. In the East, the direct "let's-get down-to-business" approach used by Westerners appears rude. Introductions are necessary through mutual acquaintances. Time must be taken to develop social relationships before business can be discussed. Maintaining relationships and fulfilling social expectations have a high priority. There is less need for the legal and contractual obligations that are part of American culture. Consequently, in the collectivist society of Japan there about as many lawyers in the entire country as there are in the metropolitan area of Washington, DC.

MASCULINITY . . . VERSUS . . . FEMININITY

The archetype of a masculine culture is the warrior hero who is fiercely competitive and domineering. Although gender is likely to determine roles, managers of either sex are expected to act in the manner of a stern father. In feminine cultures roles are less likely to be based on gender. It is more important to relate than to compete.

The traits of masculinity and femininity, however, are not always mutually exclusive. In Middle Eastern cultures masculine traits are held in high esteem, but hospitality is also highly regarded. Japanese society is highly masculine in its division of roles by gender, yet the feminine orientation of social harmony is also esteemed.

CROSS-CULTURAL ADJUSTMENTS

When a traveler goes to a foreign country many of the obvious differences are a delight. A tourist, unlike an expatriate, typically spends no more than a couple of weeks touring before returning home. The sense of disorientation caused by cultural differences makes itself felt after the first flush of newness wears off. Familiar cultural cues are missing and new ones must be learned. Feeling at home in a culture comes from mastering the subtle, cultural cues that pervade a society but are seldom referred to or discussed. It can take as much as two years and several cycles of emotional dissatisfaction and disorientation before an expatriate learns and masters these cues.

CULTURAL ICEBERGS

The iceberg metaphor of consciousness developed by Freud also describes a culture; many significant aspects are unstated or unseen. Most social customs embody ways of relating and communicating that are below the threshold of conscious awareness. These cues are neither better nor worse than those of another culture: they are just different. For example, the personal space reserved by Westerners for social interaction with friends is approximately two to four feet from the body. If someone moves into that space or closer to conduct a business conversation, the Westerner is likely to show signs of discomfort.

A familiar story of cross-cultural difficulties is how a Middle Easterner pursued a Britisher around the room, innocently attempting to close the distance necessary in his country to establish personal rapport. Neither side could understand why there was such mutual discomfort and confusion. Sharing a common culture makes it easier to relate to others. Anyone who has had the experience of meeting a fellow countryman in some remote corner of the globe knows the instant rapport engendered under those circumstances.

DIFFERENT VALUES

Some people travelling overseas for the first time seem to have trouble understanding how other cultures could have the audacity to be different from their own. They assume that everyone shares or should share the same values and even language.

They are surprised, even upset, when the evidence is embarrassingly contrary to that assumption. In your own travels abroad you may have seen this happen:

A tourist asks the store clerk a question. The clerk does not understand because he does not speak the tourist's language. Frustrated, the tourist keeps raising his voice, assuming that if he talks loud enough he will be understood.

The way different cultures regard time can also be a source of frustration.

A German woman living in Panama felt insulted that her South American friends and associates never arrived on time. It was frustrating to her that no seemed as concerned as she was about sticking to a schedule or providing fast service. Learning not to take these behaviors as a personal affront was a major adjustment.

Some cultural adjustments are unexpected and a bit comical.

Two Australians hailed a cab in San Francisco. One of them hopped into the front seat. The cabby was horrified. The Australians were puzzled by his reaction. They did not know that in urban areas jumping into the front seat of a cab seemed like a threat.

Adjusting to a different culture can also take place even when the language is supposedly the same.

An American trainer working in Australia produced a hilarious uproar when he tried to adjourn a meeting. He innocently used few words that in the local vernacular meant an act of fornication instead of signaling an end to the meeting. When the same trainer worked with a group of Asian women he was somewhat peeved by the amount of giggles they indulged in. It took a while before he realized their giggles were not due to a lack of seriousness, but actually a sign of embarrassment.

NONVERBAL GESTURES

It was noted in Chapter Four, "Communication Skills", that non-verbal gestures can make up as much as 80% of face-to-face communication. However, the meaning of certain gestures changes when you change countries. For example:

- Holding the thumb and forefinger of one hand in a circle, or making a fist and raising the thumb towards the air means "A-okay," in North America. But, some Mediterranean cultures consider this hand signal insulting.
- Pointing an index finger at the head or tapping it lightly can be a compliment. The gesture is a way of saying, "that's using your head." But in Europe, the gesture has exactly the opposite meaning implying the person is crazy or stupid.
- In North America, clasping ones hands is perceived as statement of victory, especially if the hands are waved over one's head. In the Russian culture, the gesture is an offer of friendship.
- The movement of the head to indicate yes or no are gestures usually considered universal. Yet in India these gestures are easily confused by a foreign visitor. To the uninitiated Westerner the Indian can appear to be shaking his head "no" while saying "yes".

Another potential miscommunication is the loudness of one's voice.

In parts of the Middle East the loudest voice belongs to the person with the highest status. When meeting with a foreign visitor an Arab might speak more softly than normal to show respect. The foreigner compensates by speaking louder, irritated by Arab's lack of forcefulness. The Arab responds by speaking even softer to show more respect, and the cycle continues until both sides become exasperated by each other's behavior.

DEVELOPING TRUST

If teamwork is based on trust, developing that trust in a cross-cultural context is especially challenging. People, no matter where they are from, tend to be suspicious of behavior that does not match their expectations. This suspicion can occur over the most innocuous circumstances as several American tourists found out while they were breakfasting at an inn in the English countryside.

The tourists were mystified that their requests for a glass of water were ignored or met with wary looks until they discovered the problem. "Water is for cutting whiskey," their British waiter reproached them after they made another futile request during breakfast. Since consuming water with a meal was not the local custom, the waiter did not believe the explanation of the thirsty travelers that they were going to drink the water "neat" without an alcoholic dilution.

Members of a cross-cultural team bring their unconscious expectations of how things are done with them to the work environment. If they share a vocation or sport, the common experiences and jargon provide a flag of understanding the team can rally around. Without that understanding a miscommunication can become a cultural land mine as the following stories illustrate:

An expatriate American, after a month spent living in the Far East, invited her Asian coworkers over for dinner. She worked hard to prepare a nice meal. No one showed up. When asked why, her coworkers finally admitted they had not known her long enough to accept the invitation, but could not decline out of politeness.

Another expatriate, an American accountant working in Iran, thought he had a good working relationship with his Iranian counterpart. But for several days running the man was moody and brusque. Finally, the North American found out what had gone wrong. The previous week he had made the farewell remark, "Give your wife a kiss for me," to his newly married associate when the man left for a long weekend. "If anyone else had said that," his counterpart told him later, "I would kill him."

CULTURAL DISCONTINUITY

The damage from a cultural "faux pas" can usually be alleviated by explaining that the perceived offense was due to cultural ignorance. It is those unknown and often unconscious differences that trip up a cross-cultural relationship. When one action has no context in another culture, a discontinuity is created that breaks the rapport between two people. Situations in which it is difficult to ask a direct question or get a direct answer require a high tolerance for ambiguity. Western cultures place a premium on clarity and getting to the point. Asian cultures stress the importance of saving face and maintaining harmony. Direct discussions on difficult topics are avoided. "Yes" does not always mean "yes," and a lot of other responses just short of "yes" may actually mean "no." Adding to the confusion, "no" may not really mean "no."

A study of cross-cultural negotiating styles was conducted by John Graham, a business professor at the University of Southern California. Graham found that the Brazilian businessman tendered over forty "no's" in thirty minutes of negotiating.[3] An impressive contrast to the Japanese average of 1.9 "no's" or the American average of 4.7 "no's" in the same time frame. Brazilians were the most vocal "naysayers" when it comes to negotiating business deals, but there was no evidence they end up with fewer deals.

CULTURAL FILTERS

Cultural filters are unconscious assumptions and communication patterns that affect how we interact with the world around us. These filters help you make sense of your world. The most important part of a cultural filter is usually below the threshold of awareness.

They remain invisible or transparent as long as we interact with someone from the same culture. When a person is unaware of how her assumptions impact her interactions with others, misunderstandings are more likely to result. The futurist, Joel Barker tells a story that illustrates what happens when the message sent is not the message that is received.[4]

> A young man was amusing himself by racing along a country road in his sports car. As he approached a curve a car came swerving out of it in his direction. The woman driver leaned out her window and yelled, "Pig!" at him as they sped past each other. "Cow!" the young man shouted back, returning her taunt before she was out of earshot. How could she call me that, he fumed. She was in my lane! Self righteously, he shifted gears and flew around the curve, only to run right into a large pig crossing the road.

Filters are mental habits formed from generalizations of specific experiences. However, generalizations are not always valid. Like that woman who yelled, "pig", the reasons for a person's behavior are seldom observable. The chart below shows why:

Cultural Filters

OBSERVED
BEHAVIOR

MESSAGE   MESSAGE
SENT   RECEIVED

CULTURAL FILTERS
(not observable)

TRAITS

CUSTOMS

NORMS

VALUES

BELIEFS

Cultural filters are like trip wires: the ones you know about are easy to step over. It's the ones you do not know about that cause problems. For example,

> The employer of the Asian American thought she communicated the message, "You're doing okay, just make a few changes," when giving the employee feedback on her job performance. The employee was upset to the point of quitting because the message which she interpreted was, "You have dishonored yourself."

CULTURAL BLINDNESS

Because of cultural filters the members of one culture are sometimes blind to certain phenomenon that cause another group a great deal of difficulty. Most of us never even notice the width of a door, but a person in wheelchair can not escape noticing it. Given the multitude of cultural idiosyncrasies it is useful to follow a few multicultural guidelines such as:

- *Make no assumptions.* In some cultures people address each other formally, especially anyone considered to have a higher status. Before making assumptions it is a good idea to ask how the person would like to be addressed. An eighty-year old woman was surprised and not pleased that the young receptionist at her doctor's office addressed her by her first name. The woman knew that no disrespect was intended, but the unwanted familiarity still seemed disrespectful. The principle, make no assumptions, applies to many situations. When in doubt, ask.
- *Verify Mutual Understanding.* "Yes" can mean a lot of things besides yes, such as, " I understand you" or "I am paying attention." Since assumptions differ about what words or gestures mean, it is wise to verify your understanding.
- *Be Aware of Nonverbal Messages.* Most facial expressions mean pretty much the same to everyone in the human race. Sin-

cere expressions are not usually under conscious control. A simple frown or smile and all the gradations in between are usually interpreted the same regardless of race, class, or gender. Although it is true that some nationalities smile more than others, especially when nervous, facial expressions can say as much or more than words. Interestingly, many gestures, including insulting gestures, vary between cultures.

- *Communicate Good Faith and Acceptance.* Groups comprised of different cultures should have a lot to talk about. However, people tend to socialize with others who are most like themselves. The less communication there is the more likely a miscommunication will occur. Reaffirming the common purpose, and a sincere desire to make things work, keeps the small problems that arise in any situation from becoming big ones. It takes a little more energy to find commonalties with others who are apparently different, but the payoff is worth it.

- *Know Your People and Yourself.* Getting to know others is done by taking the time to show some interest in who they are and what their opinions are. Knowing yourself comes from watching and observing how your biases and attitudes affect your behavior. The more you know what you are feeling and thinking in the present moment the more conscious and aware you are. A person with a high degree of awareness is more likely to be perceptive to the subtle clues that others present during an interaction. Knowing yourself and others will help you avoid potential problems.

- *Keep an Open Mind.* Many people ignore or discount any evidence that is contrary to one of their preconceived ideas. This is the attitude that says, "Don't confuse me with the facts. My mind is made up." According to the ancient Greeks, the only true wisdom is to know what you do not know. At one time or another it is wise to question everything, including long cherished beliefs, assumptions, bias, and judgments. The conclusions we jump to about someone because of his appearance or behavior are often wrong.

Those who stereotype others usually complain the loudest when they are stereotyped.

CULTURAL SENSITIVITY

Cultural sensitivity is the ability to keep track of the verbal and nonverbal impact of an attempted communication. Cross-cultural breakdowns occur because the implicit aspects of a communication are not taken into consideration.

An American woman working in Indonesia was mystified that her Oriental boss was not responding to her memos. In her culture the effort expended in putting her ideas in writing was evidence of a diligent conscientiousness. She was not aware that in the context of a collective/high power distance society sending a stream of memos showed a disregard for personal contact and status. A memo going from the subordinate to the superior does not acknowledge the status differential between them, especially if it is taken as telling the boss what to do.

Communication works when it is done in the style and context appropriate to the culture it takes place in. When sender and receiver share the same culture the implicit implications of a communication are more likely to be understood.

Mickey Schulhof, who held the post of vice chairman of Sony, USA, was said to understand Japanese not because he mastered the actual language, but because he understood the significance of what was left unsaid. This is an important skill in a culture that often communicates indirectly to avoid conflict and save face.

CULTURAL STEREOTYPES

A cross-culturally adept manager has some sense of how people will be predisposed to respond in a given set of circumstances. In the Myers-Briggs Type Indicator (MBTI) a person's preferred approach in dealing with the world corresponds to his particular psy-

General Tendencies and Stereotypes	
North American:	pragmatic, impatient, straight-forward, legalistic, linear time, idealistic
European:	status and class conscious, authority valued, worldly, linear time, cynical
Asian:	maintain harmony, dedicated, hardworking, face saving, emotions controlled
Middle East:	emotions valued, religious, fatalistic, highly hospitable, eloquence valued
Latin American:	emotions valued, sensual, fatalistic, authoritarian, nonlinear time, pride
African:	kinship and friendship valued, traditional beliefs, nonlinear time

chological type. In the same way, cultures are identified by the preferred approach of their members towards interacting with the world. The chart above (drawn from a variety of sources including Casse, 1983) presents the general tendencies of six different cultures. Naturally, any list of cultural traits will be skewed by the cultural biases of the person compiling it. This chart reflects the biases of a North American viewpoint.

Despite the ease with which people stereotype each other, human behavior has a way of defying categories. The cultures of Asian and African countries differ from each other just as much as European cultures vary from one country to the next. The information provided by the above chart is useful only as a rough approximation of general tendencies expressed in various cultures.

FAMILIARITY BREAKS STEREOTYPES

Many professionals are surprised how the stereotypes about another culture do not hold up after they have worked with people from that culture. Western trainers are often impressed that the responses of non-Westerners to team building (using experience-based activities) are much the same no matter what country the training is conducted in. After working with Europeans and Asians, a North American trainer remarked that she was struck by how much people from different cultures had in common despite their differences. As trust builds, in Singapore or in France, it becomes acceptable to go beyond the bounds of politeness and speak one's mind.

A female trainer from the United States always thought of Australian men as being on the far edge of sexism and the English as being overly reserved. Both of her biases toward these two groups proved wrong when she conducted training programs in their respective countries. There were some behaviors at first that seem to confirm her biases, but as she got to know the people in her classes, her actual experiences contradicted her initial assumptions.

EAST MEETS WEST

Making the effort to understand is the first step to creating more understanding. This point seems obvious, yet somehow it is frequently overlooked as the following story indicates:

A Japanese businessman and an Australian associate had been in the same company for fifteen years, however they never developed any degree of closeness in their working relationship. Both men managed departments in the same division although they were geographically separated. During a planning session on a joint project the Australian tried to lighten up the atmosphere with some boisterous and comic gestures. His antics failed to warm up and involve the Asians on the team including his Japanese counterpart. Since the English language skills of the Japanese businessman were functional but not fluent the team facilitator urged the two men to try to relate to each other non-verbally. The Australian put his hand out to shake hands. The Japanese responded, but the tone of the relationship between the two men remained the same. Then the Japanese gave the Australian a lesson on how to bow and present a business card. Improperly giving or receiving a business card is considered rude in Japan. The card must be presented with the printing towards the recipient. Both hands must be used to hand the card over to the recipient who uses both hands to receive the card. The recipient must thoroughly scrutinize the name, address and phone number of the card before putting it way. The atmosphere in the group became more friendly and informal as the other members applauded the efforts of the Japanese businessman to educate the Australian. The lesson only lasted a few minutes yet it made a big impact on the level of rapport between the two men. The willingness of the Australian to learn was the sign of respect and cooperation his counterpart had been looking for.

CULTURAL SENSITIVITIES

Certain behaviors carry a world of meaning that varies from one culture to another. In the society of the American southern belle it is a serious faux pas to walk around smoking a cigarette or to drink a beverage from a can or bottle. Women of this class show their good breeding by smoking only when they are seated and never drinking beverages without the benefit of a glass. One of the female members of the British royal family failed to heed these nonverbal mannerisms of good breeding on a visit to Texas. After she left town, Princess Margaret was denounced by the local wags as a woman who could never be a southern belle. This denouncement even became the title of a popular book on the subject of southern etiquette.

There are many behaviors that seem normal in your home country but may be considered offensive in another culture.

In France, a group of Americans got off a bus and headed toward the local rest room. Much to their amazement, the restroom, a large room with separate stalls, was a unisex affair. They decided to bear the pain of full bladders rather than suffer the embarrassment of using a bathroom frequented by both men and women. The French in the group had a good laugh about the difficulties their American friends imposed upon themselves.

An American businesswoman was working with a group of Asians in Singapore. The group spoke English, the language used to conduct business in that country, but had trouble understanding a particular point she was trying to make. She asked one member with good English language skills to translate what she was saying into Chinese. The man replied he would be glad to, but that it would not help most of the group. "What about our team members who are Japanese, Filipino and Malaysian?" he asked. The trainer felt provincial that she could not perceive the differences between the various nationalities.

One woman with a group of Americans on tour in England pulled off her boots in a teahouse and began bandaging the blisters on her feet, a medical procedure she never would have done in public back home. Her companions were ready to crawl under the table after observing the looks of the local patrons in response to such an unusual sight.

AUTHORITY AND INDIVIDUAL INITIATIVE

According to the popular theories of participative management, the more power is shared within an organization, the more productive the organization will be. Societies like Japan, which seem highly authoritarian, can also be highly participative in the emphasis placed on building consensus and harmony between members. Turkish orientation towards authority is similar to other high power distance countries found in South America. Obligation to family authority is high compared to the American focus on the individual. However, this obligation is accompanied by more personal warmth, whereas Americans associate authoritarian relationships with an absence of personal warmth.

Americans differ from many other cultures in the amount of faith placed in the individual. The offshoot of this faith is that American managers expect their subordinates to exercise a high degree of personal initiative.

Another belief popular in North America is that any man can rise from humble origins to occupy the highest office in the land. For a politician or even a Supreme Court judge, these humbler origins can be an asset. Interestingly enough, this concept is also cherished by Chinese communists.

CULTURAL RESISTANCE

Any new idea is bound to come up against some resistance. A typical response to a new program is, "This stuff is fine for where you come from but it won't work here." And, in all likelihood, it will not work unless local conditions are taken into consideration.[5]

Participative management did not go over well in a factory in Puerto Rico (Barrette & Bass, 1973). Much to the surprise of consultants running the program, the workers began quitting. The workers thought the company must be about to go out of business since their supervisors had started to ask them what they should do. Along the same lines, a study of leadership in India found that authoritarian leadership produced a higher level of morale and productivity than non-authoritarian leadership. A study conducted in Peru found a similar relationship in the preference for authoritarian leadership, as long as the worker had a low level of interpersonal trust. When the Peruvian workers developed a high level of interpersonal trust, they preferred a more egalitarian relationship with their supervisor.

FINDING COMMON GROUND

Cross-cultural teams need to spend some time taking an inventory of their differences before they tackle their common tasks.

Raising the issue creates a context to deal with the issue more easily if it comes up later on. One way to get this discussion going is to talk about what it is like for an outsider to work in a foreign culture and the difficulties that have to be overcome.

You can start the discussion by sharing your own experiences and ask if others had any similar experiences, setting a tone appropriate to the development of the group. A sense of belonging is tough enough to achieve even when everyone is from the same culture.

Multicultural groups should look especially hard at the purpose that unites them and affirm the shared values, symbols, and traditions that define who they are as a group. Developing this common ground helps to strengthen the cohesion of the group.

One multinational company had divisions that were Swiss, German, Swedish and American. When cross-functional teams from the different divisions worked on a project the acknowledged language was not English but "bad" English. To keep people from being embarrassed by their command or their lack of it with the English language the standard for communication was made speaker friendly. A training program was developed to instill a common set of values and expectations to which all the divisions could agree.

An international development organization in Latin American was staffed by locals and managed by Americans. The local staff felt that the Americans tended to be cold and uncommunicative. The Americans were concerned about how the locals viewed them, but they were more concerned about getting the job done. The staff thought the American managers were too naive towards and trusting of the local officials, but ironically not trusting enough of their staff to fully utilize their abilities. The American managers needed to be reminded of the importance of building relationships, especially in Latin America.

UNIVERSAL THEMES

A common point of connection among individuals with diverse backgrounds helps to create a sense of belonging. This sense of belonging enables team members to discuss with each other their personal experiences and feelings about significant events within the company. One example of finding a common connection took place during a team building session for a company in Singapore.

A young Chinese manager went through the program with his staff. He had a reputation of being dedicated to his job and had advanced through the company ranks to a position of responsibility. During the program the question was raised about personal and professional commitment. The man talked about his commitment to his own personal integrity and how that commitment was supported by his company and coworkers. His depth of feeling was such that tears filled his eyes as he spoke.

Exposing himself in this way, affected his team, breaking down the normal reserve between the members. The connecting point within the group was the desire to be personally supported by other members; a universal theme that transcends cultures and countries.

CROSS-CULTURAL PROGRAMS

There are a number of cross-cultural training programs in Washington, D.C. that prepare executives for working overseas.

- The National Association for Partners in Americas conducts cross-cultural training programs for business leaders in North and South America.

- The International Counseling Center runs several conferences on cross-cultural issues each year and provides contract training to international organizations.
- The Society for Intercultural Education Training and Research (SIETAR) maintains a list of members who conduct cross-cultural training. The Society also conducts a five-day workshop to certify trainers in cross-cultural communications.

CULTURGRAMS

Brigham Young University produces a four-page summary on the culture of a country, which they call a culturgram. Culturgrams have been written for most of the countries in the world. They offer a quick way to prepare for a visit to a part of the world that is unfamiliar. To obtain a copy you can visit your local library or contact Brigham Young University.

15
Benefiting from Diversity

Broderbund

E pluribus unum—
from the many, one.

Motto on U. S. quarter

The discussion about diversity seems to increase each year. Emigration is changing the ethnic composition of the workforce not only in the United States but also in Europe and Asia. Before 1924, when Congress enacted restrictive immigration laws, emigrants poured into America bringing with them a polyglot of customs and traditions from the countries of Eastern Europe. A large proportion of the population entering the workforce in the early part of this century spoke English as a second language if they spoke it at all. The fledgling science of industrial psychology got its start, in part, by researching the issues that arose over assimilating these new workers.

THE DIVERSITY DEBATE

Internationally, a debate exists whether a diverse workforce helps or hinders productivity. Some Japanese believe the lack of diversity among their workers contributes to their economic prowess. People of different cultures and values can be hindered by their differences when they work together. The creed in America is that diversity is a positive force. A person with a different perspective can make a unique contribution, increasing the range of available resources and ideas. According to a study conducted by Warren Watson, a professor at the University of North Texas, both views have some validity. Watson compared the work of 19 teams that were "culturally homogeneous" against the work of 17 teams that were diverse. The teams, composed of four or five graduate students, were given the same tasks. At first, the non-diverse teams out performed the diverse team. Over a period of 17 weeks, the diverse teams improved to the point their work was nearly as good as non-diverse teams. The diverse teams had to strive more to create understanding and cooperation, but they clearly showed more potential for creativity and problem solving.[1]

BOTTOM LINE

Watson's study has important implications for American industry. The main rationale, for a diversity training program, as with any training program in the corporate world, is its contribution to the bottom line. The more diverse a work team, the more impact multicultural skills will have on productivity. Companies that learn to manage a diverse workforce, and teach their employees multicultural skills, will have a competitive edge over other firms which continue to do business as usual. The model presented on the next page diagrams the relationship between multicultural skills, cultural diversity and organizational performance.

Teams have to do more than appreciate their diversity to benefit from it. The ability to benefit from diversity becomes increasingly important when you consider the prediction made by the U.S. Department of Labor: after the year 2000 between 80 to 85% of the people joining the workforce will be from groups currently considered minorities.

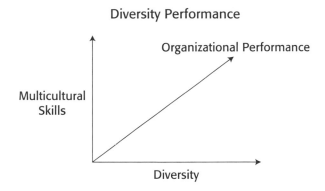

During the 1990's, the percentage of Caucasian males in the workforce was estimated to be 44% to 47%. Within twenty years it will be half that amount.

E PLURIBUS UNUM

Differences in our national culture stem mainly from influences that are generational, racial, and ethnic. Gender, sexual orientation, religion, and physical ability are also important. Because of these differences, sharing the same nationality with someone does not mean we share the same basic values, beliefs, and language.

The ways people communicate, handle conflict, give feedback, and participate in a group are affected by our cultural and physical traits. Ironically, teamwork is based on the identification of what we have in common including, values, goals, norms, and language. A team is built on the willingness of its members to create a shared culture. A diversity program, properly designed and implemented, lays the groundwork for this process. Acknowledging and respecting differences reduces the potential for ethnic strife. The acceptance, understanding, and appreciation of our differences clear the path towards acknowledging the similarities that bind us together.

CULTURAL UNDERSTANDING

The more entrenched our differences become, the more a conscious effort is required to build a bridge between them. The adage about personal communication, "misunderstanding is the norm and understanding the happy accident," points out the inherent shortcomings of a common language.

When Caucasians converse, the listener usually looks at the speaker while listening. With some African Americans the reverse is true (Watts, 1987). The listener looks away, glancing back occasionally at the speaker.[2] Because of cultural differences, one speaker might think that he is not being listened to, while another may wonder why the listener is looking at him so much. Even when you think you understand why someone is acting as he is it is wise to ask. The following questions might help create more understanding when communication is confused by diversity or other related issues:

- Here is what I hear or see.
- This is what it means to me.
- Is that what you are trying to tell me?

You might also learn something useful by asking:

- What do I need to know to understand you better?
- What can I tell you that will help you understand me better?

DIFFERENCES CAN'T BE IGNORED

Some managers insist they run a colorblind operation and treat everyone in the same manner, as they would want to be treated. However, a person's culture and values affect the intent and interpretation of every communication sent or received. Ignoring a person's cultural background increases the potential for a miscommunication. The following incidents reveal some of the mishaps that occur between different cultures:

An emigrant from Russia was nearly in tears after filling out a job application. The application required that she list her accomplishments, an act considered by her ethnic group to be crude bragging.

An emigrant from West Africa was asked, not infrequently, if the people in her homeland really lived as they were depicted in Tarzan movies. The woman, raised in a large, cosmopolitan city, felt belittled by these questions even though they were asked in a friendly manner.

A Native American elder tried to discuss a community issue with a government official. The elder was shocked by the lack of respect the official showed by looking directly in his eyes. The official wondered to himself why the elder seemed displeased with the conversation and redoubled his effort in what he thought was a sincere and straightforward manner.

An Asian emigrant was singled out by her supervisor and praised in front of everyone else for her accomplishments on the job. The employee reacted with a great deal of embarrassment and did not come to work the next day.

SOME DIFFERENCES SHOULD BE IGNORED

The performer Cher sings a popular song about not enough love and understanding between people. Diversity is not just about understanding each other. It is about acceptance. But acceptance comes from understanding. Treating people as less than us because they are not like us is the taproot of prejudice. And prejudice is fed by ignorance or a lack of understanding. The impact of prejudice affects those who differ from the norms accepted by society in the areas of sexual orientation, gender roles, physical or mental ability, and size.

A very overweight woman hid her snacks from her coworkers. Someone would be sure to make an unkind comment or raise an eyebrow if she was seen eating a candy bar. Even when she wasn't eating the looks she got from some people made her feel awful.

A lawyer, confined to a wheelchair, was frustrated by narrow doorways and corridors in his workplace that slowed down his movement. Some people were impatient to pass him and brushed by as if he were an inanimate object.

Two lesbian women who lived together as a couple were afraid to be seen together too often. If their employers found out they were gay it might hurt their careers. If people in the neighborhood found out, they might be targeted for abuse or even physical assault.

A man who was four feet tall was always aware of how others reacted to his height. He tried to make people feel comfortable by making jokes at his own expense. The strain of dealing with the issue was exhausting because it never let up from day to day.

CREATIVE DIFFERENCES

Does everyone look, dress, talk, and act the same way in your office? To what extent are personal differences accepted? A relentless demand for conformity can numb the spirit and the mind. Xenophobia, the fear of outsiders, is really the fear of differences. This fear kills the creative urge because the creative process works best in an environment that is open to, accepting of, and even curious about differences.

KNOW THY SELF

Some diversity programs ask you to identify your own prejudices. But they do it in an indirect manner. In some programs the participants are shown pictures of people and asked to come up with a name and biography that reflects who they think those people are. The participants discuss the pictures in small groups. After they present the made-up biographies they are given the actual biographies of the people in the pictures.

As you might expect the process is something of a set up. A man in one picture whom one group dubbed Poncho, the outlaw biker, turned out in real life to be John, the successful writer of children's books. The homeless woman in another picture is in real life a lawyer. The moral of the exercise is that judging by appearances tells more about the judge than it does about the person being judged. Snap judgments can keep us from getting to know who a person really is.

DEALING WITH THE PAST

In a business environment people keep a certain level of reserve. The public self, the person we present to the world, is not always congruent with the private self, where our true thoughts and feelings reside. Diversity programs ask participants to take a look at the inner realm of the private self, since this is where our attitudes and behaviors are shaped.

Some diversity programs use the techniques developed by the therapeutic self-help movement known as Co-Counseling. According to Co-Counseling philosophy, nearly everyone has felt the "oppression" of different "isms" such as ageism, racism, or sexism. Unexamined beliefs form the root of the "isms" that have afflicted human relationships for as long as we have been dealing with each other. The more unknown and different the "other" is, the easier it is to project the disowned side of our own personality upon that "other." Damage occurs when a young person internalizes an oppression and ceases to believe in his or her own self worth. During the diversity program, dyads or small groups are formed in which the participants share their experiences of oppression and how it affected them. By sharing the traumas of the past it is possible to free oneself from its binding influence. As you might expect, these kinds of programs can be emotionally challenging.

CURIOSITY EXERCISE

Curiosity is nonjudgmental. We are seldom curious about those we judge. The curiosity exercise is used in some diversity programs to foster more understanding. In order to be curious you have to forgo your judgments. The exercise starts by asking the participants to self select into similar groups. The participants are asked to choose a category such as sexual orientation, age, race, gender, or nationality. Once they are in their groups the participants discuss some of the following questions:

- What it is like to be a member of your group?
- As a member of your group what are you most proud of?
- Are there any questions you have of the other group(s) that you always wanted to know but hesitated to ask?
- Where did you get your opinions about the other group(s)?
- How have these opinions affected you?

After discussing these questions among themselves each group asks and then answers a question in turn from another group.

PAIN

If you spend any time listening to people talk about how they have been discriminated against one point keeps emerging. Few non-minorities really grasp how pervasive, insidious, and painful racism is. If you are not the target of it, it's not likely you will see it. But just because it is not on your "radar screen" does not mean racism or some other "ism" of gender, age, or size, is not there.

Given this kind of reality it can seem that those who respond by saying, "but look how things have improved," are only reassuring themselves. At the other extreme the "hypersensitive, quick to take offense, and quicker to get rich by being a victim," mentality needs no encouragement in today's litigious world. One point most people could agree to is the need for more compassion and understanding. If we really could walk a mile in someone's shoes and know what he or she had been through we might find more admiration instead of condemnation.

NO HONEYMOON

The cost of not dealing with diversity issues can dramatically hurt the bottom line. Nissan Motors paid out millions of dollars because of lawsuits over sexual harassment. The bad publicity and poor morale affected sales and productivity. Denny's Restaurants took a similar hit from a charge of racial discrimination from black Secret Service agents who received poor service. Starting a diversity program, however, is no guarantee that everyone is now going to get along. Things may seem like they are getting worse as they move towards getting better; a state called the "healing crisis" in the medical field. In situations where there is suppressed hostility, providing a context for discussion can unleash a lot of bottled up energy. Skilled facilitation by program trainers who can manage the process is the first and last requirement. Understandably, just the idea of discussing diversity in a racially mixed group will make most managers nervous. What if people leave more upset than when they came in? Hoping to avoid a meltdown some managers will want to create a two-tiered training. Staff in one program and management in another. But if one group is racially diverse and the other is not that setup can generate even more frustration. Obviously, discussion about diversity can be more beneficial when it takes place in a diverse group.

COMMUNITY HEALING

It is difficult to change attitudes and behaviors when the source that feeds them is beyond the realm of the intellect. There are archetypes deep in the human psyche that affect us more than we realize. They are best accessed, if they can be touched at all, through emotions, myths, and ritual.

Coat and tie programs held in air conditioned classrooms seldom reach the place in the human mind and heart where profound meaning and change reside. The following is an account of the author's experience with one of the best diversity programs he ever attended:

Malidoma Somé[3] is an African Shaman from Burkina Faso. He currently lives in Oakland, California and leads workshops in the United States. His approach to healing the pain of discrimination is based on African tribal customs. To heal a community the community must be willing to engage in ritual and ceremony. The first part of the workshop is spent letting people tell their stories. Men and women from all backgrounds and races share how discrimination or other "isms" have touched their lives. After the stories have been told each person goes into the woods to gather a bundle. Sticks, grass, spider webs, a dead moth, are some of the items a person might wrap together as a bundle. Along with those items the intention is made that the bundle contains the pain, anger, humiliation, guilt, and anything else, which the person wants to let go. From the meeting room door to the fire pit outside a pathway with arches is constructed and decorated. According to Somé, the subconscious mind takes note that something significant is about to happen when it passes through an arch. Somehow it responds and opens up to a deeper level of awareness. When the preparations are complete, one by one the participants leave the meeting room. Slowly, they walk along the pathway to the fire pit. For a few minutes they stand by the fire and when ready toss their bundle and everything it represents into flames. When they return they are welcomed back with song and dance. After the ceremony the room radiates happiness, fellowship, and a very tangible sense of accomplishment.

16
Business Games

Maxcomm Associates

Why must anyone seek for new ways of acting?
The answer is that in the long run the
continuity of life itself depends on the
making of new experiments. . .

J. Z. YOUNG
BRITISH BIOLOGIST

Does your organization need to lighten-up? Are too many employees taking themselves and their ideas too seriously? Why not
try having everyone stand in a circle and then sit on each other's
laps. "New games" such as a giant "lap-sits" without chairs have
been done with over a thousand people at one time. These games
are activities that help the members of an organization regain their
sense of perspective and have fun doing it. The games got their
start back in the heyday of student anti-war protests. Stewart Brand,
the founder of the Whole Earth Catalog, decided a format was
needed that would allow people "to experience the source of their
views within themselves." Many gatherings, political or business,

simply ended in more entrenchment of opposing points-of-view. Through games that created opportunities for cooperation Brand hoped to open a space for genuine dialogue between conflicting groups.[1]

BUILDING COMMUNITY

Encouraged by the results achieved through "new games," Brand started the New Games Foundation as a means for community building. The foundation evolved into an organization that consulted with corporations and human service agencies, tailoring training sessions according to their needs. Although the foundation is no longer in business many trainers and consultants have continued to develop and use new games in an organizational setting. The games are not debriefed at any great length, but are mainly done for their own sake. The games strengthen the primary relationship and alliance between group members. When people have fun together it generates a sense of community that lasts long after the games are over.[2]

Many of these games are used as "ice breakers" to energize participants at the beginning of a training session or business meeting and get them moving and laughing. Playing helps move people out of their intellects into their bodies and emotions. As the individual becomes engaged in the process of having fun, creativity and problem-solving abilities are enhanced. The following are some examples of "new games":

Animal Call

Participants are divided into groups or pairs, blindfolded (or asked to close their eyes), and individually given the name of an animal. Making a reasonable facsimile of their animal's mating call, participants of the same species try to link up with their group or partner. The trainer's job is to keep people from bumping into trees, walls, or each other. Once they find their group or mate the participants take their blindfolds off and cheer the other "animals" on in their search. The last participant to find his group or partner earns a round of applause.

Yurt Circle

Participants need to depend on each other to accomplish this task. The group stands in a circle, almost an arm's length apart and holds hands. A count off by "yag" and "doa" or in English "one" and "two" designates those who will lean out and those who will lean in. Slowly, coached by the trainer, the "yags" lean out and the "doas" lean in and then vice versa. The more people lean in either direction, the more their weight must be balanced in the other direction for the circle to remain upright.

Rock-Paper-Scissors

A good example of a "new game" where there is some friendly competition is Rock-Paper-Scissors. Two teams are formed of ten or more members. The teams face each other a few feet apart in two parallel lines. Behind each team, twenty or more feet away, is the boundary of a safety zone. On the count of three, each team presents their extended hands in the form of a rock, paper, or scissors. Just as in the children's game, rock breaks scissors, scissors cut paper, and paper covers rock. The losing team must beat a hasty retreat to their safety zone before the opposite team tags them.

Tagged members join the other team or they can form a cheering section on the sidelines. Before each match, both sides conduct a quick huddle to decide on what symbol they will present. The game continues until all the members of one side have joined the sidelines or the other team (Fluegeleman, 1981).

COMPETITION VERSUS COLLABORATION

What makes a game a game, according to Berine De Koven, a researcher in the nature of play, is the conjunction of a goal and the resistance against achieving it (Fluegeleman, 1976). In the workplace you compete individually for position and recognition, at the same time you must cooperate collectively so your department can compete for market share or bureaucratic influence. This paradox is modeled in a game. Just as in real life, your opponent is also your partner. The participants can choose to compete with other teams or collaborate. Even though it reduces the overall level of success, most groups automatically compete. The choice to compete is made out of habit rather than any conscious decision that weighs the pros and cons of competition versus collaboration.

However, in the last few years many trainers have noticed a shift towards more collaboration when team-building games are played. The reason could be what has come to be known as the "hundredth monkey" phenomena. A critical mass is reached when enough people embrace a new behavior. That critical mass acts as a catalyst, causing a shift in the behavior of the entire society.

TEAM-BUILDING GAMES

Team-building games are ideal for a team with eight to twelve members. Smaller groups may lose the dynamism and energy that a team provides. A group of fifteen or more can be difficult to manage unless broken down into subgroups, each with its own qualified facilitator. The activities are experience-based and heuristic. The learnings come from the group discussion held afterwards as well as from the experience of doing the exercise. Presented in a light-hearted spirit of fun, the activities provide a stimulus for serious learning and insight when the team rehashes what it did or failed to do.

Some team-building games are described below:[3]

Blindfold Trust Walk

The team is divided into pairs. One of each pair is blindfolded. The other acts as a guide, leading the blindfolded person around the office or an area outside. The exercise can be done in silence if the pair are given time to develop a set of nonverbal signals before they begin. A nice addition to the exercise is for the blindfolded person to touch some objects like a tree or park bench. After each person takes a turn being blindfolded a discussion is held. Team members frequently comment on the deeper levels of trust and sensitivity they feel has developed between them. Allowing someone to lead you requires significant trust and communication. If two partners can develop a system that allows them to achieve that level of trust in the woods, what do they need to do to achieve the same results back at the office?

Knots

This exercise is best done when the business dress for the day is jeans or other casual attire. Its purpose is to create a sense of group accomplishment in a way that is fun and enjoyable. The group circles up. Everyone reaches across the open space in the circle and grasps the hand of another person across from them. With their free arm, they grasp the hand of the person next to them. From then on it is up to the group to figure out a way to untangle themselves and recreate a circle without letting go of anyone's hand. People climb over, through under and around each other before they clear up the tangle. Finally, it is down to a smaller knot of three or four people still tangled up. Everyone gives encouragement and suggestions. "Let's try this," someone suggests and to everyone's surprise, it works. The team gives itself a round of applause as it stands again in a circle.

Continuous Improvement

This exercise is a good way to illustrate two key points of effective group work. The first is that all of us together are smarter than each of us separately. The second is the ever-present potential for more improvement. Have the group of six or more people stand in a circle. Toss a tennis ball to someone in the circle and ask him or her to toss it to someone else and so forth until everyone has had a chance to catch the ball. The last person to catch the ball will toss it back to the first person to toss it. Then challenge the group to repeat the same sequence of tossing the ball from one person to the next. If the team does not think they can do it point out that each team member only has to remember to whom they threw the ball. Once the team has the sequence mastered start tossing more balls into the circle and watch the fun level escalate. The second learning is that continuous improvement is always possible provided all the options for task performance are considered. Collect all the balls except one and challenge the team to reduce the time required to move the ball around the circle in the same sequence. The analogy to producing a product or document is obvious. Step out of the circle and time each attempt the group makes. Some teams will figure out though trial and error a way to move the ball around in less than a second. During the debrief discuss the assumptions that affected the teams "productivity." Ask the team how their assumptions limited the options they tried for continuous improvement.

Blindfold Square

After a group has loosened up with some of the previous exercises it is likely to be ready to attempt an event that requires focused planning and problem solving. Each team member is blindfolded and given his mission. Somewhere in the open area or room is a length of rope. Once they find the rope they must organize themselves into a structure with four equal sides. (If the group is looking for more of a challenge have them form a five- or six-sided figure. Or with two ropes they can form two squares and create a pattern like the one on an argyle sock.) The process of decision making is highlighted when the team is asked by a facilitator if they are ready to take off blindfolds and assess the results of their efforts. Some groups argue with each other like the proverbial blind

men trying to describe an elephant before they take their blindfolds off.

The Great Egg Drop

This exercise is a an excellent tool to illustrate the dynamics of
competition and cooperation between small groups. It also provides the chance for the natural ham in all of us to come out and
act outrageous. The tone set in the initial presentation of the exercise will affect the way it unfolds and the type of learning that
can be gained.

Divide a large group into smaller teams. Each team is given ten
or twenty drinking straws, some masking tape, and one egg. The
task is to build an airborne egg retrieval device for NASA. The
device must allow the egg to land safely on the ground or floor
after being dropped from a height of eight or more feet. Once the
teams have constructed their device they make a marketing presentation and conduct a test flight in front of the other teams. A
successful test flight (the egg does not break) and the best presentation wins the contract.

All the various factors provide plenty of material to highlight
the group dynamics of each team. Watch out for the tendency of
some team members to take over and disregard the input of other
members. Exercises that involve physical or construction activities often bring out gender issues.

Another version of the Egg Drop highlights the importance of
cooperation among seemingly competing groups. In this story line
a nonprofit organization is trying to save an endangered species.
The only way to retrieve the eggs of the species is by dropping
them from the nest to the ground below. Your group is on site and
has been asked to construct a number of retrievers for this task.

Each team is given a different amount of resources to build their
device although the difference is not made obvious. Some items
in the kits provided are useful and some are not. Do the teams
share resources and ideas on how to build their retrievers? Did the

teams compete with each other when cooperation would have been more productive? If they failed to cooperate, why?

BOARD GAMES

A number of board games are marketed for team building and diversity training. Some games use structured roles, dice, and playing pieces, to pit the wits of the individuals or teams against each other or against the game itself. Others have more free flowing scenarios and are facilitated by the vendor. The value in playing a board game is the learning and insights generated in a discussion about the outcome of the game and the behaviors of the participants. Since the board games on the market are likely to change frequently, the best way to see what is available is to pick up a recent copy of "TRAINING: The Human Side of Business" or the "Training & Development Journal" and look through the advertisements. Some popular board games include:[4]

- The Compact Team Game offered by Games Teams Play, Compact Training Company
- The Diversity Game offered by Quality Educational Development, Inc.
- Eagles Flight and Gold of the Desert Kings offered by Eagles Flight
- Simgames by Thiagi, offered by Workshops by Thiagi
- The Looking Glass Experience offered by Leadership in Action at the Center for Creative Leadership

TEAM-BUILDING SIMULATIONS

Simulations are games in the usual sense of the word but the subject matter is more serious. The participants are given a scenario such as being lost in the wilderness or facing a severe storm at sea. Critical decisions must be made by the players as a group. An unwise decision could have drastic consequences if this was a real

life event. As the players get into the game the imaginary consequences generate heated conversations. The game is debriefed just
like other problem solving-activities. Insights are gained by discussing the interactions between the players. The discussions
should be led by an experienced facilitator, who can help the team
examine the approaches it uses to solve problems, share resources,
conduct planning, and make decisions.

TEAM-BUILDING VIDEOS

Given the pervasive presence of television in our lives it is inevitable that team building would be offered on video tape. Most
of these videos are about twenty to forty minutes in length. They
usually have a plot involving situations in the business world that
are resolved using management principles taught in most business
schools. A few videos, featuring some well-known personality, try
to get their message across in the pep talk format. A video, like a
board game, has a certain advantage in its ease of use and relative
low cost. Although the initial price may be as much as $800 there
is no limit to the number of times you can use it.

Videos are an excellent way to introduce a topic and provide
material for a group discussion. As a stand-alone training program,
a video is too passive to have the impact of more interactive learning formats. Most companies will let the potential client review
the video for a fee before paying the full purchase price. As with
the board games, it is a good idea to check with a recent copy of
"TRAINING"[5] or the "Training and Development Journal"[6] to
see what is available on the market.

A few of the many companies you can contact include:[7]

- CRM FILMS
- Films Incorporated
- Video Publishing House
- AMA Video.

Section V
The Challenge of Change

17
Team Killers

Stream

Nothing can stop the man with the right mental attitude from achieving his goal; nothing on earth can help the man with the wrong mental attitude.

THOMAS JEFFERSON

The fellow who thinks he knows it all is especially annoying to those of us who do.

HAROLD COFFIN

Why do some teams fail when they have so much going for them? The members are saying the right things and everyone is putting out vast amounts of energy, yet nothing works like it should. During the lifetime of any team there will be periods of frustration and little apparent progress, no matter how talented the members. Certain behaviors and attitudes are obstacles to high performance. Successful teams are aware of these obstacles and take the actions needed to overcome them.

When you can name a problem or a troublesome behavior it loses some of its power to disrupt the collective effort. The purpose of this chapter is to identify some of the blocks to teamwork and help you find solutions. One of worst self-inflicted wounds is to blindly continue to do what does not work. Potential solutions, obvious in hindsight, are never discovered because no one took the time to analyze what was not working and why.

TURF ISSUES

You have seen it before. Large egos, scarce resources, covert agendas, and conflicting interests, are some of the conditions that prevent a sense of unity. As was mentioned in Chapter Six, "Conflict and Negotiation," conflict is often situational. Employees with different responsibilities can easily end up at loggerheads when each jealously guards the prerogatives and agendas of his own position or department. Teamwork begins when the members of the different departments focus on where they support instead of constrain each other. Divisive issues obscure the larger purpose. To find that larger purpose, ask the essential question: "What goals do we all support?"

Defining common goals that everyone can pledge allegiance to is the starting line. If people first agree on where they are going as a group they are more likely to agree on the means that will get them there.

THEY . . . to . . . WE

Some organizations polarize themselves into two opposing camps: union versus nonunion, professionals versus support staff, department X versus department Z, or management versus everyone else. Each group perceives the other to be the "they" that is the source of its woes.

$$\text{"We"} \longrightarrow \text{"They"}$$
$$\text{"They"} \longleftarrow \text{"We"}$$

As long as an organization is divided against itself, gridlock is inevitable. Even when there are no active recriminations, the constant use of "they" in everyday conversation indicates a potentially troublesome split. As mentioned in Chapter Six, "Conflict and Negotiation," gridlock is broken when two opposing groups shift their perspective and begin to look together at the problems and challenges they face, instead of seeing each other as the problem. This shift from blaming to problem solving happens when people point their fingers at the problem instead of each other. You can tell right away when you are in an organization with a unified spirit; employees at all levels of the company use the pronoun "we" when they talk about "their" company.

Participatory organizations are alert to opportunities to narrow the gap between separate and competing interests. Even seemingly small and symbolic measures help shift the mentality and language of "they" to "we." In some companies, physical space, such as the layout of the parking lot, office partitions, and eating areas, are arranged to minimize differences in status. Use of first names and dress-down days are encouraged.

At Quad\Graphics, a national printing firm, the people in the front office and those back at the presses, wear the same uniforms. Male managers don a coat and tie when they go meet with clients. When they return, the managers put on a blue work shirt with their first name stitched over the front pocket, the same type of shirt worn by the hourly employees in the plant.

CLASS WARFARE

A few conflicts are predictable. One of them is the friction between the professionals and the administrative/clerical persons who support them. The administrative people complain that they are taken for granted and treated like kids. The professionals wonder why the administrative staff does not seem to have the same sense of urgency or focus they do. The administrative people want to know what is going on but are frustrated that no one tells them. The professionals grouse that the support staff is just not motivated.

Some organizations minimize and even avoid this type of class conflict by emphasizing that everyone is a professional and should be treated that way. Gore & Associates, Inc., the maker of Gore-Tex fabric, has an egalitarian corporate culture. Gore traditionally does not assign job titles to any of its associates. This does not stop some employees from using their imagination. Poking fun at titles one woman went so far as to give herself the moniker, Supreme Commander. In this kind of culture everyone is considered and treated as a valued member of the organization. Gore goes even further by encouraging managers not to give orders. Just as you would with any adult, managers make requests of associates instead of dictating or commanding. Gore's egalitarian philosophy requires executives to forego typical perks like special parking, and executive dining and wash rooms. What the managerial ego forgoes in losing a few perks is more than offset by the ideas and energy fostered by Gore's approach to building an organization.

FEAR OF FAILURE

The onslaught of multiple deadlines in the business world often generates tremendous pressure to get things done. The survival of one's personal reputation hinges on the degree of success achieved. This pressure can act as a disincentive to be creative and take chances. The learning curve of a new approach usually results in mistakes. The damage "mistakes" can inflict on one's reputation heightens the disincentive toward innovation. The following story may be apocryphal, but it illustrates how the ideal corporate culture would respond to proactive mistakes:

> A manager made a mistake that cost his company nearly a million dollars. He started cleaning out his desk thinking he would be fired. His boss called him to his office and started talking about his next project. "I thought you were going to fire me," he blurted out in surprise. "Are you kidding?" his boss replied. "Not after I've invested so much money in your education."

The fear of failure has kept more than one team from realizing the synergy of a group performance. Trying to avoid mistakes, managers often perform tasks they should delegate. The price of a participative environment, at least initially, is more mistakes. Innovation is more likely when people have some leeway to take risks without the limiting fear of repercussions. In an environment that encourages initiative, errors of commission (risk taking) are always more acceptable than errors of omission (carelessness and apathy). The fear of failure is tied to other fears that impose conformity and prevent people from challenging the status quo. The resulting "group think" can bind an entire company to outmoded concepts and beliefs.

Senior management often preaches the virtue of risk taking. Just as often they fret that there are no takers. The problem is that people always pay more attention to what people do than to what they say. If management confuses retribution with holding people accountable a culture of risk avoidance is the natural outcome. Perhaps the senior manager who forgave his subordinate in the above story used to be a Jesuit. According to the Jesuits, the true faith is best supported by the creed, "It is better to ask forgiveness than to ask permission."

SHARING THE GLORY AND THE BLAME

The aphorism, success has many who claim parentage, but failure is always an orphan, must have been written with office politics in mind. Grabbing for the glory if a project looks like a winner, or passing the buck when the outcome is in doubt, reduces the level of cooperation and the potential for eventual success. Predictably, if the project runs into trouble, some people will be back on the sidelines wondering aloud whose idea this was in the first place. Assigning blame seldom solves any problems. In a team effort, the team members share the blame when things go wrong and expend their energy on problem solving. When things go right everyone on the team shares in the glory and rewards of the success.

A government team was kicking off a high visibility project. The members were highly motivated but nervous. Success was not a certainty. If "the wheels came off" how would the project leader hand out the blame? His supervisors would want to know by name who screwed up. During one of the initial meetings the team members discovered they were all veterans. Swapping war stories they recalled one of the axioms of military service: Never leave anyone behind. Units that remained effective when others fell apart under fire or cut off behind enemy lines were the ones that carried their wounded out with them. At the end of the meeting the team affirmed that they would look for solutions instead of scapegoats. If someone did make a major goof everyone shared responsibility because it meant they failed to give that person the input, coaching, or feedback he needed to succeed.

MANAGEMENT BY INTIMIDATION

Some managers attempt to motivate their employees by scaring them. Shame, blame, and guilt, administered verbally or in writing are the tools of their "tradecraft." The signs of a psychologically unhealthy company are written on the faces of the those who work there; lower levels of cooperation, trust, and morale; higher levels of hostility, fear, and discontent. As soon as you walk inside the office door you notice the atmosphere has an uncomfortable and heavy feeling. Employees model how they treat each other and their customers based on how they are treated by their boss.

The culture of an organization is self-perpetuating. The more fear there is in an organization the harder it is to get people to work together cooperatively and creatively. Heavy-handed managers seldom ask for the ideas and opinions of their subordinates because of a strongly held belief that no one knows as much as they do. Their philosophy, "my way or the highway," destroys initiative. Subordinates are quick to notice if the boss has the habit of shooting the messenger. Consequently, not only are problems hidden, but solutions as well. The heavy-handed manager is always looking for someone to make an example of what not to do. Instead of employee of the month, the motivational program is dog of the month. Even though everyone does his or her best to avoid the doghouse someone will be selected. There are times a manager should show anger or displeasure, but a good manager does not abuse her power by going beyond disciplinary actions that are firm and fair.

Derogatory language, even behind closed doors, undermines the confidence of employees who are afraid to set limits or fight back. Heavy-handed managers do not realize the impact their behaviors and even their unspoken attitudes and moods have on others. They seldom see the light and change their ways without the help of a forceful intervention. If an epiphany does occur it can usually be traced to the conjunction of a personal and professional crisis.

DIVIDE AND CONQUER

One of the most common fears in the workplace is losing one's job to someone else in the organization. It can be unsettling when those with less seniority seem to know more than you do about the newest trends in the business. If a subordinate or associate does too well they might get your job while you get the door. Some managers try to deal with their fears through the strategy of "divide and conquer." They limit the information they distribute, giving one subordinate one part of the picture and another the other part. Hoarding information creates a bottleneck only they control. Failing to educate and coach their subordinates keeps them from looking too good, giving the manager a false sense of superiority and job security.

Effective leaders let go of tightfisted control and do what they can to set up their people for success. This means the noise level may go up, since the manager who shares information and works participatively is going to hear things he or she may not want to hear. If you know your people, their strengths and weakness, you can tailor their assignments so they do the tasks they will excel in. A manager who manages in this fashion creates an environment where everyone has the opportunity to learn from others.

FEAR OF MENTORING

When fear and misguided self-interest prevent older employees from mentoring newer and younger ones, the organization is systematically destroying its future. Productivity in a team is dependent on the willingness to share procedures, tips and other job related information. This sharing diffuses power throughout the organization in a way that encourages everyone to contribute to the collective effort.

The nuances of running a business are difficult to transfer through books or videotape. The level of skill that makes for exceptional performance often is nurtured initially by some form of mentoring. Leading-edge companies encourage more senior employees to mentor new or junior members. Organizations that do not actively encourage mentoring are engaging in a mild form of self-sabotage. For example, in one American steel mill, new employees were practically ostracized for the first six months of their employment. The new workers did the same work but were paid less. Older workers told the newer workers as little as possible out of fear that the new worker might some day take their job. Eventually, the mill, like many others in the "rust belt," went out of business.

Mentoring does not have to be an accidental process. The Wall Street company, Dow Jones, started a program called Quad Squads. The mentor, a senior manager, Meets with and counsels three junior employees from other departments. The "squad" benefits from the counsel of the senior member and the opportunity to build relationships and exchange ideas with each other.

Other companies use a similar format that matches senior professionals and employees with a year or two of experience with new arrivals. The new arrivals are exposed to the spectrum of corporate knowledge and professional contacts. The programs help minorities and women gain entrance to the "old boy" or "old girl" networks.

SCARCITY VERSUS ABUNDANCE

The story about the steelworkers points out that hoarding information can create a "lose-lose" situation. Holding on to what they have, insecure persons treat others as potential rivals instead of associates. In a group, the belief in scarcity instead of generosity results in hanging separately instead of hanging together. An old Russian joke illustrates how this attitude creates a self-fulfilling prophecy.

> A peasant received a visit from an angel. His prayers have been answered, the angel announced and whatever he wants will be granted. The peasant was overjoyed until the angel added that whatever the peasant asked for, his nearest neighbor will receive twice as much of the same blessing. The peasant pondered this for a while and then told the angel, "All right, poke out one of my eyes."

People who feel secure in themselves make good mentors because they encourage and even celebrate the professional growth of their subordinates. Successful organizations become precisely that because their leaders were willing to work themselves out of job. These people know that in helping their associates and subordinates succeed they are helping themselves succeed as well. They have faith that there is enough success and opportunity out there for everyone. Companies recognize that the people most worthy of advancement are those who are supportive of their colleagues; even the colleagues they may be competing with for a promotion.

TOXIC TEAM MEMBERS

A few people in any organization will show up with an especially large bag of psychological issues. They often end up feeling ignored, unappreciated, and trapped in a dead-end job. Eventually, they seek an outlet for their frustrations by venting them on a suitable target. Nit picking, faultfinding, foot dragging, and rumor mongering are some of the many passive-aggressive activities that serve to perpetuate the grievances that produced them.

Since these team members save up their bad feelings like green stamps, the motto one trainer frequently repeated to her classes in Washington DC was, "Burn the past daily." Toxic team members act, in part, the way they do because no one confronts them about the impact of their behavior on others. Since they are usually good at making critical and caustic comments, others fear their wrath. Trying to cope, some teams invest an outsider with the responsibility to reform the errant member—a strategy that seldom succeeds. Firm yet compassionate coaching is a leadership responsibility that cannot be transferred or abdicated.

> A simple test to determine if someone has the aptitude for teamwork is suggested by Blotnick in his book, *The Corporate Steeple Chase*. Ask the person in mind if there is anyone in the organization whom he admires and respects. If the answer is an emphatic "no" and that person has been around at least six months, he is not likely to be a team player.[1]

SETTING LIMITS

Occasionally a team member will take on one or more of the roles listed below on a full-time basis. If there is no consequence for dysfunctional behavior, no one says a word to the person, the behaviors will probably continue. The leader's job is to define the behaviors that are not acceptable, explain the impact they have on others and the consequences if the employee chooses to continue to act in a dysfunctional manner. If the behavior continues the leader has the unpleasant but necessary task of enforcing those consequences. The roles include:

- *Cynic.* Nothing works and never will.
- *Complainer/Victim.* Not poor me again.
- *Martyr.* I do more work than anyone around here.
- *Blamer/Fault Finder.* It's always your fault.
- *Put-down Artist.* Let's laugh at your expense.
- *Judger.* She's no good.
- *Paranoid.* They are out to get me.
- *Saboteur.* He deserves to fail.
- *Terrorist.* I am going to intimidate you.
- *Avoider.* Not my job.

Trying to counsel someone on his attitude is risky. He might respond, "I don't have an attitude problem. You have a perception problem." Attitudes are internal mental states. Although they affect a person's words and deeds, only words and deeds are observable. Attitudes are not. Focus on observable behaviors. According to the theory of cognitivative dissonance; change the behaviors and the attitudes will change as well.

SPIN CYCLE

You may have heard the adage that what you focus on grows stronger in your life. Negativity begets more negativity just as success can foster more success. When the emotional atmosphere is toxic the stories people tell each other reflect that negativity. Lots of blame and anger with very little acknowledgement and gratitude. If you graphed on a pie chart all the stories people in a dysfunctional workplace are thinking about (or even telling each other) it would look like this:[2]

Story Pie Chart
The ratio of positive to negative stories at work:

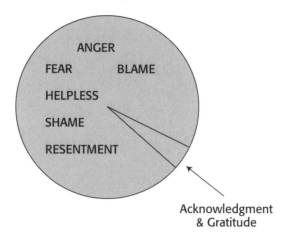

Acknowledgment
& Gratitude

Negativity grows stronger by feeding on itself. One way to break out of the downward cycle of negativity is to find and tell the stories that express the positive elements of acknowledgment and gratitude (see Chapter Eight, "Team Building On-The-Run). Given the tendency to dwell on the negative some people have this may take a near heroic effort. But if the sliver of positive elements can be widened to a wedge, the effect will be restorative. There are examples of success, teamwork, and compassion in every working group. Find them, create them, talk about them, write about them, and refer to them. People want to be with winners. Give them the opportunity.

DEALING WITH CHALLENGING PEOPLE

Have you ever thought about a coworker? "I can't stand that guy. He must be out to get me." With the possible exception of Will Rogers ("I never met a man I didn't like") most people have. The difficult person seems to work overtime to make your life miserable. No matter how much you try to be nice or reserved or professional he or she still manages to push those emotional hot buttons that upset you the most.

When these people do upsetting things it is natural to get upset. But instead of looking for a way to get even, the Dalai Lama suggests we should look for the opportunity the situation provides for our development. One of the verses from *Eight Verses for Training the Mind* states:[3]

When I see beings of a negative disposition
or those oppressed by negativity or pain,
may I, as if finding a treasure,
consider them precious, for they
are rarely met.

Of course, you're thinking that is easy for the Dali Lama to say, but in my world I have to deal with "beings of a negative disposition" every day. If you are willing to look for the opportunity in those encounters there are several "power tools" discussed below that might help you in dealing with a difficult person. Other tools will be found in Chapter Six, "Conflict Management." Using these tools is simple. The hard part is remembering to use them when you need to. These tools are especially appropriate where it seems nearly impossible to even have a conversation with the person about the issues between you. The tools are:

- Centering
- Full Responsibility
- Personal Treatment

Centering

It is difficult to find outer harmony when you have lost the connection to your own inner sense of harmony. If the feeling of alignment with others is lacking and nothing you try is helping to bring it back it may be wise to find a quiet place where you can sit comfortably for a few minutes and do the following:

- Take several deep breaths.
- Close your eyes and go inside.
- Notice and accept your feelings especially anything that is disquieting.
- Let your attention go to and be with any sensations in your body.
- Don't judge or analyze.
- Keep your awareness on those feelings and sensations and continue to breathe deeply, inhaling and exhaling slowly.

Notice after a few minutes how your mood has shifted. When you go back to work you may find the world around you looks much friendlier.

Full Responsibility

The fastest way to resolve the issues inherent in dealing with a difficult person is by taking full responsibility for all of your feelings. This is a radical approach. It is tempting to believe our emotional reaction to the difficult person is emanating from that person and the situation we find ourselves in. The fact is the source of those uncomfortable feelings is in ourselves. It was always inside of us and will remain there unless we decide to change.

Full responsibility is claiming full ownership for your emotional life. Why do this when it is so much more convenient to blame and hold other responsible? By taking responsibility you can take control of your life. Owning our collage of thoughts and feelings enables us to change them. Until you take that step you are likely to abdicate your power and remain vulnerable to what others do and say, no matter how inconsequential. Blame is a faulty thought process that undermines personal power. We feel helpless because we believe we have no choice about how someone makes us feel.

The first step in regaining personal power is to alter your thought process when the person in question is not around. In effect, you are creating a new thought process that helps instead of hinders you. Find a private place and imagine the difficult person and his behavior. Then:

- Experience your reaction.
- Write down your reactions. Use a lot of adjectives to describe your feelings.
- Vocalize this reaction with sounds and noises that express how you feel—tear up the paper or beat a pillow if you need to get physical.
- Focus on the feelings—where do they take you mentally and emotionally? How do they change?
- See yourself dealing with the person or situation in a way you feel good about.
- Remember to keep breathing—many people hold their breath when under stress, real or imagined.
- See or affirm good things happening for everyone.
- Don't forget the power of letting go of having to be right.

When you come into contact with your nemesis you may be surprised how he no longer provokes the same reaction. The predictable behaviors that used to seem so troublesome, if they still occur, now provoke a knowing smile. After clearing the emotional charge you have improved your ability to handle the situation from a place of choice. Personal power is the ability to choose your response.

Personal Treatment

Carl Jung, the Swiss psychologist, stated that the reason we sometimes have a strong reaction to a person is that he reminds us of some aspect of ourselves. Often, what we love or hate about others is what we love or hate about ourselves. The shadow we have disowned and denied insists that we acknowledge its presence by projecting itself onto someone we have to deal with. The difficult person is actually here to help us because he or she represents a part of ourselves that needs healing.

You may respond with thanks but no thanks to the above proposition. It seems much easier to change departments or try to get the other person fired or try to ignore him. The problem is no matter where you go, you take yourself with you. The characters may change, but the same drama will continue like a summer of endless reruns. This is because people will be to you as you are to yourself.

FORGIVENESS

One of the keys to freedom is forgiveness. Forgiving someone is possible when you forgive yourself, especially that part of you that has been so hard on yourself. On some level that difficult person (no matter how much of jerk he seems to be) is just an aspect of yourself that needs forgiveness and compassion. After you have let go of any intense emotional reaction you have to that person center yourself in a quiet space, think of the person and:

- Ask that the situation be resolved and healed.
- Send the person and yourself light, love, and appreciation.
- Turn everything over to your higher power, however you define it, and let go and go on with your life.

Emotional detachment does not mean you don't care or you become passive. Forgiveness does not stop you from setting boundaries or acting forcefully when you need to. However, holding on to a particular result or resentment somehow keeps our higher or subconscious mind from fully assisting us. Letting go lets the higher mind produce the results that are best for all concerned. The more you can see the part you played in creating the situation the more you can resolve it. The final steps of letting go and forgiving can be the toughest part of this process. But if tomorrow turned out to

be the last day of your life on earth would you want to leave behind a load of petty grievances?

SCAPEGOATING

Some teams attempt to avoid the problems of a difficult or toxic
member by carefully selecting their personnel. The men who run
a U.S. Navy nuclear submarine go through a battery of tests and
interviews before they are selected for duty. There is no place to
discharge a disruptive team member when you are submerged un-
derwater for a month or two.

The screening process does not mean personnel problems and
conflicts do not occur. Even in the most elite group, people sometimes project what they disown in themselves on to the most hapless or unsociable member. That person becomes the collective
butt of jokes or hostile and resentful remarks. Unconsciously, the
scapegoat finds himself acting in ways that gives others what they
need to justify their words and actions.

Scapegoating is seductive. Faulting someone can artificially
boost your own self-esteem and provide an outlet for feelings of
anger and shame. This practice conveniently puts the burden of
changing on others, since any change for personal and professional growth is a challenging process. It also gives a sense of safety.
As long as everyone is on the other guy's case they are not going
to be on yours. The alert manager will intervene when scapegoating
starts to emerge by naming the behavior and explaining why it is
unacceptable. Groups that need to create a scapegoat are acting
against their own "enlightened self interest."

Affirm the norm that everyone on the team is on-the-team,
which means they are given the feedback and encouragement they
need to do their best. Poor performance on the part of one member is also a reflection of the performance of the group. The team
should consider what they do to create or contribute to this situation and what they can do to support every team member so he
or she can excel.

PERSONALITY CONFLICTS

Just about every manager has had to deal with two employees who just cannot get along. They tar each other with the worst possible judgments. When something occurs between them the emotional reaction is out of proportion to the content of the incident. The manager may be able to negotiate an uneasy truce but inevitably the periodic blowup reoccurs. The issues may differ but the pattern of conflict is usually the same. Depending on who is complaining about whom, the diagram of the pattern looks like the typical triangle of conflict:[4]

Conflict Triangles

Manager as Rescuer

Employee *A* as Victim   Employee *B* as Persecutor

As soon as the manager takes sides a perceptual shift occurs. In the case below the manager intervened on the side of Employee A. From Employee's B perspective guess what happened. The answer is in the second Conflict Triangle below:

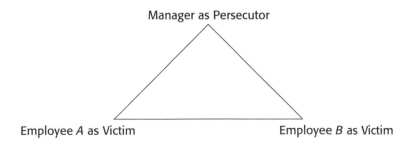

Manager as Persecutor

Employee *A* as Victim   Employee *B* as Victim

TRUTH OR CONSEQUENCES

The more the manager takes responsibility for resolving the conflict the less the two "victims" will take responsibility for their roles in creating the breakdown. The words or deeds that led to resolution are generated by the acceptance of responsibility. The lack of trust in the triangle of conflict turns the roles between victim, persecutor, and rescuer into a game of musical chairs. The process of Communication Roulette, described in Chapter Four, "Communication Skills," the potential for emotional damage over a simple misunderstanding. Each employee sees the other's actions as having negative intentions. The first step towards finding a solution is in prevention. A team ground rule for dealing with conflict includes the injunction; if you have a problem with someone discuss that problem with that person. Use the communication techniques in Chapters Four, "Communication Skills" and Six, "Conflict and Negotiation," to reach a mutual understanding. If the situation is too sensitive try the techniques in this chapter for dealing with a difficult person. If the two people are still feuding, contact a professional mediator and use her skills to help resolve the issues. Whatever the approach used it is important that people be accountable for the results they produce.

A manager had two direct reports who never seemed to agree on anything. The manager did everything he could think of but the intensity of the issues between them continued to increase. Morale and productivity began to slide. His boss started asking him what was going on. Finally, he called each man separately into his office and delivered an ultimatum. "I am not going to let this department suffer the consequences of the conflict between you and your colleague. You both must bear those consequences unless you learn how to work with each other." The direct reports began treating each other in a professional manner. Within a few months the feud was an artifact of the past.

By imposing a common goal on the two combatants, even if it meant making himself their common enemy, the manager above forced them to find a solution. In an ideal world all the participants in a conflict would have enough "emotional intelligence" or maturity to keep the issues in perspective. When people are mature enough to accept responsibility there is no need for a manager to hold them accountable. Instead of complaining to a third party about each other they would first talk to each other and see if they could work out a mutually acceptable solution. In many cases just a good dose of active listening is enough to resolve a problem before it escalates into war.

CYCLIC DILEMMAS

When times are tough and the bottom line is suffering the survival of the business seems to depend on achieving results—now. Under stress people regress to their most basic patterns of survival. Unhealthy organizations become even more unhealthy because they revert to or do more of the behaviors that allowed them to cope in the past, no matter how inappropriate they are to the present. An environment of fear grows by feeding on itself. Heavy-handed leaders respond to pressure by "kicking ass and taking names." Struggling for results, some bosses become more controlling, manipulative, or abusive. Others are too busy fighting other fires to spend any time managing the people who work for them.

Micromanaged or ignored, the workers become even more cautious, apathetic, resentful, or even disruptive. As the situation continues to deteriorate both sides react self-righteously. Respect and trust are defeated, paranoia and blame prevail.

The resulting emotional damage lowers morale and reduces communication, which in turn hurts productivity, which in turn lowers morale even more. No one talks about it, but the situation has everyone feeling scared and helpless. Breaking the cycle does not happen until people can put the problems on the table and start talking about them. Real problem solving occurs when people take ownership for the problem and responsibility for the solution. This kind of breakthrough is more likely to occur if there is forum for respectful and authentic communication facilitated by a third party. For more details in setting up that forum see Chapter 10, "Organizational Development."

OTHER KILLERS

So why don't employees, the ones who are not toxic or stressed out, do what they are supposed to do? They are good people, intelligent and capable. Yet the job is not getting done the way it should. What to do? According to Ferdinand Fournies, a business professor at Columbia University, the reason why employees do not perform is seldom ability or aptitude. Fournies believe the reasons tend to be less obvious than most managers believe.[5]

Employees do not do what they are supposed to do because:

- They don't know why they should do it.
- They don't know how to do it.
- They don't know what they are supposed to do.
- They think your way will not work.
- They think their way is better.
- They think something else is more important.
- There is no positive consequence to them for doing it.
- They think they are doing it.
- They are rewarded for not doing it.
- They are punished for doing what they are supposed to do.
- They anticipate a negative consequence for doing it.
- There is no negative consequence to them for poor performance.
- There are obstacles beyond their control.

Setting standards, giving clear directions, explaining why and how, checking for understanding and agreement, providing resources, giving and receiving feedback, enforcing consequences, acknowledging and rewarding performance, and removing obstacles are some of the actions a manager can take that will turn the "also-ran" employee into a winner.

THE HAPPY FEW

It is axiomatic that more can be accomplished by a smaller group of happy, motivated workers than a larger group of unhappy, disgruntled workers. The attitude of some "unhappy campers" shifts when the work environment becomes more participative. People are less likely to complain about the decisions they helped to make. However, there are people who are never going to participate in a positive manner, no matter what management does or does not do. It is always easier to criticize than it is to help create results. Attitudes are contagious. Many observers have noted the links between team morale and productivity (and related factors such as health, safety, absenteeism and turnover). Because of this link, productivity goes up when workers with toxic attitudes change or leave.

For example, the air traffic controllers' strike of 1983 resulted in a significant percentage of federally employed controllers losing their jobs. Even with fewer controllers, the productivity of the Federal Aviation Agency went up. The controllers reported that the absence of their more contentious and embittered colleagues made it easier to work without sacrificing safety.

The saga of one small company, Coeur Labs, replicates the experiences of larger organizations like the Federal Aviation Agency. Coeur, a manufacturer of surgical equipment, was losing money. Productivity was low and labor-management relations strained. Even relationships between workers were marked by shoving matches and bad feelings. Employees felt the existing quotas were too high. Management thought they were too low. The company instituted "rap sessions" so workers could express their concerns and negotiate for changes. Eventually, the workforce was reduced to 17 from a high of 24 workers. Those that stayed were team players. As morale improved so did productivity; going from 65 percent to 100 percent of capacity.[6]

PEER COACHING

If you ask someone if he would like some feedback it is quite likely that he will say no if he says anything at all. The connotations are just too heavy. But ask that same person if he would like some friendly coaching and you might get a different response. People know that even a person who is recognized as the best in the field can still benefit from good coaching. To paraphrase an old saw, look behind a great athlete (or a great businessperson) and you will find a great coach.

It is also true that those that need coaching the most are the least likely to seek it. You can not help someone improve unless he wants it too. But most people will readily accept coaching if they see it is offered with the intention to help them win. Not everyone can find a mentor at work to help them move up the corporate ladder. However, many employees would receive some valuable coaching from their peers if they just asked.

COACHING FOR SUCCESS–BEING A COACH

Use the following guidelines when being a coach:

- Check your intentions—you want the other person to succeed
- Invite the person's participation or ask her permission.
- Help the person define what she wants to do, be or have.
- Help the person define what gets in the way.
- Deal with observable/changeable behavior.
- Be specific—use examples—avoid absolutes and judgments.
- Help the person define the behaviors/actions that will produce the desired results. Include when and how in the plan.
- If necessary—explain the consequences of behaviors that do not produce the desired results, "That's a problem because..."
- Use "I" statements "I feel, believe or think that . . ."
- Make suggestions for the desired behaviors (explain why it's important, refer to the big picture or the stated goals).

- Check for understanding and agreement—be liberal with encouragement and appreciation, and be patient and helpful.

COACHING FOR SUCCESS – BEING COACHED

Try the following to improve your personal and professional performance:

- Be clear on what you want to do, be or have.
- Reflect on where you need to develop (how you get in your own way).
- Seek coaching in those areas; to get it you have to ask for it.
- Keep an open mind; be curious.
- Take responsibility for how life/people are treating you.
- Listen; don't defend, deny or explain.
- Breathe before responding.
- Ask questions; seek to understand
    "What else do I need to know . . . ?"
- Paraphrase the coach's suggestion/direction/idea.
    "So what you're saying is . . ."
- Notice your reactions objectively without acting on them.
- Avoid withdrawing from or dismissing the process.
    "I'll think about what you said . . . or I'll give it a try."
- Be open to suggestions and change; so what if you are not perfect, who is?
- Experiment—do something differently!
- Allow for some awkwardness and confusion as you try new behaviors and skills; be patient with yourself and your rate of progress.
- Acknowledge yourself for every step that you take.

18
Managing Stress

University of Utah

No challenge—no life.

PUNDIT SHARMA

The statistics tell the story. Eighty-nine percent of the people on the street believe they experience high levels of stress. Seventy-five percent of workers say their jobs are stressful. Forty one percent of that group go on to say they have a strong need to reduce stress. With all that stress it is not surprising there are 12 million alcoholics in this county and 25 million people with high blood pressure. More than 230 million prescriptions for tranquilizers are filled each year. If you want a "stress-lite" you may have to consciously create it.

WHAT IS STRESS?

For some people stress is their reaction to whatever is bothering them at the moment.

For the more scientific-minded, stress is the nonspecific response of the body to any demand for change. Much of the impact of that demand is determined by evaluation of it and reaction to it. A person's attitude is the balance point between the vicious cycle of distress and the virtuous cycle of "eu-stress."

CRUISING SPEED

People and airplanes have something in common. Both work better and longer at cruising speed instead of top speed. Working under constant stress adds a double load to the nervous system. People end up exerting twice the energy just to stay in the same place. The sources of stress are physical, interpersonal, and situational. Some stress cannot be avoided, but you can adjust your own attitude to minimize its impact. Since mind and body are related, physical problems have emotional implications and vice versa.

HEALTHY BALANCE

Stress goes hand-in-hand with challenge and change. For most people the lack of challenge can be as stressful as too much challenge. Personal and professional growth can be stressful, but so is the lack of it. Finding the right balance in attitude and action results in the highest level of personal productivity.

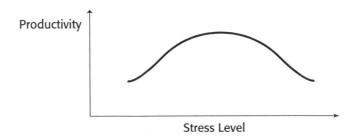

GENERAL ADAPTATION SYNDROME

According to Hans Selye, an expert on stress, there are three stages that lead to an overload of stress. Selye calls these stages the General Adaptation Syndrome: The stages are:

- Alarm Reaction
- Resistance Stage
- Exhaustion Stage

The alarm reaction is the first response to a stressful incident. Some people confront the situation; others try to avoid it. The second stage is marked by the constant expenditure of energy used when the situation remains unresolved. If the situation is never dealt with effectively or if it is one of those situations that no one could resolve it will continue to be a drain. The results of that drain could lead to exhaustion. This stage can adversely impact a person's health. At this point most people will find a way to come to terms with the situation. For some the solution will include spiritual or emotional counseling; for other it might mean finding a new career or moving to a more agreeable climate.

SOURCES OF STRESS

Some of the sources of stress at work are:

- Physical
  - ✓ faulty ergonomics
  - ✓ unhealthy ventilation
  - ✓ lack of exercise
  - ✓ poor lighting
  - ✓ extremes in temperature
  - ✓ excessive noise
  - ✓ lack of physical space
  - ✓ toxic smoke or materials

- Interpersonal
  - ✓ heavy-handed management
  - ✓ toxic team mates
  - ✓ mistakes and criticism
  - ✓ conflict or rivalry in a cutthroat culture
- Structural
  - ✓ new people or new management
  - ✓ downsizing or reorganization
  - ✓ deadlines
  - ✓ new tasks, equipment or workloads
  - ✓ legal and regulatory.

INHOUSE HAZARDS

Some hazards in the workplace are inherent in the design of the building. The principle villains are a lack of fresh air and limited spectrum lighting. Poorly maintained air conditioning and heating systems strip the air of negative ions and load it with mold, bacteria, and other airborne particles that are unfriendly to the human body. Most office buildings have tinted windows that are sealed shut. Lighting comes from florescent bulbs which emit an extremely limited spectrum of light. Deprive people of exercise, fresh air and full spectrum light; overload them with large doses of sugar, caffeine, and fat, and the results are predictable: more sickness, fatigue, and depression.

The unhealthy culture of an organization can be a source of physiological stress that has a bottom line impact. A "healthy" company (physiologically, socially and financially) is a reflection of the people that work there. Creating a healthy company takes inspired leadership that appreciates the linkage between a healthy balance sheet and healthy corporate culture. Is the stress level in your office going off the chart? The best way to tell is to pay attention to your body and your emotions. A thorough assessment examines both objective and subjective measures. Some objective measures to look at are:

- Turnover
- Terminations
- Sick leave
- Absenteeism
- Grievances
- Accidents
- Health care claims

Tracking the above measures can help justify the action that needs to be taken to bring about an improvement. Other factors are more subjective, such the number of smiles, the amount of laughter, and the emotional tone in the interactions between people. If the stress level is too high, start looking for the factors: physical, interpersonal, or situational, you can change in a positive way.

STRESS BUSTERS

Some people cope with stress in ways that only make matters worse. Indulging addictively in drinking, smoking, or drugs are ways to avoid unpleasant feelings. When used obsessively, even television, sex, or food can be a means for avoidance. Bickering and complaining are also attempts to relieve tension. Most addictions are progressive. Job performance, personal relationships, and health lose their importance compared to the addiction. Workers who show signs of substance abuse should be referred to an employee assistance program for counseling and treatment.

Measures for dealing with stress in the workplace include:

- Provide healthy snack food and spring water instead of the usual sodas, candy, and coffee.
- Establish a smoke free workplace.
- Clean A/C vents and filters.
- Provide indoor plants and fountains.
- Provide indoor gyms and showers.

- Provide full spectrum lighting.
- Install untinted windows that open.
- Offer employee assistance programs.
- Offer employee wellness programs.

ALL THAT JAZZ

One company in New York City with 85 employees brought in a tap dance coach to give noontime lessons in tap and jazz dancing. The company constructed a stage where employees could take the dance lessons and exercise. According to Ralph Guild, President of McGavren Guild Radio, "Not only is it simply great fun, but the byproduct of stress reduction is beneficial for all of us." Besides tap dancing, other measures for dealing with personal stress include:

- Practice some form of regular exercise and stretching—even if it's just a walk around the block or a few stretches in your chair.
- Remember to breathe more deeply more often—especially during a stressful situation.
- Find daily quiet time to meditate, pray, or just focus on being aware and centered.
- Lighten up, laugh and keep things in perspective; the line between the absurd and the tragic is paper thin.
- Do the best you can and then let go—there are things none of us can control so why wear yourself worrying about them?
- Look for the gift in everything. The situation or person that is causing you stress has something to teach you. What is it? How could you see this situation differently?
- Develop a support system of peers to confide in.

CONSCIOUS BREATHING

Breathing is something we forget to do when we are feeling anxious. If you breathe deeply you will change your physiology. It is difficult for your body to be tense and breathe at the same time. You can prove this to yourself by holding your breath and tensing up. Now try to stay tense while breathing deeply. . . See!

- Breathe in all the way.
- Let your belly expand as you breathe into it.
- Breathe all the way out.
- Let the belly contract as you breathe out.

This process works best in loose fitting clothing. The out-breath should take longer than the in-breath. Notice how you feel after a few breaths.

MAGNIFICATION

When a stressful thought, feeling, or memory persists, the harder you try not to think about it the more it keeps coming to mind, uninvited yet unavoidable. And the unpleasant feeling and/or image associated with the thought keeps returning. Try something that is counterintuitive. Instead of trying to get the feeling or image to go away, invite it in and do the following:

- Make it bigger.
- Exaggerate it.
- Amplify it.
- Make it faster

Paradoxically, magnification can create a mental and emotional shift that integrates the difficult feelings and alleviates the inner distress.

REDUCTION

Magnification can take the edge off a stressful thought. Reduction will smooth it away. Bring the image of the stressful situation or person to your mind's eye. Then take that image and:

- Make it smaller.
- Make it farther away.

- Make it dimmer.
- Put it in a box.
- Make yourself bigger.
- Put the box out of sight.

This technique helps people feel better. It enhances the sense of personal control by offering a new perspective.

SELF COMPASSION

A major source of stress is the inner critic. We make a small mistake or suffer a slight setback and part of our psyche won't stop beating us up for our lack of perfection. The judgmental self talk of the inner critic goes on and on in an endless loop. Breaking that loop requires a conscious act of compassionate affirmation. Stop the inner nagging by taking a mental timeout.

When life presents another learning opportunity that's a bit bumpy, say to yourself: "Hey, this is *nooo* big deal . . ."

The end of the world is not here yet so reassure yourself that:

- This too shall pass.
- Everything is working out.
- I don't have to be perfect to be good enough.

WHAT I LIKE ABOUT THIS IS . . .

Say you're stuck in traffic. The freeway is a parking lot. You're late for an important meeting. Now you're going to be really late. Who hasn't had that experience? You're stomach could be starting to churn just thinking about it or the all the traffic you will face on the drive home. Try seeing things differently. Ask yourself the simple question, "What do I like about this (situation, issue, person)?"

Dwell for a few minutes on the fact that you enjoy the music on the radio or that it is nice and warm in your car compared to the cold weather outdoors or that it's great to have a few minutes by yourself to think about things. Notice how you feel after a few minutes of looking at the bright side of life. Studies have shown that changing your thinking like this is beneficial to your physical and emotional health. It might even help you think of some creative solutions. The tenser we become the less effective we are intellectually, emotionally, and physically. You might not be able to clear the traffic, but at least you will show up in a more effective frame of mind. The next time you are upset, even if the issue is more serious than a traffic jam, try this technique. Try it right now on some issue or person that has been a source of irritation in your life. It works.

LETTING GO OF FEAR

Fear is a major source of stress. Most fear is about what might happen, not what is happening right now. The human mind has the uncanny ability to focus on the future and especially a future that we don't want. There is an old saying that whatever we think about will grow stronger in our lives. The only thing that is real is what is happening right now. The only way to change the future is to change what we are thinking and doing right now. The future is unknowable and the past does not matter. Both are beyond our grasp. All we really have is now—right now.

SURRENDER TO THE WORST

One way to handle fear is to surrender to the worst. Check in with yourself and identify what you are feeling. When you are feeling a lot of stress this may take some fortitude. Many people would rather medicate themselves with things like alcohol or television then feel their feelings. Sit quietly and identify your feelings. Feel the fear. After a few minutes you might feel the feelings begin to ebb and even disappear.

If the fear persists imagine the worst that might happen. If it is getting fired, let yourself be fired in your mind. Do not resist what you are fearful about. Surrender to it and to the fear behind that fear, like losing your house. Feel the sense of peace that comes from allowing yourself to fully experience your fears. Remember to keep breathing. People hold their breath when they are afraid.

YOU HAVE WHAT YOU WANT

Think about what you really want. If the fear is about losing your job imagine having the job you want. Affirm that you are living abundantly and working with confidence and true security. Write down some brief affirmations in the present tense that define what you really want to be, do, or have, as if this is the way it is for you right now. Post them where you can see them or carry them around and repeat them during the day. Feel what it would be like to already have what you want. Notice the difference these new thoughts make each day when you focus on them.

HEART LISTENING

There is wisdom in the heart. We know much about using and developing the mind, but very little about how to access the wisdom of the heart. In *Freeze Frame*, Doc Lew Childre describes a simple technique for dealing with stress by listening to the heart. When you are dealing with a difficult situation do the following:[1]

- Sit quietly—take a timeout.
- Think of a loved one or a positive, fun experience.
- Focus on the heart . . .
- Ask yourself the question, "What is the best course of action, one that will minimize future stress?"
- Listen to your heart.
- Pay attention to whatever words, feelings or pictures come into your mind.

The heart is more than a muscle that pumps blood. Learning how to listen to your heart can help you develop greater emotional maturity.

19
Managing Change

Team Building Associates

*The more rigid the system
the more likely it is to
collapse under pressure.*

ILLIYA PRIGOGINE
NOBLE PRIZE LAUREATE IN CHEMISTRY

*Never be afraid of trying
something new. Remember,
amateurs built the ark,
professionals built the Titanic.*

UNKNOWN

*If you want to make enemies,
try to change something.*

WOODROW WILSON

Name one major industry that has not been affected by significant change over the last five years. Stumped? If not, maybe you just returned from a long space flight. Change has come from every possible direction including:

- Increased regulation (in some industries)
- Decreased regulation (in other industries)
- Globalization
- New technology
- The Internet
- Customer demands
- Mergers and consolidations
- Divestitures and breakups
- Marketing and media

- Transportation
- Workforce diversity
- The environment
- Telecommunications
- Break up of the Soviet Union
- Demographics
- Privatization

A detailed list would be a book in itself. The president of a billion-dollar division for Mobil Corporation said during a management meeting that he had seen more change in the last year or two than he had seen in his entire thirty-year career in the industry. And this statement was made three years before Exxon and Mobil announced their plans to merge.

Change may not be inevitable but it is certainly ubiquitous. The political, social and economic arenas listed above offer ample proof for anyone who needs it. Yet the necessity for adapting to change is frequently denied, ignored, or resisted. Because of this denial many organizations have found themselves struggling against the tide of global competition, new technology, and the increasing demand for low-cost, high-quality services and products. These pressures are forcing the private and even the public sectors to "reinvent" themselves through restructuring and downsizing. The pyramid that represented the corporate hierarchy is getting flatter as the world's economy becomes more global. More is required, in terms of quality and productivity, with fewer resources. This achievement can be realized only by tapping the full potential of the workforce. One way to unleash that potential is to replace a hierarchical and autocratic culture with one that encourages teamwork and participative decision making. However, the successful introduction of a new culture in any organization is always a daunting task.

FEAR OF LOSS

Managers who want to instill more teamwork into their organizations need to anticipate the resistance they will meet. Even if the change is obviously a great idea there is no guarantee others will embrace it. People do not fear change but they do fear loss and change is often perceived to be a loss. This phenomenon is illustrated by Annie Dillard in her book, *Pilgrim At Tinker Creek*. When surgeons in the nineteenth century first discovered how to perform cataract operations they restored the sight of a number of people who had been blind since birth. Instead of celebrating, many of the newly sighted found the change intensely distressing.[1]

An observer at the time noted:

> A disheartening number of them refuse to use their new vision, continuing to go over objects with their tongues and lapsing into apathy and despair.

One young woman described by her father in a letter to a doctor:

> . . . carefully shuts her eyes whenever she goes about the house and she is never happier or more at ease than when, by closing her eyes, she relapses into her former state of total blindness.

From the perspective of a sighted person this account illustrates how emotional acceptance of change may not occur as fast as intellectual acceptance. A person can intellectually accept something: seeing is a wonderful gift; while still harboring emotions that need to be resolved: giving up the familiar is scary. The internal conflict between the emotions and the intellect produces inaction and despair. Acceptance can take time even when the change seems beneficial.

BREEDING ELEPHANTS

Organizations, like any objects at rest, have inertia. Trying to change a major corporation or government agency is like the old joke about breeding elephants. There is a lot of noise and fuss at a high level and you have to wait eighteen months before anything happens. The larger and more complex the organization, the more time and effort it takes to overcome that inertia. An organization in transition is like a plane climbing towards cruising altitude. The faster the rate of the climb the harder it is to stay on your feet. According to Kurt Lewin, organizational change has three phases:[2]

Three Phases of Organizational Change

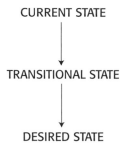

As the rate of social and technical change accelerates, organizations, as well as individuals, will spend more of their time in a transitional state. And getting into a transition state is not as hard as getting out of it, as the former leader of the former Soviet Union, Mikhail Gorbachev, might testify. According to some observers the trend today is change that just does not let up. Instead of three phases organizational change now has two:

Two Phases of Organizational Change

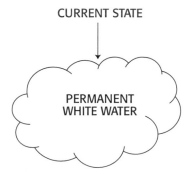

Another government figure by the name of Nicolo Machiavelli, who lived in the city-state of Florence in the early 1500's, also had some ideas about change. Machiavelli wrote in his book *The Prince*:[3]

> *It must be remembered that there is nothing more difficult to plan, more doubtful of success, nor more dangerous to manage than the creation of a new system. For the initiator has the enmity of all who would profit by the preservation of the old institutions and merely lukewarm defenders in those who would gain by the new ones.*

Machiavelli believed that men love novelty and sometimes change things for the sake of change. A soldier by the name of Petronius Arbiter, who lived in Italy in 210 B.C. had ideas about change that sound surprisingly modern.[4]

> *We trained hard . . . but it seemed that every time we were beginning to form up into teams we would be reorganized. . . . I was to learn later in life that we tend to meet any new situation by reorganizing; and a wonderful method it can be for creating the illusion of progress while producing confusion, inefficiency, and demoralization.*

EXPECTATIONS

The prospect of change creates expectations. Many times our expectations are not realistic since most situations have a way of not being as good nor as bad as they first seem. When a major change is about to occur here are some questions to ask yourself or your team:

- What are your negative expectations?
- What are your positive expectations?

- Are these expectations realistic?
- What new opportunities does this change offer?

The necessity for change seldom arrives without some prior warning. Blocking those warnings out or discounting them as unimportant is a form of coping. Anxiety results when the warnings are too strong to be discounted or ignored, but nothing is being done about them. The resulting sense of helplessness leads to feelings of guilt or panic. If these feelings remain bottled up in a person they can turn into depression and withdrawal.

THE GRIEF CYCLE

According to Elizabeth Kubler-Ross, there is a necessary cycle of grief people go through after suffering a profound loss. Some of the stages defined by Kubler-Ross in this cycle include:[5]

- *Denial.* "It won't happen."
- *Anger.* "How dare this happen."
- *Bargaining.* Trying to change the situation.
- *Guilt.* "Why did this happen (or not happen) to me?" These feelings can occur for both survivors and casualties.
- *Depression.* The less emotions are dealt with the greater the depression.
- *Identity Crisis.* "Who am I now?"
- *Acceptance.* Coming to terms with the circumstances and adjusting.

New opportunities for personal and professional growth occur after a person has moved through these stages and come to terms with what happened. A lingering depression can result if a stoic denial or withdrawal is used to avoid coming to terms with difficult emotions.

DEALING WITH RESISTANCE

People need an opportunity to express their reactions to any significant experience of change. When an organization is in transition the initial stage of a team-building program is often spent addressing the emotional impact of change. Mergers and acquisitions mean new ways of doing business, maybe even a new identity. Sometimes people cannot come to terms with and accept those changes because they have not dealt with the emotional side of change in a healthy way. Unable to legitimatize and express the natural feelings of grief, anger and fear, they stew in a bitter brew of self-pity, blame and resentment. Their resistance goes underground, leaking out in passive-aggressive behaviors and negative attitudes. The key question is:

> *How do we help people move through the cycle of grief or resistance to a place where they are emotionally and mentally ready to deal with the changes that will or have occurred?*

There are no easy answers, but this question must be asked by those who are planning a change initiative. Management can and should help people make that first step towards adjustment. Training in personal and organizational change management is an important part of the process.

Change cannot be sugar coated. If it is bitter that should be acknowledged. However, people move forward when they believe they have something to move forward towards. If something has been lost there are two choices that are mutually exclusive: 1) Stay stuck in grief or resentment. 2) Work to replace the loss with something comparable or better. People who have a strong sense of self-efficacy will go for the second choice.

GUIDELINES FOR PLANNING CHANGE

According to Bill Liggett, a consultant who helps organizations implement Total Quality Management (TQM), a company has to be committed to the change process if it is going to succeed.

Two-thirds to three-fourths of organizational change initiatives based on TQM or "reengineering" fail. Reasons for this lack of success can be enumerated by putting a *Not* in front of each of the guidelines listed below. Guidelines for a successful change process include:[6]

- *Communicating your reasons for making the change.* Employees appreciate getting the "big picture" and the reasons for why something should be done. What may seem obvious and redundant to the denizens of the corporate suite might be enlightening to those on the shop floor or even in the office down the hall. When people know the "why" they are more likely to get involved in the "how." Workers will be more open to change if offered evidence that the benefits justify the effort. Sell the program to middle management before trying to sell it to the rest of the organization. Keep on selling it.
- *Having a convincing rationale.* Following the latest fad won't do it. The fact that you may go out of business if productivity and innovation do not improve is more compelling. Workers at Johnson Wax resisted at first the move towards working in teams. "We had a record year in sales and profits," they said, "Why fix it if it ain't broke?" "We have to," management replied, "Our competitors did better than we did. Unless we continue to improve they will take our market share and our jobs."
- *Doing your homework.* In most organizations you will find people who have been there, done that, and ate the tee-shirt. Talk to them and find out what went wrong the last time those guys upstairs tried to change things. Find out what went right when change was successful. Learn from others, especially their mistakes. Give people some reason to think that maybe this change will be better managed than the last one they went through.

- *Requesting everyone's cooperation and support.* Even in the military, compliance is not automatic. Resentment, foot-dragging, and countless ploys can thwart your best efforts. Work to defuse this resistance before it arises because it will occur. People will give a surprising amount of cooperation if you make a sincere effort to ask for it.

- *Involving those who are going to be affected.* Ask for personal opinions and suggestions. Interviews, focus groups, and general surveys are some of the means to collect information. Large group gatherings based on Harrison Owens's Open Space model or a Future Search Conference are powerful formats for drawing upon the collective talent of up to several hundred people at one time and place. Newsletters, E-mail, videos, and memos are other ways to get the message out and receive feedback. A change program has a better chance of succeeding if it is designed and planned with the involvement of all concerned parties. Employee involvement does not always require a fancy process. According to the consultant, Robert Rosen, one company building a new plant posted the blueprints so employees could comment on them. The changes resulted in a better design that improved the workflow after the plant was built.

- *Creating a change management team.* The team members should represent a cross-section of the organization. They plan, organize, coordinate, and troubleshoot the change process. They might start by surveying the workforce, talking to people at every level, assessing reactions and answering questions. Appoint respected opinion leaders to the team and give them the resources, management access and guidance they need to do their job. Their input will prove invaluable.

- *Keeping the faith.* A change program stays alive only if top management stays involved. Frequent program status reports, acknowledging those who have made progress, and keeping the topic on the agenda during meetings, are some of the many things management can do to show commitment and keep the process moving. Half measures communicate this is just another other one of those management schemes that will soon be overcome by events.

- *Making only promises you can keep.* Practice "safety first" when it comes to promises about the future. The conditional promise will be regarded as a binding agreement. Any benefit that is given on a temporary basis will soon become permanent in the eyes of the receiver. Nothing destroys credibility and breeds resentment as fast as a "promise" broken or a benefit taken away, even for reasons beyond your control. During any change process more things are not under your control than expected.

- *Communicating—Communicating—Communicating.* Communication is only communication if it is both ways. Listen to what people are saying and address their concerns and reactions. During times of change there is no such thing as too much communication. Anticipate that the organizational rumor mill will operate on overtime and at unbelievable speeds. Withholding sensitive information that affects everyone is seldom a complete success, especially in a large organization. Some of it will leak out causing even more confusion and angst. Let the troops know what is known and what is not known. Keep them informed. No one likes bad news, but people like even less being held hostage to uncertainty.

- *Managing expectations.* Before you know it expectations can rocket out of sight over how good or bad it is going to be. Do frequent reality checks. Practice rumor control. Don't let unrealistic expectations turn into cynicism.

- *Managing emotions.* Expect that people will be experiencing various degrees of FUDD: fear, uncertainty, doubt, and despair. Anticipate those fears and put as many to rest as you can as soon as you can. Reassure people that they will succeed.

- *Listening.* The best way to manage emotions and expectations is to listen to people's concerns. Let them know you really understand their point-of-view. Most resistance to change is based on legitimate concerns, even if those concerns are shortsighted. Show your understanding by discussing those concerns and responding to them.

- *Communicating with symbols.* Symbolic actions, logos, or fixtures, like any picture, are worth a pile of words. When military units go through a change of command, the departing commanding officer (CO) hands the new CO the unit flag in front of the assembled troops. This very visible action says it all. In one merger of two competing companies, the hourly workforce traded their hats (with the old logos) with each other as a show of solidarity before the hats with the new logos arrived.

- *Being prepared for the long haul.* Most change management experts agree that if a major organization is not prepared to spend five or more years implementing the change process it should not bother doing it all. It is tempting to think the new program will constitute a quick fix. Real change takes time, training and follow through. When the initial results fail to match inflated expectations some will instigate junking the program without giving it a chance to succeed. As Rosebeth Moss Kanter, a professor at Harvard Business School, has said, "Everything looks like a failure in the middle."[7] An indicator that the desired change has taken hold is when there is agreement at every level that, "This is the way we do business."

- *Conducting training.* Training programs based on accurate needs assessments are essential for success. The classes help employees master the new methodologies and provide a forum where concerns and problems can be discussed. Employee training pays off. According to the *Wall Street Journal*, Japanese and German firms spend four to six percent of their operating budgets on training. Most North American firms typically spend about 1.5 percent. Only a small percentage of progressive companies spend twice that amount.

- *Aligning goals and values with actions and rewards.* If you preach teamwork yet reward individual performance over group performance guess which behavior will dominate? If you want individual initiative and risk taking yet run off anyone who makes a mistake how are people going to conduct themselves? If you want trust and openness yet frown on any frank discussion of sensitive issues what kind of atmosphere will result? One word: cynical. Not a productive or fun place to work. Organizations work best when the stated goals and values are aligned with its actions and rewards.

THE BIG FOUR

Organizations that have been most successful in changing their culture have four things in common:

1) Strong leadership that pays attention to the human side of change
2) In-depth training programs that provide the skills needed to make the new culture work
3) Long-term commitment to make the change successful based on measurable goals
4) Frequent, on-going conversations between management and staff about the progress of the change initiative and the related issues it has generated.

Change programs are not limited to downsizing. Mergers, new plants, technology or products, creating self-managed work teams, and introducing consultative or total quality management are all major changes that require new knowledge and skills.

CUSTOMER FOCUS

In the business world one impetus for change has been the recognition that everyone should have a customer. That customer can be internal or external. They could even be your fellow team members. The fact that you provide a service or product they need makes them a customer. Your success can be measured by how well you meet your customer's needs. If we are active in getting feedback from our customer, chances are we will also be active in making changes that will improve our service to that customer.

THE LONG MARCH

Given the avalanche of change our society has experienced, it would seem that most people would accept the need for change as inevitable. You have to change in order to deal with change. Don't bet on it. If senior management wants the people in their organizations to change they better be determined.

> One government agency with 5,000 employees has been making a major effort to create an environment of consultative management. Employees, union representatives, and mid-level supervisors with many years of service were used to an authoritarian style of management. Many of them did not believe management was serious about creating a more consultative environment. Newer employees with less than a year or two of service were the ones most open to the change. It took more than two years, $1.5 million and thousands of employee hours invested in training programs, to make significant progress towards a consultative environment.

TRADE-OFFS

A certain amount of resistance should be expected when employee involvement programs such as consultative or participatory management are introduced into a workplace. These programs ask managers to share power and workers to take on more responsibility, shifts that can take considerable persuasion and training. Each new style comes with a tradeoff. For example, consultative decision making takes more time and energy. The payoff is that the decisions are generally of higher quality and easier to implement, since they engender more support by the people who have been consulted.

The changes may be beneficial, but they come with an emotional as well as an economic price tag. Productivity is likely to drop at first as people struggle to learn new ways of doing things. Morale may suffer even if the workforce understands the reasons for the changes. One manager going through a change process compared the experience to dancing with a bear: you do not get to sit down when you are tired.

OVERCOME BY EVENTS

Most change programs are not killed by intentional acts of sabotage or managerial fumbling. The bureaucratic way to resist a proposed change is to drag your feet until the condition known as overcome-by-events sets in. Chances are if enough people resist for long enough the program will eventually die from lack of attention or changing circumstances.

Turnover or retirement can also take away the people who kept a program alive. Harried supervisors naturally feel mastering a new approach like consultative management undermines their authority. Cynicism sprouts like a field of weeds when senior management espouses a philosophy that mid-level managers fail to support. The discrepancy between the way things are supposed to be and the way they are, leading to statements like, "What's the use of trying, things will never change." The irony of this statement is that both management and the workforce are pointing the finger at the ubiquitous "they" as the reason why "change can't happen here."

PROACTIVE APPROACH

When things are going reasonably well few teams or individuals take time to think about making changes. Usually, it takes a crisis brought on by failure or new conditions before an organization will do any corporate soul searching. Yet seldom does an organization escape being forced to adjust to the inevitable vicissitudes of the business world. The best time, however, to conduct an assessment is when things are going well.

As business writer, Peter Townshed said, "If it ain't broke, break it!" Most major problems give hints of their pending arrival well in advance. The reactive response ignores or denies the problem until forced to take drastic measures that have drastic consequences. The proactive approach minimizes the potential problem while it is still on the horizon.

WAKE UP CALL

Complacent organizations are usually victims of their own past success. Self assured, they disregard any new concept labeled "not invented here." Like IBM or General Motors, a complacent organization makes significant changes only when forced to by huge losses that leave no other choice. As one team-building consultant put it in a discussion about changing a corporation, "If I can wake them up to the fact that they have problems they need to deal with, then I've done half my job." New work teams, a change in leadership, or a reorganization provide opportunities to instill the agreements that foster teamwork within the group. You have their attention, so to speak, during those crucial periods.

HUNDREDTH MONKEY

Systems Theory states no part of a system can exist in isolation. Change occurs when there is significant discrepancy between output, input, and the demands of the environment. Change in one sector creates changes in the other sectors because the system will seek to regain a state of equilibrium.

Pull on one leg of a chair and the other three have to come along. The principle of the Hundredth Monkey Theory is similar. Scientists noticed that the monkeys on one island in the Pacific started washing roots they dug up before they ate them. After a significant number of monkeys on the island had adopted the custom, they noticed that the monkeys on other islands also began to wash their food. This happened even though the monkeys on the different islands had no physical contact. This story about the monkeys may be fabrication. But the theory itself rings true. When a critical mass of people adapt a new behavior that behavior soon becomes an accepted norm for everyone else. If enough people sign on to the new way of doing business even the most resistant manager will have to change as well. A story from the upheaval in France during 1848 illustrates a similar point:[8]

During the disturbances in Paris a man spotted a friend following a crowd as it moved in mass towards the barricades. The man called out to his friend, to warn him and to ask why he was following that mob. "I must follow them," his friend yelled back, "I am their leader."

20
Team Leadership

The Learning Company

*Leadership can not be taught—
it can only be learned.*

HAROLD GRENEEN, CEO ITT

*Leadership is not wielding authority—
it's empowering people.*

BECKY BRODIN

One of the paradoxes of human behavior is that it takes strong leadership to build strong teams. Yet strong leadership can discourage others from exercising the level of initiative that produces outstanding teamwork. Ironically, a strong leader is also someone who can let go of control and empower others to practice her leadership skills.

In a team environment, the leader's job is to provide the group with what it initially cannot provide for itself. Without strong leadership the team may lack the confidence and direction it needs to get organized. As a team matures the members learn how to pass the baton of leadership between each other, encouraging the more introverted members to contribute their ideas and opinions. Leaders, who feel secure in themselves, develop their subordinates by risking the potential mistakes they might make. Teamwork and leadership may seem contradictory, but they are actually complementary halves of the same whole, the art of managing people.

FIVE MANAGEMENT STYLES

A lot has been written on the different leadership styles. Here are five basic styles of managing others based on the experience of the author. Managing others is never tidy. Effective managers can work with any style to achieve the results they desire. These five styles are:

- *Directive* ----------------- tells
- *Persuasive* ---------------- sells
- *Consultative* -------------- asks for input
- *Facilitative* ---------------- asks questions
- *Participatory* -------------- joins or delegates

Directive

Directive leadership is highly authoritarian; the decision making and problem solving is done by the leader. Information is tightly controlled and communication flows one way, from the top down. Standards are set and enforced externally and worker activities are closely supervised. The authoritarian style is the norm in hierarchical organizations with centralized planning, clear lines of authority and numerous rules and procedures. People do things because they are told to do them. The directive style is best suited for teams that deal with crisis situations or happen to be in one. However, team members that are skilled and motivated may feel they are being micro-managed.

Persuasive

The persuasive leader takes the time to explain why a task needs to be performed. He "sells" as well as "tells" others what to do. His authority is based on his ability to motivate people by understanding and appealing to their needs and values. Like a coach, a skilled, persuasive leader gives encouragement, direction and feedback to his players, however, the persuasive leader is still the authority who makes the decisions and sets and enforces the standards of performance. Teams going through the initial stages of "forming" respond best to the persuasive style of leadership.

Consultative

The consultative leader asks team members for their input on major decisions. The leader is interested in what others think and encourages a dialogue over major problems and decisions that affect the team. The consultative leader motivates others by taking into consideration their opinions and desires. Vision, guidance, and direction are still the responsibility of the leader. The consultative leader makes the big decisions, but is more likely to delegate selected areas of planning and problem solving to the team. This management style is best used in teams that are experienced and skilled in their work, but need some direction and encouragement.

Facilitative

The facilitative leader does not provide the answers. This leader focuses on the questions. She knows that most people have the experience and knowledge they need to get the job done. What is needed are the kind of questions that help people, individually or collectively, bring out and apply the full diversity of their resources. The leader facilitates the interactions of the team members with each other.

Participatory

The participatory leader asks the team to plan and supervise its own work. Although the leader represents the team at other levels of the parent organization, decision making and problem solving on major issues are dealt with by the entire team or delegated to selected members. Leadership functions are often shared or rotated between the team members. This style works best with technically and interpersonally competent team members who are highly motivated and know each other well.

CATALYTIC LEADERSHIP

Participatory leaders act as catalysts. They do not tell people what to do as much as they ask people what needs to be done. They know how to make people feel important by giving them a sense of ownership on more than one level. Ricardo Semler, the president of Semco, a manufacturing company in Brazil, has all of his employees vote on major decisions. Semler believes that corporate success means not making his own decisions and that he can trust his employees with issues critical to the destiny of his company. Since employees receive 22 percent of all company profits they prosper when the company prospers. So far, Semler's approach has produced a highly successful company that people do not want to leave.[1]

RIGHT STYLE FOR THE JOB

There is a saying that when you only have one tool, a hammer, everything looks like a nail. Many leaders just have one style. They may have gotten pretty good at it, but it is the only style they ever use. Good leaders do not limit themselves to one of the five styles. Situational leadership postulates that the most effective style of leadership depends upon the nature of the task and the capabilities of the people being led. For example, a captain of a ship during a storm gives orders expecting immediate obedience. When the ship is safely in port that style of management would not be the most effective. If a new navigational system must be selected a better decision will be made if the captain encourages discussion and debate about the options.[2]

An effective leader knows that different groups require different styles of leadership. Using Tuckman's Stages of Group Development the following table suggests the best leadership and decision making style for a particular group:

Appropriate Leadership Styles

Development Level	Leadership Style	Decision Style
Forming Group	Directing and Persuading	D-1 Decisions
Storming Group	Persuading and Consulting	D-2 Decisions
Norming Group	Facilitating	D-3 Decisions
Performing Group	Delegating and Participating	D-4 Decisions

CHANGING TOOLS

For many managers it is a revelation that they need to use other tools besides their favorite hammer. One manager in a government agency would often hear his employees say, "Just tell us what to do." He was good at consulting and delegating, but there were times he needed to be directive and make more D-1 decisions (Chapter Nine, "Decisions and Problem Solving"). A manager in the corporate sector got similar feedback:

During a management meeting a team of senior financial executives discussed how they wanted their team to function. The Vice President, the team leader, stated firmly that people who worked for him should be able to do their jobs so he would not have to. He expected his direct reports to do their work and not take up any of his time. That's why he hired them. Some of the managers appeared to be uncomfortable with that expectation. The facilitator saw a "teachable moment" and outlined the different leadership styles to the group and how the best style depended on the situation. The Vice President agreed that his style was to delegate. "But there are times we need you to do more coaching and directing," his staff interjected. Based on the feedback the Vice President agreed to broaden his leadership repertoire.

WORKING YOURSELF OUT OF A JOB

The increasing competence of a work group goes hand-in-hand with increased self-management. This self-management is possible because, over time, the leader steps back and shares or delegates more of the decision-making functions. Competent leaders work themselves out of a job by developing their people. The outcome is a team that has learned how to assess its effectiveness and adjust its own activities. Paradoxically, learning to self manage as a group takes a lot of directing and coaching.

ROLE SHIFTING

In the early stages of a team's development the team leader needs to provide extensive direction and control. He has to work pretty hard because he is taking on most of the roles that give shape and definition to the group. As the team members gain more understanding and confidence in each other and the requirements of their work, they can start to take on many of those roles.

In participatory management there is the flexibility to seamlessly switch from one role to another. Tasks are shared and people do what it takes to get the job done without the arbitrary divisions of titles and positions. People take on or give up certain roles in response to the demands of a situation, and the particular skills each person has to offer. Role rigidity collapses into role flexibility; role clarity becomes fuzzy if not ambiguous. For some it's confusing and troublesome. What keeps things from sinking into chaos is the ability of the members to communicate with each other. When people know each other a lot can be said with just a word or nod. The greater a person's role versatility the more influence he is likely to have within the group. Positive team roles are listed below. With the possible exception of the first three or four, the only limit to what you can play should be your own initiative, talent, and desire.

- *Chief:* tells you what to do, makes the decisions.
- *Judge:* evaluates performance, disciplines or fires.
- *Santa:* hand outs rewards and recognition.
- *Cop:* enforces the rules and standards.
- *Organizer:* makes plans and assignments.
- *Facilitator:* manages the agenda and the flow of ideas, asks the right questions.
- *Time Keeper:* keeps track of the schedule, presses for closure.
- *Energizer:* relieves stress with humor.
- *Morale Booster:* acknowledges and praises others.
- *Coach:* teaches and gives encouragement.
- *Devil's Advocate:* weighs cons versus pros.
- *Technical Guru:* high tech handyperson.
- *Politician:* knows how to navigate the organizational maze.
- *Recorder:* documents action items and decisions.
- *Communicator:* disseminates information and updates.
- *Observer:* points out the behavior of the team in an objective manner.
- *Innovator:* thinks up new ideas and better processes.
- *Historian:* recounts organizational history, stories, and myths.
- *Therapist:* has a sympathetic ear and helpful feedback.
- *Peacemaker:* harmonizes differences, resolves conflict.
- *Socializer:* build relationships, brings people together.

- *Trouble Shooter:* loves to define a problem and fix it.
- *Prophet:* inspires with the vision, goals and values.

EVERYONE IS A LEADER

You may wonder where the role of "leader" is in the above line-up. With the possible exceptions of chief, judge, and Santa all the other roles can be shared. Everything a team member does which has a positive influence on the rest of the team is an act of leadership. Even in the role of timekeeper you can lead by letting the team know it is time to move to another task. Before starting a project or meeting, some teams find it useful to appoint members to specific roles such as facilitator, timekeeper, or recorder.

During a team activity, leadership in a high-performance team will emerge based on who has the most inspiration or ability in relation to a particular task. Some leaders participate in team meetings as a contributor and appoint one of the team members to facilitate the meeting. This keeps the biases of the leader from overly influencing others. In a high-performance team the leader can leave for an extended period of time without affecting the team's performance. People may not even notice she's gone.

NEW TEAM LEADER

A new team leader who is also inexperienced in leading teams often has to deal with a dilemma. If she has a new team she may need to be directive. And if she has an experienced team she may think she needs to be directive to show she is in charge. Yet it is difficult to be directive if you do not know how to direct or what directions to give. If there is someone around the new leader can go to for good advice the problem will take care of itself. But if a trusted advisor is not available the leader needs to be able to use the other leadership styles. If she and the other team members are new to their jobs the most effective style may be facilitative or even, at times, participatory. Most new leaders think they have to have all the answers. What they really need to have are the questions that will lead the team to the right answers.

BORDER PATROL

An important part of the team leader's job is to address, and even define, the boundaries between the team and the rest of the organization. In a new or developing team the leader will be focused on managing each team member. As the team develops, the leader is concerned with managing the relationships within the team. In a team that is ready for participatory management the leader spends more time on managing the relationship of the team to the rest of the organization. Individuals have the freedom to manage themselves and their relationships with each other.

BALANCING ACT

A study of 18,000 managers was conducted by the consulting firm, Teleometrics, Inc. The study found that the managers could be divided into two groups: those that were afraid to use their power as managers (about a third of the subjects) and those that wielded power without regard for the emotional consequences (the remaining two thirds). The first group was overly concerned with being liked. The feelings and concerns of others were put ahead of the work that had to be done, a typical trait of "Feelers" according to the Myers-Briggs Type Indicator. The other group, dubbed John Waynes, consistently put the corporate mission ahead of any human concerns; something MBTI "Thinkers" are prone to do.

The Manager's Dilemma:

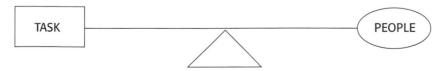

People versus task performance is the manager's dilemma. If the human element is not acknowledged and taken care of the workers will suffer. But if the human element is given precedence over the mission, the work will suffer. Ideally, the manager finds a way to balance both—the demands of the mission (get the job done on time) and the personal needs of the workforce (such as time for family).

PARTICIPATION ON THE BELL CURVE

The Participation Bell Curve offers a graphic display of the range of participation on a team.

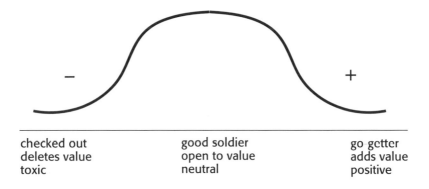

checked out	good soldier	go getter
deletes value	open to value	adds value
toxic	neutral	positive

In every organization there are people who are catalysts for progress and innovation. The natural enthusiasm they exude persuades others to get "on-board" and participate. Their counterparts are the "unhappy campers." At their best they are retired on the job and at their worst they are on a crusade to "get even." In between the two extremes are the majority of workers; the "good soldiers," who do what is expected of them. One group adds value, the other reduces value, the third is neutral yet amenable.

MOVING THE CURVE

Because input determines output, a group of go-getter's will always outperform a group of good soldiers who, in turn, will outperform a group that has checked out.

A team will be the kind of team it decides to be. In a team with high morale and good esprit d' corps, most of the members will be to the right of "Good Soldier" on the Bell Curve. A team that is falling apart experiences the attitudes and behaviors that emerge on the left side of the curve. The leader's job is to create a climate that enlists everyone's full participation—moving the team to the right side of the curve.

Active listening and team dialogue are two potent tools for moving the curve. Put a copy of the curve on a flip chart and ask:

- Where are we on the curve as a team?
- Where do we want to be?
- What do we need to do to get there?

The last question is a tricky one. The temptation to engage in the blame game can be overwhelming for some groups. Preempt that temptation by asking people to focus on what they can do themselves rather than what they would like others to do. This approach is covered in more detail in Chapter Seven "Ground Rules and Agreements" in the discussion about Circle of Concern versus Circle of Influence.

POWER QUESTIONS

Where a person shows up on the Participation Bell Curve is always a personal decision. Ironically, many employees are unaware that they made this decision or that they even had a choice. People often check out of the group effort without realizing it or why. They also do not understand the impact their lack of participation has. It is worth having a discussion about why people check out. The place to start is to ask: What causes you to check out?

Some of the answers might be:

- My ideas are ignored.
- No one asks my opinion.
- When I speak up I feel teased and disrespected.

- I cannot get a word in the conversation.
- Lack of sleep caught up with me.

The next question is naturally: What will it take for you to check back in? Just the act of asking for a person's participation, and letting him know it is needed and appreciated, will go a long way towards getting it.

ALL ABOARD

Every team needs full participation to perform at its full potential. However, everyone has an off day and people understand that. Sometimes just acknowledging the reason for the checkout is enough for some to get back on board. For others it may take some active listening and problem solving. Full participation is more likely when people feel they can say what they are really thinking without retribution. A few people will raise the proverbial bar so high that it just not possible to address (much less resolve) their grievances.

Those individuals, especially the toxic teammates described in Chapter Seventeen "Team Killers," always find plenty of reasons to withhold their full participation. They may even abuse those who have a positive attitude. Too often the toxic people get away with creating a hostile workplace because nothing is done. Anger, or the threat of it, can even intimidate the boss. Dealing with that anger, especially for the MBTI "Feeler" (see Chapter Eleven "Different Work Styles") may not be easy. However, the leader's job is not always easy or pleasant. Start by setting standards for the respectful workplace. Enforce those standards with coaching, counseling, disciplining, and if none of that works, termination.

LEAD, FOLLOW, OR GET OUT OF THE WAY

The old military admonishment, "lead, follow, or get out of the way," applies to every team member, especially those who expend their energy finding fault instead of finding solutions. This is also true for the leader of a team that has reached its full potential. Sometimes the best thing she can do is get out of the way.

DEALING WITH SETBACKS

Like a person, a team has it moods. Given the vicissitudes of the business world no endeavor is free from setbacks and frustrations. Capable leaders are sensitive to the collective, emotional life of their team represented by the ebb and flow of morale. A few influential members who are disgruntled or withdrawn can adversely affect everyone else. Especially in new groups, the cynics can set a tone that keeps the group from coming together as a team. Setbacks, internal friction, and other sources of frustration and disappointment take a toll on a person's participation.

When personal needs for approval, inclusion, and influence are not met satisfaction with group membership decreases. Under these conditions the "Good Soldiers" will start checking out. Instead of waiting for the drop off a good leader can do a lot to compensate for the inherent frustrations on any job with just a few supportive and encouraging words that remind people they are valued and important.

When setbacks occur it may seem the team has little control over what happened. A functional team, however, has a great deal of control over how it responds, emotionally and operationally. A functional group will openly discuss the problem and make adjustments based on the collective assessment. There is value in talking about a problem if listening also occurs. Just acknowledging there is a problem and guiding a discussion about it in a constructive manner can reframe a frustrating failure into the obligatory period of trial and error that is the precursor to success.

THE MICRO-MANAGERS

Leaders fall into three camps: those who delegate too much too soon, those who never delegate enough, and everyone else in between. In a large bureaucracy the tendency is for the micro-manager to rise to the top. The key to getting results is to stay on top of every detail. This approach works well for someone who is managing himself and his own project. However, true to the Peter Principle, strengths that got a person promoted can prove to be a liability at a higher level of responsibility.

The environment in most organizations is adverse to mistakes although plenty of them occur anyway. The way to avoid mistakes that would make the careerist look bad is to keep as much of a project under his direct control as he possibility can. Delegation is equated with risk, meaning mistakes, which cause the delegator to look bad. The lack of delegation, however, creates work for both the micro-manager and the people who work for him. The micro-manager needs a lot of information to stay on top of every aspect of every activity. This has a cascading effect. If the leader does the senior manager's job the senior manager ends up doing the junior manager's job; the junior manager in turn does the support person's job, who in turn will hang out at the water cooler, complaining to the other poorly utilized staff about how messed up things are. Ironically, in spite of heroic efforts to get the job done or perhaps because of them, people get tired and stressed and end up making mistakes that make them and their managers look bad anyway. Is there a cure?

> An agency was proud of it accomplishments. In terms of results they were among the best. But the frantic pace was taking its toll. Some of the managers felt things could not continue at the level of stress and conflict they were experiencing. They believed their management team leader was a workaholic who micro-managed by working night and day. The professional staff throughout the agency voiced a similar complaint and asked for more delegation from their managers. Interestingly enough, the department in the agency with the best morale and the best performance was the one where the manager delegated to his staff and gave them the coaching they needed to handle more responsibility. They were also the only department that reported themselves to be comfortable with their workload unlike everyone else who felt overloaded to the breaking point. Based on the feedback

from the staff and an example of how to make the system work the managers in the agency started making some changes in their management styles.

LINKING FOR RESULTS

The micro-manager spends a lot of effort controlling the work of each individual subordinate. The opportunity for synergy is lost because the manager remains the focal point of the information flow between the different subordinates. People do their work more or less isolated from each other.

Management by Isolation

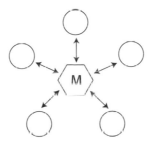

The effective manager facilitates the flow of information between the different members of her team. Even if her subordinates are a working group she still encourages the exchange of ideas between them. Information is never bottlenecked and the collective resources of the team are bought to bear on common problems. Instead of working in isolation people are linked together as the need arises.[3] Managing and participating in this network both draw upon all of the leadership and team skills covered in this book.

Management by Linking

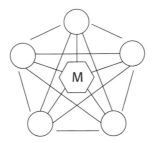

CRISIS MANAGMENT

No matter what style they prefer most managers will eventually put on their firefighter's hat and go into crisis management mode. The cycle quickly gets vicious. There is so much happening that is urgent but not that important that there is little time to focus on the issues that are important, but not really urgent. It does not help that the new marketplace mantra is faster, better, cheaper; all with fewer resources. More and more time is spent reacting to the latest problem instead of anticipating and resolving the problems before they explode into a minor disaster. People run faster but the amount of ground they cover keeps slipping. The irony of it all is that as the need to stop and figure things out becomes more desperate the less time there is to do it. Is there a solution to workplace mania?

A consultant was making a sales call to a potential client. He noticed the frantic even frenetic pace in the office. "It's always like this," he was told. "Let's slow things down," he replied. "It may be hard to believe, but the world will not fall apart if you slow down and catch your breath." He got the job. Working together with the managers and workers he helped the organization set priorities and learn to renegotiate impossible turnaround times without losing customer satisfaction.

MID-COURSE ADJUSTMENTS

A team leader or member seldom goes wrong by asking a few questions to help refocus the energy of the group when it begins to ebb. The resulting discussion could prove crucial to maintaining the momentum of the group effort.

A team leader noticed that the enthusiasm of his team for a project that was waning. He called a meeting and explained his observations and concerns in general terms without naming anyone. He then asked the team a question, "How do you want to accomplish the outcomes you have been tasked to achieve?" Issues and concerns were raised that had been brewing but had not been discussed. At the end of the meeting the team had greater clarity and agreement on what they were doing and how they were going to do it.

GRIDLOCK

The desire to be the dominant member of a group leads to what psychologists have termed "alpha" behaviors. Asking an adult to do something, instead of giving a direct command, is a common courtesy. Many people equate telling others what to do with dominance. The downside to participative management and self-directed work teams is the possibility of power struggles. Until the members master the team concept a gridlock can result over the most trivial concerns.

A team, with several outspoken members, argued most of the morning during an off-site meeting over the issue of when to take a coffee break. The group broke for lunch and then resumed the argument when lunch was over.

Even when the topic is more substantial than a coffee break, many conflicts are only proxies for the real issues, such as: Who is in charge? How are we going to make our decisions?

You can break the impasse by posing questions, such as:

- What is the principle behind this issue?
- What are we really fighting about or for?
- In the general scheme of things will this issue still be important five minutes, five hours or five days from now?
- What are we trying to accomplish here?
- What is our common purpose?
- What are some of things we do agree on?

LEAD BY CHALLENGE

Some leaders turn their people into "go-getters" by offering a vision that is compelling and challenging. The power of challenge works with a vision or mission that is inspirational. The lack of a compelling vision can lull an organization into complacency. According to Edward Land, founder of Polaroid:

> *The first thing you naturally do is teach the person to feel that the undertaking is manifestly important and nearly impossible. This draws out the kind of drives that make people strong.*

Putting a man on the moon in ten years was that kind of challenge and NASA responded by doing what had never been done before in nine years. However, you do not have to go into space to find a challenge Mr. Land would approve of. Bringing a new product to market in record time, winning a large contract, or producing a high quality, low cost product, are big enough challenges for most teams. Chapter 21 "Structural Reinforcement" covers process mapping, a technique used by teams to improve productivity.

SO WHAT ARE YOU GOING TO DO?

Teams or individual team members sometimes get into trouble when they fail to ask for the help they need to accomplish a difficult task. However, think before you rush to the rescue. You can rob others of their opportunity for growth by too quickly taking on their troubles. Instead of kicking the problem upstairs, see if it can be solved at the level it originated. For example, on hearing about a certain shortfall in production a manager might respond to the production supervisor who reported the problem:

> *Your team has got a challenge all right. What are you going to do about it? Get back to me with at least three options and your team's recommendation.*

A team that does not automatically pass the buck masters a higher degree of self-reliance and confidence. Of course, there are times when it is wise to take the problem upstairs and ask for assistance. Waiting until things are out of control creates problems that can be avoided. Knowing when to ask for help takes discernment and judgement, traits developed from experience instead of a book.

REAL PEOPLE

According to the authoritarian paradigm of leadership the leader has to be perfect. General George Patton, for example, could never be wrong. Once he put salt in his coffee from an unmarked container thinking it was sugar. When one of the officers on his staff pointed out what he was doing, he replied, "I like my coffee this way," and proceeded to drink it to the last drop.

Effective leaders have enough confidence in themselves to acknowledge their humanity and their imperfections. They know how to listen to others, to ask questions, and to admit when they are wrong. These leaders keep their people informed and explain their motives, letting others see who they are underneath the title and the business suit. Because they are authentic with their feelings and their motives, saying what they mean, meaning what they say, and doing what they say they will do, people trust them.

SHOOT THE LEADER

It is human nature to blame someone or something besides yourself for your frustrations. Whether deserving or not, the leadership of an organization at all levels can expect to be assigned that role. The degree this happens depends on the ability of the leaders to maintain their credibility during periods of stress. John Bion, one of the founders of the Tavastock Method, noted in his research into human dynamics, the disposition of a group to turn on its leader. Teams become highly participatory, in part, because the members encourage rather than disparage acts of leadership. One of the blocks to participatory management is the shoot-the-leader mentality found in some groups. No one wants to contribute to leading the team if that means subjecting oneself to a barrage of criticism.[4]

Follow-the-leader groups become shoot-the-leader groups because of the lack of willingness of the members to take personal responsibility for their own experiences and feelings. During times of stress leaders need hefty amounts of self-confidence if they are going to maintain the confidence of their subordinates. Good leaders know how to consult with and keep their people informed. They explain the rationale for all major decisions, especially those that are difficult or unpopular. They realize that not everyone is going to be happy with them no matter what decision they make. However, strong leaders have enough inner acceptance that they can deal with overt or covert forms of disapproval.

LEADER FEEDBACK

According to Scott Adams, the author of the cartoon strip, Dilbert, "If bosses were aware of their impact on others there would not be so many bad ones." Good leaders want to know what their people are thinking and they know when and whom to ask. They seek feedback and use it.

> During an off-site meeting the Executive Vice President of an Engineering firm urged his managers to be frank with him. "Let me know when you think I am full of it," he said several times. "I tell the President (of the company) he's wrong and why I disagree when I think he is screwing up. He tells me I'm the only direct report who does that and he is glad I do." The other managers nodded but their expressions said, "Yeah sure." Finally, during the last session one of the managers took a deep breath and told his boss the issues he had working with him. The Vice President said little in response except he appreciated the feedback and would think about it.

When people find they can talk to each other about sensitive issues without repercussions or defensiveness the amount of trust deepens. The place for disagreement and feedback on business decisions is in team meetings. Feedback on personal style and related interpersonal issues may be more appropriate in private, one-on-one. Even with the most approachable leaders, employees will hesitate to give them the feedback they need. As a leader you may have sensed on occasion some dissatisfaction in your own team. Out of politeness or fear of a negative reaction, people are just not going to tell you what is really going on. One technique is to ask your subordinates to share their feedback with a third party (often an outside consultant) you both trust. Chapter Ten "Organizational Interventions" discusses this option in greater detail. Obtaining useful feedback on your own takes good timing, finely tuned questions, and a degree of trust that can only be built up over time.

THE "IMPERIUM"

The ancient Romans believed that leadership was a divinely inspired gift from the gods that literally descended on a man when it was needed. The moment the divine inspiration alighted, the chosen man would know what to do. Using that knowledge he would unerringly guide the legions in battle or speak the words in the Senate that would bring glory to the Roman people. This inspiration they called the "imperium," a Latin word that also means command, authority, and power.

The councils of the Native Americans used a similar approach. When pressing questions needed to be addressed the men gathered together in a lodge with their chief. Smoke from smoldering sage and sweetgrass was used to acknowledge the seven directions and purify those in the circle. An elder would implore the Great Spirit and the tribal ancestors for their guidance. A talking stick was placed in the center. The elder or warrior who felt inspired to speak would pick up the stick and speak from his heart about the issues facing the tribe. No one else would speak while he held the stick. The guidance they sought might be spoken through the chief or it might come through any of the men in the lodge. When it did come everyone would know it and affirm his or her understanding through a ritual that honored the source of the wisdom.

Like the Romans and the Native Americans, participatory teams hold a space (both organizational and psychological) that encourages inspiration to strike. This inspiration could hit any one of the team members in the office or during a meeting. When it does the team listens, evaluates the idea and responds. Leadership does not need to be limited to one person. Like lighting, inspiration can keep striking. Anyone can have a piece of the puzzle. Presenting new ideas or encouraging other to do so is a definite act of leadership.

BURIAL OF THE GREAT CHIEF

Leadership in management circles is cited as the *a priori* factor for corporate success. Leadership from a person like Lee Iacocca or Winston Churchill can be crucial, but so is the sense of initiative and responsibility that comes when people learn to think for themselves. The following Native American story from *Red Earth: Tales of the Mic-Mac Indians* is instructive:

> As long as the Mic-Macs could remember, there hadn't been a chief as brave and as wise as Ulginoo. He led the tribe to many victories over their enemies and he was the most cunning hunter of all. When he felt that his time was up, he told he people to bury him only lightly because he would soon ride again and lead them anew. But they held counsel and after a long debate decided to bury Ulginoo really deep and to put heavy stones on his grave. They reasoned that if Ulginoo would come to life again, the young men of the tribe would look up to him and follow only his advice. In the end, the tribe would perish because the young men had not developed any initiative of their own. Thus all agreed to prevent Ulginoo from rising again and to let him rest deeply in the good red earth.

21
Structural Reinforcement

Maxcomm Associates

Simple, clear purpose and principles give rise to complex intelligent behavior. Complex rules and regulations give rise to simple, stupid behavior.

DEE HOCK

Team-building programs are more likely to produce lasting change if that change is supported by the organizational structure. The culture of a business and the structures that reinforce it will prevail in the long run. If no one ever bothers to ask, "Is there a better way?" processes and procedures become sanctified by their own longevity.

Empowered work teams, teams that can make decisions and solve problems, require an empowering organization. A bureaucracy, however, is inherently adverse to any decentralization of decision making and problem solving. Centralization is part of the bureaucratic "immune system" that reduces risk, assigns responsibility, and protects turf. The task of senior management is to balance the needs of the team—freedom to innovate, with the function of an organization—maintenance of order and control.

DECENTRALIZATION

The amount of inertia in a large organization is generally proportional to how centralized it is. If a team is constrained by layers of bureaucracy and rules, the good ideas it generates (as well as the bad ones) go nowhere. Decentralized organizations recognize that those closest to the problem can do the most about it. Decentralization moves decision making and the responsibility for results down to the level responsible for performing the task. Bureaucratic organizations respond to problems by tightening control and enacting more rules in the belief that these are adequate substitutes for good judgement—a mistake many large corporations make over and over again. For example, IBM lost huge amounts of market share in the late 1980's because the manufacturer was unable to react to changing market conditions as a result of its penchant for centralized decision-making. IBM personal computers were kept underpowered and overpriced so as not compete with the sales of mini- and mainframe computers. Sales were lost to companies who were willing to build and price their computers in a way that the much bigger IBM would not.

Hewlett-Packard, like IBM, was another major producer of office automation products with a solid but aging product line. Realizing it had a problem, Hewlett-Packard went though a major change process in the mid-1980s in an effort to increase innovation and reduce the time it took to get new products to the market. As one manager put it:[1]

> We needed several things: a higher sense of urgency, a streamlined decision making process, and a hierarchical structure that cut across fundamental and organizational boundaries.

Hewlett-Packard found the agility it needed by giving new product design teams more freedom to cross organizational lines. Instead of making all their parts the teams broke with the past by contracting out for selected components. The results from throwing away the rulebook were products, like a desktop laser printer, that led the marketplace.

David Osborne and Ted Gaebler in their book, *Reinventing Government*, point out that wherever they found participatory organizations they also found teamwork. One is not really possible without the other. These organizations encourage or even require employees to be involved in the decision-making process. Decentralization provides more opportunity for:

- *Flexibility:* The ability to quickly respond to changing conditions.
- *Involvement:* Participation leads to a sense of ownership and commitment.
- *Innovation:* The best ideas come from those closest to the problems.
- *Pride:* Those responsible for the outcome are credited for the results.
- *Leverage:* Giving guidance and goals instead of micro-managing.
- *Initiative:* Instead of ignoring problems people see what needs to be done and do it.

Decentralization is not a laissez-faire form of management where employees just do whatever they please. People are accountable to their jobs, to their coworkers and to their bosses. According to the consultants, Osborne and Gaebler, ". . .organizations that decentralize authority also find they have to articulate their missions, create internal cultures around their core values, and measure results."[2]

TEAMWORK STRUCTURES

Just as hierarchical organizations are centralized, organizations that encourage teamwork tend to be decentralized. Three structures that foster teamwork through decentralization are:

- *Matrix*. Boundaries between departments are flexible and cross-connected. Members with different skills work together as needed.
- *Ad hoc*. Similar to the matrix organization but departmental boundaries are more fixed. The person is assigned to a cross-functional team on a full-time basis for a limited period of time.
- *Self-Directed*. The team manages itself without an appointed leader.

NETWORKING MATRIX

The networking of computers has multiplied their utility many fold. Networking has also accelerated the exchange of information between employees and managers and leveraged everyone's' effectiveness. The ubiquitous "org chart" that listed functions and the people responsible for them in an orderly sequence of lines and boxes, no longer represents the reality of all the interoffice networks. Just as information can now come and go from every point on the compass so can teamwork.

The matrix organization is composed of flexible networks of interdependent teams creating an organizational chart that looks more like a spider's web than the typical pyramid. Matrix management takes the rigid frame out an organization, softening the boundaries between various departments and tasks. Interdisciplinary teams with the required skills and resources are structured and then restructured to fulfill each new or evolving requirement.

In a bureaucratic culture, positions within the hierarchy determine the task that is performed. In the matrix organization, titles no longer take priority over the task and the results that need to be achieved. As Charles Savage, author of *Fifth Generation Management*, describes them, "Instead of mutually exclusive task and department assignments . . . (matrix) . . .enterprises blend the talents of different people around focused tasks."

The drawback to this arrangement is the potential for confusion around lines of authority/responsibility and chain-of-command. If everyone is responsible, no one is accountable and important tasks are not completed. Reporting to two or more bosses or dealing with divided loyalties will cause difficulties. Making it work takes constant communication and clarification between all the parties that are sharing resources and people. Until it all gets sorted out we are talking about *a lot* of meetings. Meeting management, team problem-solving, and decision-making skills are critical. Without these skills most groups will continue to stumble about, generating more heat than light as they try to get organized.

A government agency was reorganized into the matrix management configuration. Everyone was on at least two if not four or five teams. Most of the teams operated on a permanent basis. Some members were "core" team members (technical or managerial types) and others were "expanded" team members who performed support functions such as procurement and financial management. The people were on cross-functional teams, but they also still reported to a head of a functional department. Getting the system off the ground took a lot of meetings. People, especially the "expanded" team members, found themselves in meetings all the time. This created a major bottleneck because they had little time left over to do their procurement or financial tasks. The resulting internal friction was extremely stressful for everyone. Since a support person, in effect, had several bosses who did they owe their loyalty to when everyone was tugging on them at the same time? The "we-they" blame game between the technical and support people started to get ugly. In hindsight the solution was obvious. The heads of each functional department had to sit down together and come up with a mutually agreed upon system for prioritizing the work. Not everything can be a priority when resources are limited. By talking to each other frequently, help-ing each other out when they could, being flexible when they couldn't, the department heads could coordinate the flow of work and resources between the teams. This kept small prob-lems from growing up into major crisis.

AD HOC TEAMS

Ad hoc, cross-functional teams are the life blood of today's orga-nization. Its members are drawn from a number of different de-partments within an organization to work on a short-term project. When their project is completed the team disbands or reshuffles in order to undertake the next project. The impact of an ad hoc team does not end when the team disbands. Because they have crossed department or functional lines the former members of the ad hoc team help create more understanding and cooperation when they return to their old departments. Employees who get a chance to "see what those other guys do" gain a new perspective on the rest of the organization.

FINDING THE COMMON GOOD

Most problems are bigger than one or two teams or divisions. The solutions are like pieces of a puzzle that are divided up between various groups. Cooperation across organizational lines is needed to put those pieces together. Ad hoc teams succeed best when they develop a loyalty to each other and the goals of the team. This can mean subordinating the interests and agendas of the de-partments they came from, for those of where they are.

Executive teams frequently struggle with this issue of divided loyalties. The members are usually less willing to subordinate the interests of their departments for some common good, since the interests of their subordinates create a natural pressure group. The "B-word," bonding, may be needed before the members will will-ingly compromise for the common good.

SELF-DIRECTED WORK TEAMS

Self-directed work teams are frequently found in the manufacturing sector. The concept is simple. The people directly involved in a task can make better decisions about how to perform their task than the people who are indirectly involved. In autonomous teams, those that manage themselves, major decisions are made by consensus or majority vote. Team members are cross-trained and the various administrative and technical tasks, including leadership, are rotated. As a team, the members are recognized and rewarded. Also as a team, they rate each other on performance and teamwork. In the case of one manufacturer, team members even determine the hours they work and the wages they earn.[3]

This approach to teamwork requires extensive training in the basic skills covered in the first section of this book. The members of a self-directed team need to know how to communicate and listen to others, resolve conflicts, solve problems and make decisions as a group. Creating self-directed work teams is easy. Getting them to work together productively can be like hanging wallpaper with one hand. Companies typically plan for a five-year transition. Rather than converting one of its existing plants, General Motors started with a shovel; building an entirely new company in Tennessee called Saturn Corporation.

The self-directed work teams at Saturn are producing results. The absentee rate is 2.5% compared to an average that runs as high as 14% at other GM plants. The quality of Saturn cars is considered the best among all American manufactures and equal to those produced by Japanese.

Managers should look before they rush to reorganize their company into self-directed teams. Some people will have a hard time adjusting to the team concept. Others think they will be making decisions that impact the entire plant. Companies have experienced anywhere from a twenty to a forty percent turnover in personnel. As in any major sea change, it takes heroic amounts of communication, training, and skilled leadership to smooth the waters.

PROGRAMS AND PRACTICES

Programs and practices to promote a healthy and participative workplace are becoming more widespread. The trend has been to combine a number of these different practices into a systematic approach that encourages a healthy workplace and a higher level of employee retention. These programs and practices include:

- Employee Training Programs
- Special Purpose Committees
- Company Web Sites
- Shared Databases
- Peer Reviews
- Employee (360 Degrees) Feedback
- Customer Feedback
- Team Rewards
- Flexible Job Descriptions
- Cross-Training
- Family-Friendly Policies.

EMPLOYEE TRAINING PROGRAMS

Training pays off. The more employees know, the greater their technical and interpersonal expertise, the more power they have to succeed. Some companies offer informal classes after work or during the lunch hour. Others with deeper pockets have campuses devoted solely to training which employees attend for days or even weeks at time. The "little dragons" of Asia attribute part of their economic boom to the high value their culture places on training and education. In Singapore the government urges all companies to set aside five percent of an employee's time for training.

The first American auto maker to introduce self-directed work teams was General Motor's Saturn Corporation. Team building is such a high priority that the factory in Tennessee even has its own in-house ropes course. Frequent classroom training is also conducted in both technical and interpersonal skills. Five percent of an employee's work time or about 92 hours each year is set aside for continued training.

Other successful companies also follow this standard for employee training. Corning, Inc., obligates around five percent of an employee's work hours to training. Since it began investing in its employees through training, Corning's return on equity increased six percent in five years. Many high-tech companies believe continuous employee training is essential for their company to keep its competitive edge. Motorola, for example, spends over $70 million a year on training through its own university.

SPECIAL PURPOSE COMMITTEE

A special purpose committee can play an on-going or a temporary role in an organization. Membership is drawn from different specialties and departments. Purposes include problem solving, conflict resolution, quality of life, labor relations, affirmative action, compensation, or just about any other issue that is a common concern.

The committee acts as a forum for gathering and exchanging information and concerns about the issue, problem solving and recommending policies and procedures. The auto parts manufacturer, Donnelly Corporation, wanted to create greater employee involvement. The company formed "equity committees" staffed by a cross-section of workers. Each committee has its own topic, such as wages or grievances, and makes its recommendations by consensus.

COMPANY WEB SITES

Web sites dedicated to the topic of change and improvement provide a forum for employees or customers to share information and experiences. It is quite appealing to find out what others are thinking on a topic of mutual interest. The chat room is a meeting place where people can discuss the latest corporate initiatives. Although email does not offer complete anonymity it can still foster the free and open expression of concerns, gripes, and suggestions from employees or customers depending on how it is set up.

The email data can be compiled and analyzed for trends by comparing the content over a period of time. If a lot of people have the same gripe about a product or program it is obviously a smart idea to take corrective action. In one small firm, anyone with a major gripe or a brilliant idea can email the company president. The president reads the messages and replies by email to the sender. Administrative, logistical, and travel functions are increasingly being conducted through the corporate web site. You can order supplies, update your 401K plan, and arrange a trip—all by spending a few minutes at your computer.

SHARED DATABASES

Web sites containing the latest articles and memos on change, teamwork, and other relevant topics are an effective way to disseminate information. The databases include reports and studies conducted in-house. Some companies have their managers file a "lessons learned" report after they have finish a project or program so others in the company will benefit from their experience.

PEER REVIEWS

Team members, from executives to factory workers, should be accountable to each other and the common objectives that brought them together. Peer pressure has always been a powerful motivating force. People do not want to let their teammates down. Setting collegial standards through peer review recognizes the importance of team accountability. In the Fibers Division of Du Pont, the input from the team in the area of teamwork, counts for about twenty-five percent of an employee's rating. Not everyone welcomes the concept of peer review. When told they were going to start doing peer reviews, employees in one government agency objected. "We can't rate each other," they protested. "We are not experts in what the other person does." However, the team rating does not need to be about technical expertise. The employees in the agency were told they would rate how well their fellow members communicate, cooperate, and support the team effort. Training was conducted in the skills that support teamwork so the team would know what to evaluate.

In some organizations information used for peer review is provided in written form to the team leader. Negative comments that have not been validated by the leader nor discussed with the team member are not included in the employee's evaluation. As a general principle, if there are any surprises for the employee in the evaluation they should be positive ones.

EMPLOYEE (360 DEGREES) FEEDBACK

In just a few years 360 degrees feedback has become a widely used tool for professional development. 360 degrees mean getting feedback on your performance from peers, subordinates, and superiors. The feedback is given a without attribution to encourage honest and frank responses. There are a number of computerized systems on the market that compile and present the feedback. One of them, TeamView/360, provides feedback on both team and individual performance. It is available from Jossey-Bass/Pfeiffer.[4]

CUSTOMER FEEDBACK

In some organizations it is easy to forget why you are there. The most successful organizations never lose sight of that ultimate reason for every job—to serve a customer. That customer may be internal or external. It could be another organization or even a nation. It could be your boss and your coworkers. In a team-based organization most workers have multiple customers. If you are really concerned about customer service you will gather feedback

---

Customer Service Survey

1) On a scale of ten to one (10 best . . . 1 worst) how well are we meeting your needs with the service (or product) we provide?

2) What could we do to better meet your needs?

---

on your service to the customer. Initiative. Listening. Responsiveness. Three words that describe good customer service. The hallmark of a bureaucratic organization is the lack of a meaningful yardstick for measuring customer satisfaction. If you work in a bureaucratic organization try something radical. Identify your clients and ask them how you are doing.

A department in Westinghouse spent many hours preparing quarterly reports. After working late to get the tedious and time-consuming reports in on time the manager decided to follow-up and see what impact all this work was having. He picked up the phone and asked, "That report we just sent in . . . did it meet your needs?" Much to his surprise he was told, "Yeah, thanks, but we really don't need all that information you guys provide." The next quarter a much streamlined report saved everyone time, effort, and money.

TEAM REWARDS

The American ethos of the rugged individual, encourages us to stake out an achievement we can point to as our own. But an undue concern with garnering personal "kudos" can be detrimental to the collective effort. Rewarding the team as a group reinforces those values that foster teamwork. Recognizing and acknowledging the team's accomplishments builds that all important sense of pride in the team. In addition to announcements, plaques, and other forms of public commendation, financial rewards are given to the team as a bonus that is commensurate with the collective achievement. If the team comes up with a new process that saves the company money or a product or patent that generates additional income, the team shares part of the profits or savings. The team members decide among themselves how the money will be divided.

FLEXIBLE JOB DESCRIPTIONS

Job descriptions for production workers in some companies seem as difficult to amend as the U.S. Constitution. The lower the worker is on the pay scale the more specific the details of the description and the less freedom there is to innovate. A common problem related to job descriptions is that people often feel overloaded and wonder if they are doing someone else's work in addition to their own. To help resolve this conflict the need was identified in one organization to define the job descriptions in terms of required outcomes, team resources and access to other groups. In order to make these changes the team should meet to more clearly define the roles of each member and the needs they have of each other. Clarifying roles and needs can be facilitated by calling a meeting and asking the team members some of the following questions:

- Describe what you do.
- What are your most significant responsibilities?
- What do you need from others in your department to do your job?
- What do you need from others outside of the department or organization to do your job?

The difference between the "empowered" worker and the ordinary worker is that empowered workers manage themselves to achieve the results they are responsible for. Ordinary workers just do what they are told. Within certain parameters, empowered workers make up their own job as they go along, focusing time and attention on the projects that seem most interesting and rewarding.

CROSS-TRAINING

Cross-training enables workers to be cross-functional. Both are essential in order to blur the boundaries imposed by a narrow job description. By its nature, matrix management requires team members to be willing and able to do other jobs besides the one they were hired to perform. Most of this training can be conducted on-the-job. Those with the knowledge and skill in some area instruct others until they can do the task on their own. Small businesses especially benefit from this investment in employee time. The attitude of ownership is one that says, "the more we learn about each others work, the more we can help each other and our business." Tutoring an employee in a new task affirms that employee's potential.

Most employees are excited by the opportunity to learn and increase the scope of their activities. When a senior employee or manager tutors someone she is almost sure to act as a mentor to that person. Inevitably, they both have the opportunity to learn useful things about the organization and each other.

Self-directed work teams have to embrace cross-training. Because of shared roles and responsibilities a person's job can change every few weeks or even day-to-day. Workers stay interested and involved because they are constantly learning and doing new things.

FAMILY-FRIENDLY POLICIES

Balancing the conflicting demands of family and work is tough enough for the traditional, one wage-earner family; an arrangement that constitutes only ten percent of American households. When both parents work, a condition found in two-thirds of American households, or in single parent families, the demands are at least twice as great. In most organizations, one- to two-thirds of employees struggle with this issue. Programs that ease this burden benefit the organization, as well as employees and their families. Some of the more popular pro-family policies include:

- *On-site Child Care:* Parents bring their pre-school children to a licensed day care center that uses space provided by the corporation.
- *Family Leave:* Government regulations require unpaid family leave for 90 days be provided when a family member is sick. This includes maternity leave for mothers and fathers. Progressive companies provide some income maintenance during the leave.
- *Flex-Time:* Flex-time allows employees to set their hours. It can also include provisions for working at home (telecommuting by fax and email) or working part-time. Sabbaticals for ten-year employees are also offered.
- *Get a Life:* Many workplaces impose peer pressure to work late. Others may not say anything, but anyone who leaves before five o'clock should feel guilty. The workaholic lifestyle is not only encouraged, it is expected. In contrast, healthy workplaces believe employees are more productive if they live a balanced life.
- *Wellness Programs:* Companies are offering special classes to their employees on health, nutrition, weight loss, stress management, and family issues. The improved health of employees reduces overhead costs and raises productivity. The Wellness Council of America is happy to provide more information on work site health-promotion programs.[5]

22
Process Improvement

Broderbund

*If you can't describe what you do as a process,
you don't know what your are doing.*

W. EDWARD DEMING

Starting in 1993, the United States enjoyed one of the longest running business expansions without inflation in recent history. Many factors, like globalization and emerging markets contributed to this expansion. One factor, seldom emphasized by the economic pundits, has been improvement in productivity. As expected, a significant part of this improvement comes from the investment in new technology, especially the Internet. What has not been acknowledged is the impact of continuously improving processes that involve existing technology. In other words, we are making better use of what we already have. Look closely at a successful organization with a competitive advantage and you will find continuous improvement. At the beginning of the 1990s Paul Allaire, the CEO of Xerox, described his vision of how new gains in productivity would be achieved:

I envision a time when this company will consist of many small work groups . . . tied directly to the customer with the capacity to design their own work processes and to adapt continuously as business conditions change.

Allaire realized something that other early advocates of team-based organizations seldom grasped. It is not enough to build teams. Teams do not stand alone in a vacuum. They exist as part of a larger system. They must have the charter to innovate within that system in a way that is beneficial to the client/customer relationship. It's a much overused word, but synergy is seldom found in a working group because people in those groups do not need to talk to each other. In a team people need to talk to each other. And if they do some thinking, along with that talking, they will find a better way to do what they do.

SYSTEMS THINKING

Allaire's organizational paradigm has it roots in systems thinking. The old concept of an organization was that of hierarchy with clearly defined areas of responsibility. The focus was on each functional department or division. Accounting happened in the accounting department. Marketing in the marketing department. Engineering in the . . . well you get the idea. The degree of compartmentalization meant that a decision made in one department was thrown over the transom into another department with little regard for the impact it would have. Ford's Edsal was one infamous result of that kind of thinking. Anytime there are competing processes in an organization and little or no coordination between the owners of those processes the end results will suffer.

For example, in Widget Industries three different departments have three different agendas. Sales is upset with Credit because of the tight credit restrictions. Production is upset with Sales because of the promises for special modifications. Credit and Sales are upset with production for the high rate of returned products.

Different Agendas

DEPARTMENT	GOAL
Sales - - - - - - - - - - - - - -	High Sales
Production - - - - - - - - -	Fast Turnaround
Credit - - - - - - - - - - - - -	Low Losses

As long as they continue to set their own agenda without con-sulting with each other on the overall process the conflict be-tween the departments will continue to impact customer satisfac-tion, and of course, the bottom line.

SYSTEMS THINKING

Systems thinking starts with the big picture. It focuses on the end results and what it takes to get there. The overall process, not the special interests of one particular department over another, drives each decision. Cross-functional teams are inherently part of this approach. Each process is coordinated so that the overall system produces the desired results, based on the feedback provided by the customer and the other members of the system. Each depart-ment has to subordinate its special agenda to the overarching re-sults the system is intended to produce. This way of looking at an organization and how all the different parts fit together creates the potential for tremendous gains in productivity.

For Widget Industries, this new approach is achieved by form-ing cross-functional teams with representatives from the different departments. The team members engage in a dialogue and make trade-offs that improve the output of the overall system. The pay-off in this approach for the Widget Industries includes other areas besides better productivity and profits. A few of the more promi-nent ones are:

- More involvement of employees
- Better utilization of in-house talents and skills
- Higher morale
- Enhanced customer service
- Improved career development
- Better coordination and communication.

WHAT IS PROCESS IMPROVEMENT?

Process Improvement (PI) is defining a process and making it better. The changes usually involve making the process faster, simpler or easier. Doing PI requires systematic analysis in two areas:

1) Defining the steps for producing a product or service.
2) Enhancing that sequence of steps to produce the output more efficiently and effectively.

WHAT IS PROCESS MAPPING?

Process mapping is a way to "chunk down" a complex process into a series of graphical representations. The map uses computer flow-chart symbols to diagram the steps in a process starting with the input and ending with the output. Mapping the steps helps us clarify what we are doing so we can do it better. Often that means finding out which steps we can do without.

KEY DEFINITIONS

Here are some key terms that will help you explain to others what you are trying to do when you starting talking about improving a process.

- *Process:* A series of tasks that produces a product or service, which meets the needs of the customer.
- *System:* A collection of related processes.

- *Task:* A specific individual action performed in sequence to produce an outcome.
- *Product or Service:* The outputs produced by a business process.
- *Customer:* Someone who uses and gains benefit from the product or service we provide. Her direct or indirect input determines the design and content of what she receives.

MAPPING SYMBOLS

The following are some the symbols from computer flow-charting used in process mapping:

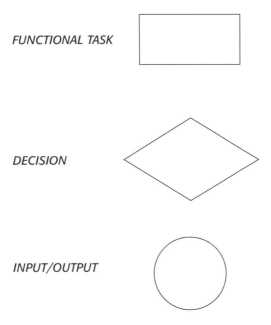

FUNCTIONAL TASK

DECISION

INPUT/OUTPUT

THREE PHASES

To minimize disruptions, process improvement is sometimes done in three phases. The phases are used when significant changes are anticipated that will cross departmental boundaries.

- *Phase One:* Map the processes conducted by a team and identify disconnects and optional improvements.

- *Phase Two:* Validate the maps and the suggested improvements by reviewing them with other knowledgeable participants. Identify additional improvements. Prepare action plans for implementing the recommended changes.

- *Phase Three:* Implement the action plans. Coordinate changes across all organizational boundaries. Measure the impact and make adjustments.

The difference between process improvement and reengineering is in the degree of radical change. PI makes incremental changes. Reengineering starts at ground zero to produce a totally new system. Odds are, if the people running the new system (the ones that are still there) need to be retrained to do it the system has been reengineered.

GROUND RULES

When you conduct a process improvement meeting it is a good idea to ask the group to set some ground rules. Some people like to call these rules SOB's, short for, Standards of Behavior. We will have more fun and be more productive if we agree to follow our SOB's. Here is a sample list.

- Participate fully.
- Take turns speaking one at a time.
- Listen carefully.
- Use friendly humor (no put-downs)
- Encourage each other.
- Share insights and ideas.
- Be on time.
- Think! There is always a better way.

PROCESS MAXIMS

Maxims are ideas or concepts that can help guide a person's actions. Listed below are ideas that will help guide a team as it begins process improvement.

- A process exists in order to serve customers by producing a product or service they need.
- Efficient processes do things right. Effective processes do the right things.
- Process improvement doesn't end. There is always a better way.
- Output is what is produced from a process. Outcome is the impact of what is produced.
- Don't let the "perfect" be the enemy of the "good."
- No process exists in isolation. It is continuously impacted by many factors that affect the input, the process owners, the customers, and other related factors.
- The whole of all the processes in a system is bigger than their sum.
- The longer a process has not been reviewed the more likely it is done the way it is done because we have always done it that way.

PROCESS MAPPING

The following page diagrams the process of making cookies. Yes/No decisions points are represented by diamonds. The starting point is the decision to make cookies and the end point is serving the cookies.

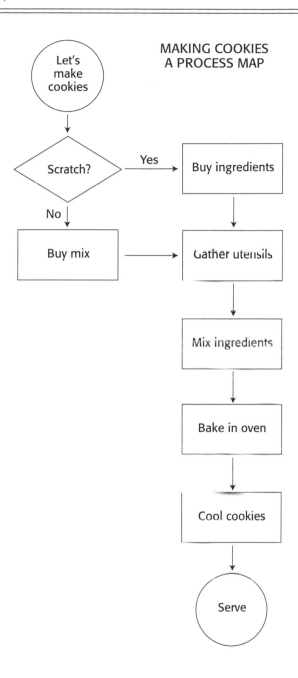

MAKING COOKIES
A PROCESS MAP

23
Forging a Vision

Stream

"Would you tell me please, which way I ought to go from here? That depends a good deal on where you want to go," said the cat. "I don't much care where—so long as I get somewhere," Alice added as an explanation. "Oh, you're sure to do that," said the cat. "If you only walk long enough."

LEWIS CARROLL
Alice's Adventures in Wonderland

Mention the "vision thing" in a corporate meeting and eyes will start to glaze over. Why? Most visions are put together as an obligatory statement that will do no more than collect dust. Yet when you find an inspired group of people they are inspired because they share an inspiring vision. This kind of vision sparks action because you can compare how things are to how you want them to be. The completed vision statement has four components that should be in alignment with each other. They are:

1) *Vision:* The ideal or impact we aspire to achieve.
2) *Mission:* The means we use to fulfill our vision.
3) *Goals:* Objective standards that measure results.
4) *Values:* Shared beliefs that define who we are and how we live our lives.

VISION STATEMENT

A vision represents the ideal for the organization and its impact in the world. It is the spiritual side of a business plan that expresses the spirit or essence of an enterprise. This statement captures in a paragraph or two what is unique about an organization and the sense of purpose that drives it. The sentiments expressed are the rationale for the business that appeal to the heart as well as the mind. They offer a personal element that employees can identify with. The vision is a corporate pole star that people can use to maintain their heading. Teams that have lost their sense of direction often lose their sense of urgency as well. The lack of any compelling purpose or agenda keeps an organization in a reactive rather than proactive state.

CARPE DIEM

A dynamic organization will change its vision as the times change. The old vision of the Library of Congress was to be "a repository of the past for the present." But the dramatic changes in information technology, fueled by the fax machine, the personal computer, the Internet and the optical disk, created a need for a more compelling vision. The new vision sought to make the Library "an active catalyst for a democratic civilization." Unexpectedly, at the time the vision statement was crafted, the Library was given the opportunity to develop an exhibit drawn from the files of the KGB of the abuses of the Lenin and Stalinist era. Documents and pictures were obtained and arranged in record time for an exhibit in Moscow to help educate the Russian people about their own past. Had the Library not acted quickly, the historic documents might have been lost during the dissolution of the Soviet Union. Organizations that articulate their vision are more likely to seize opportunities that no one could have anticipated.

MISSION STATEMENT

The mission statement is, in broad terms, how you are going to fulfill your vision. It defines the measures you will take to achieve the desired impact. A good mission statement clarifies what your company does without limiting the possibilities for innovation. It tells people what business you are really in without limiting new opportunities. For example, do you make buggy whips or vehicle acceleration devices? Do you provide telephone service or telecommunications? How an organization defines what it does can have far reaching implications for future growth.

WORKING DOCUMENT

It is common practice for senior managers to create a vision statement during a management retreat. When they return from the plush resort with the statement in hand the receptivity of the other employees is often indifferent if not cynical. These statements fail to engender much enthusiasm because people become excited about the visions they helped to create not the ones handed to them. A successful statement is forged from the thoughts and ideas gathered from every corner of the organization. It is a working document that can be updated with new input and ideas as they emerge.

TOM'S MISSION

Tom's of Maine is a consumer products company that offers an excellent example of the above process. Tom's vision is to be a company committed to the environment and to give people a better choice in the products they use for personal hygiene. Tom's mission statement was drafted in a dialogue that involved all its employees. The statement urges the company to be "distinctive in products and policies, which honor and sustain our natural world."

To fulfill that mission employees ". . . seek ways to increase the natural effectiveness of our ingredients, to reduce and recycle our packaging and to support recycling in our community." Not surprisingly, Tom's of Maine has grown into a national company since it was founded in 1974 by a young entrepreneurial couple.

TEAM MISSION

A team, just like a company, can benefit by crafting a mission statement in its own words. Without a clear purpose that everyone understands and supports, a team is just a group of people who happen to work with each other. A good mission statement defines this purpose in a way that inspires the allegiance and energy to do it. Questions that a team mission statement might answer are:

- What contribution do we make?
- How do our efforts make a difference?
- What is or could be unique about our efforts?
- What do we really get excited about?

The best statement is simple and concise. It defines the role the team plays that turn the vision and mission into a reality. One way to generate more understanding and agreement is to have the team members draw a large picture that graphically expresses their mission. A discussion about the drawing can elicit new ideas and possibilities.

MEASURABLE GOALS

Goals are standards of performance that can be used to measure success. Without a yardstick to objectively evaluate results, a team will never be able to realistically assess its progress. Teams that help define their own goals and performance standards are more likely to work harder to achieve them. Objective standards include sales, profit, production, and quality. Internal departments that have no contact outside the organization can still measure customer satisfaction. Financial performance can be tracked on a cost basis by charging internal customers for services rendered and receive charges from other departments who act as internal providers. Without ownership and some form of feedback on how we are doing, team goals have little power to motivate.

SHARED VALUES

The activities used to conduct a mission are shaped by the values the members aspire to. These values are defined by the range of interpersonal, communication and organizational skills that enable people to express who they are. Good leadership articulates and models these values in a way that inspires others to accept them. During difficult times shared values and a common sense of purpose will keep a team from falling apart. What makes values real are the actions taken to support them. At one time or another we are all faced with choices that test our commitment to our values. Integrity is making the choices that keep our actions congruent with our values.

Define the values of your team by asking:

- What kind of team do we want to be?
- How do we want to be with each other?
- What values make us more effective?
- What are some recent examples of when people's actions were based on those values?

Trust and teamwork result from values that have been internalized and expressed in countless small acts through out the day. Trust and teamwork are not something that can be added to a team like a cup of detergent to a load of laundry. Instead, these attributes are the results of values that been discussed, tested, and practiced to the point where they have become an integral part of the team culture.

HEALTHY VALUES

The management consultant, Robert Rosen was funded by the MacArthur Foundation to conduct a study of "healthy companies." Rosen discovered companies that were value-driven, tended to have healthier balance sheets than companies that always put profits ahead of people. One study, quoted by Rosen, showed companies with a people-oriented culture had on the average, a 64 percent higher, annualized growth of sales and a two percent higher profit margin than less progressive companies.

The commonality between healthy companies was their recognition of the links between the triad of "People, Principles, and Profits." According to Rosen, in his book, *The Healthy Company*, the values shared by these companies:[1]

> . . . bind people to their organizations. By creating a language of common aspirations and appealing to principles of dignity, commitment, and growth, these values help to create an identity that connects thousands of people around a shared mission.

The seven values cited by Rosen are:

1) Commitment to self-knowledge and development
2) Firm belief in decency
3) Respect for individual differences
4) Spirit of partnership
5) High priority for health and well being
6) Appreciation for flexibility and resilience
7) Passion for products or service (what we produce or provide) and process (how we work together to produce them).

Shared values create a culture. To the denizens of a culture the values that define it are as transparent as water is to a fish. But they affect how everything is done. Once they have become in-grained there is little conscious thought about their presence.

TEAM VALUES

The values that make a team the kind of team you would want to be a member of are not limited to the seven listed above. Each team needs to discover and articulate the values that create the kind of team its members want. These values are no more alive and real than the actions and attitudes taken that give them life.

During times of change, core values act like the needle of a compass: a reference point that helps people find their way. But even the best organizational values will not mean much if employees hardly know about them. Some companies print up their values and mission statements on pocket-sized, calendar cards. Large posters, videos, and pamphlets are also some of the means used to get the message out. Tom's of Maine put its vision in a two-page write-up that is enclosed with each product.

Some of the values of a high performance team include:

- Sense of purpose
- Mutual encouragement
- Mutual coaching
- Interpersonal commitment
- Collaboration over competition.

SENSE OF PURPOSE

A team exists for one reason: to do something. Team members must have a sense of purpose as to why they are working together; otherwise they won't work together in a manner that improves the collective performance. Fostering commitment to a common goal is extremely difficult if no clear and compelling purpose has been articulated. This sense of purpose (and all the elements of the vision behind it) can evolve over time as the team gains experience and confidence.

High-performance teams, teams that exceeded all expectations (Katzenbach and Smith, 1993), commonly are engaged in tasks in which the results of their efforts can be measured. The members are emotionally involved in their work because their mission is real, important, and challenging as well as measurable. Just because a group of people is called a team does not mean they will work as one. If you call employees a team without offering a measurable purpose you might end up with something less than one. The resulting cynicism and negativity can destroy the potential for continuous improvement.

As NASA discovered during its ten-year mission to go to the moon, groups become synergistic when they are trying to accomplish something they find meaningful and exciting. Every month NASA employees could look up at the night sky and see their objective. And it did not take a rocket scientist to measure the results of the collective effort. You may not be trying to get to the moon, but a sense of purpose can transform the most mundane job. This story is apocryphal but it makes a point:

> A man came upon four men chipping away on several large stones with hammers and chisels. In turn he asked each one what he was doing, "Breaking rocks," the first man said. "Earning a living," the second one replied. The third man pointed proudly toward the foundations of a large building, "Building a cathedral." The fourth man looked him in the eye and said, "We're creating a sacred place where people can find peace and community."

MUTUAL ENCOURAGEMENT

One of the biggest rewards from participating in a group is the feeling of validation and acknowledgement. Some people are self sufficient to the extent they do not need or want the acceptance of others. The majority of the human race, however, has a strong need for the validation that comes from positive, emotional interactions with those around them. A person needs to be seen and appreciated as a person and not a body that fills a position. Employees who are overwhelmed by the obligations of work and family may not have the emotional resources to give much encouragement. Competition, low self-esteem, fear, or apathy can also stop members of a work group from helping each other.

If no one can give what everyone needs the team effort suffers. Observers of human behavior have long said that a person is more likely to get the best from others if he first offers his best. What you put out will come back. How much sincere and specific encouragement are you giving to your teammates?

MUTUAL COACHING

One of best things about working in a team is the opportunity to learn from one another. The readiness to instruct and be instructed is an essential part of teamwork. New members usually need some informal instruction from their work group before they can become fully productive. Everyone loses when new members do not receive the instruction they need to get "up to speed." Can you show someone how to do a task without making him or her wrong in some subtle way? Can someone ask how to do a task without risking humiliation? In a healthy organization there is no such thing as a dumb question, nor is there any shame attached to the statement, "I don't know."

INTERPERSONAL COMMITMENT

The elements of a team: common identity, shared purpose, interdependence, and mutual accountability are present in all teams worthy of that designation. In teams performing at exceptional levels all of the members are consciously aware of these elements. This awareness is strong enough to keep the members honest with each other.

In the book, *The Three Musketeers*, there is the well-known motto of the heroes, "All for one and one for all." Exceptional teams have the same motto even if no has put the concept into words. People invest in each other when it's clear that "your success is my success" and vice versa. A high level of commitment to each other and the team's mission enables the members to deal with conflict constructively. They learn how to disagree without being disagreeable. And even if they are disagreeable they keep talking to each other until the issue is worked out. When people take a personal interest in each other and build social as well as professional relationships the collective effort gets an extra boost. As one person whose tenure on a high-performance team was one of his fondest memories put it:

> When you feel the people around you are on your side, when you realize they want you to succeed and will go out of their way to help you, the part of you that was wrapped tight with fear and "looking good" starts to relax. The more that part relaxes the more you can be creative and productive . . . you have a lot more fun too.

COLLABORATION OVER COMPETITION

Americans compete. This is so ingrained in our cultural mindset that if you put any two teams or peers together in an organization they will compete with each other. Underlying this reality are assumptions like: "Not everyone can get the promotion or the recognition. The scarcity of rewards means winner takes all. No one wants to be a loser. And nice guys finish last. So look out for number one. And get yours while you can and don't give that sucker an even break. . . . Right?"

What is lost is the distinction between healthy and unhealthy competition. Reflect for a moment on the consequences when people in the same organization ruthlessly compete with each other instead of the competition. In a world of global competition who benefits if the people in your organization refuse to share information and ideas, seldom help each other, or cheer every stumble or misstep their coworkers make? Your competition.

The lack of internal collaboration has caused more than one firm to fold. This cultural trait starts at school. We learn in the first grade that sharing information is cheating. There are only so many "A's" given out. Help others and you hurt your own chances for success. This unconscious mindset leads to "red ink" behaviors that are clearly not in everyone's best interest. But no one stops to ask if it might be smarter to compete against the competition instead of each other.

Ironically, those who would benefit the most from collaboration, senior managers, tend to be the worst offenders. They fought their way to the top and, by golly, no one is going to crowd them on their turf. Even when they are not trying to outdo or undermine each other there is rarely any mutual assistance. Management can counter this tendency by establishing a new corporate mindset, preaching and modeling to others that collaboration helps everyone win and win more.

WALKING THE TALK

Trying to implement values that determine the "reality in how you run the place," according to Paul O'Neill, the Chairman of the Aluminum Company of America, is not always easy. For O'Neill, the process has been, ". . . tortured, difficult, and aggravating because often you discover you've done things you wish you hadn't." However, executives such as, Robert Hass, the Chairman of Levi & Strauss and Company, believes the process is worth the effort because, ". . . a company's values—what it stands for—what it believes in—are crucial to its success."

Defining core values is the easy part. Living them yourself and getting others to do the same can seem like a quest for the impossible dream. Carlos Castaneda in his popular books about his experiences with a Mexican shaman talks about the difficulties of turning words into deeds.

The flaw with words is that they always make us feel enlightened, but when we turn around to face the world they always fail us and we end up facing the world as we always have, without enlightenment.

The motto, "control your destiny or someone else will," also applies to the culture of a corporation. Leave it up to chance or hope for a happy accident and it's likely the lowest common dominator will call the tune everyone else has to dance to.

If management wants a healthy culture with positive, people-friendly, values they will have to take action. Defining and disseminating those values is only the first step. There should be frequent follow-up to assess the organization's progress. Senior management should ask employees at every level how they think people are doing in implementing those values. The gap between the real and the ideal is part of being human. Without dialogue, feedback and adjustments, words will remain just words that are soon forgotten in the pressure cooker of work.

PERSONAL VISION

Crafting a personal vision statement is one way to discover principles you can use to better organize your life. This vision or mission is something you would want to do whether or not you got paid for it. The more overlap there is between the vision of your organization and your own personal vision the more obvious it is that you are where you should be. Integrity is being true to who you are and what you find meaningful. If you do not enjoy what you are doing, and it means nothing to you but a paycheck, then maybe it is time to consider a change. Knowing who you are is a part of knowing what to do with your life.

Getting clear about your own vision, mission, goals and values, forms a mental roadmap you can refer to on your journey through life. There is wisdom in the adage, "If you don't know where you're going any road will get you there."

Getting there is half the fun when you know where you are going. As the author of this book I hope to avoid the practice of preaching. My own personal vision is to facilitate organizational communication, change, and transformation. My job is to help create community by building strong, productive teams that people enjoy belonging to. I do this through conducting team-building interventions, teaching teamwork and leadership skills, and writing and speaking on these topics.

THE POWER OF ONE

A vision, and the values on which it is based, starts with the individual. To paraphrase Margaret Mead, a small group of motivated and committed individuals has changed the course of a company (or history) more than once. The example of even one person of courage and integrity can be the model for profound change—a change that originates within the individual. For example, reflect for a moment on the impact of Nelson Mandela in South Africa or even the world. Joseph Campbell, the author of *The Hero's Journey* and other works on mythology, told young people who came to him for advice three words: "Follow your bliss."

INITIATION FEE

Campbell believed it was more important to do what you really wanted to do rather than what might seem more practical but less satisfying. However, Campbell might have added that there is a price. Doing what you really feel called to do often demands a great deal of inner trust and faith. Trust in yourself and have faith in the universe or a Higher Power. Otherwise, your vision may seem too risky or impractical.

What is your personal vision?

Postscript
The New Spirit At Work

Team Building Associates

Whoever wants to reach a distant goal
must take many small steps.

HELMUT SCHMIDT

Perusing this book you've seen a wide range of activities, actions, and attitudes that have been used to fuel successful teamwork. Just a few years ago some people would look like they were hearing a message from Mars when we talked about working as a team and the skills it took to do that successfully. "There's no reason to learn this stuff," they protested, "we'll never have a chance to use it, because the boss will always make the decisions."

Today the concept of a team-based organization is more widely accepted. People still joke about group hugs, singing "Kumbaya", saying "I love you man" and other "touchy-feely" professions of forced intimacy. However, when they realize they are not going to have to pretend they like everyone, they relax and open up to learning ways to work more effectively with each other.

But their instincts are right. Something radical is happening that has as much to do with the heart as it does the intellect. Emotional intelligence is gaining recognition as an essential component of personal and professional effectiveness. People are being asked to relate to each other in a much different way than they are used to doing. A new set of values and behaviors is being introduced. A new level of knowledge and skill is being offered. The message may be couched in the languages of business and psychology, but the means are truly spiritual. The bottom line is about replacing fear with trust, competition with collaboration, strife with resolution, disrespect with respect, blame with responsibility, rigidity with creativity, in short, dysfunctional values with life-supportive ones.

Spirituality is being introduced into the workplace. Popular business books mirror this phenomena. Titles like, *Looking Out For Number One* or *Management by Guilt*, are being replaced with books like, *Creating Common Ground: The Power of Relationships at Work* or *Artful Work: Awaking Joy, Meaning, and Commitment in the Workplace* and newsletters like *Spirit at Work*.

Those who scoff that this is just pablum that panders to the angst of fifty-something "boomers" who never got over missing out on Woodstock, should consider the recent statement made by the CEO of a $6 billion company: "Our (corporate) culture is more important to us than earning per share." The CEO was Roger Sant and the company, AES, an independent provider of electric power based in Arlington, Virginia. AES even cited Mother Teresa in its annual report.[1]

> *The example of her life of selfless love gives us renewed zeal to pursue the corporate mission we have chosen: to help meet the world's need for safe, clean, reliable electricity while striving to embody and uphold our shared principles.*

AES's principles include integrity, fair dealing, social responsibility, and fun. Not bad for a power plant operator. As we move into a very uncertain future, corporate creeds that are friendlier to people and the environment will be a must. Several business alliances, like the Pew Center on Global Climate Change in Northern Virginia, stress corporate responsibility in addressing our most serious environmental threat, global warming. The fact that major corporations are signing on indicates a shift in the short-term thinking that dominates our decision making process.

Modern physics and ancient mystics both tell us everyone and everything are infinitely connected. How we treat each other, our clients, and our earth, are all related. Organizations that abuse the environment probably deal with their employees the same way. To paraphrase Albert Einstein, the kind of thinking that will get us out of a challenging situation has to be different than the kind of thinking that got us into it. And you, dear Reader, have the opportunity to contribute to that new thinking.

Chapter Notes & References

INTRODUCTION

The photograph at the beginning of this section shows a team celebrating its success in building and operating an egg-tossing catapult. The exercise was the last one in the day for a large, team building program.

Chapter 1. TOOLS FOR TEAMS

The chapter-heading photograph shows a team going through the Spider Web. An excellent activity for practicing team planning and decision making skills.

Chapter 2. WHAT IS TEAMWORK?

The chapter-heading photograph shows a team going through a warm-up activity called Witch/Watch (among other names). Two objects are passed in opposite directions around the circle. With each pass a communication must move back to and from the person who started passing the objects. Confusion and laughter result when the objects meet in the middle of the circle.

   1. Katzenbach, Jon & Smith, Douglas (1993). *The Wisdom of Teams: Creating the High Performance Organization*, New York, NY: Harper-Collins.

   2. Reilly, Anthony J. & Jones, John E. (1974). *The 1974 Annual Handbook for Group Facilitators*, San Diego, CA: University Associates.

   3. Snow, Harrison (1992). *The Power of Team Building: Using ropes Techniques*, San Diego, CA: Pfeiffer & Company, page 13.

Chapter 3. THEORIES AND MODELS

1. Owen, Harrison (1988). *Spirit: Transformation and Development in Organizations*, Potomac, MD: Abbott.

2 . Tuckman, B.W. & Jensen, M.A.C (1977, December). Stages of small-group development. *Group & Organization Studies*, pages 2(4), 419–427.

3. Brocklebank, S., & Mauer, R. (1990) Jack Gibb's theory of trust formation and group development. In S. Brocklebank (Ed.), *Working Effectively in Groups and Teams: A Resource Book*, Washington, DC: Mid-Atlantic Association for Training and Consulting.

4. Lacoursiere, R.B. (1980). *The Life Cycle of Groups: Group Development Stage Theory*, New York, NY: Human Services Press.

5. Hersey, P., & Blanchard, K.H. (1988) *Management of Organizational Behavior: Utilizing Human Resources* (5th ed.), Englewood Cliffs, NJ: Prentice-Hall.

Chapter 4. COMMUNICATION SKILLS

1. Mehrabain, Albert, (1968) Communication Without Words, *Psychology Today*, New York.

2. Nadir, R. & Luckier J. (1992). *Processing the Adventure Experience: Theory and Practice*, Dubuque, IA: Kendall/Hunt Publishing Company.

3. Robbins A. (1988). *Unlimited Power*, New York, NY: Ballantine Books.

4. Bandler R. & Grinder, J. (1982). *Reframing: Neuro-Linguistic Programming and the Transformation of Meaning*, Moab, UT: Real People Press.

5. Stanislavski, Constantin (1986). In Ray, M. L. & Myers, R. (Ed.), *Creativity in Business*, New York, NY: Doubleday Books, page 79.

6. Hendricks, Gay (1998), *The Ten-Second Miracle: Creating Relationship Breakthroughs*, New York, NY, Harper Collins.

7. Covey, S.R. (1989). *The Seven Habits of Highly Successful People*, New York, NY: Simon & Schuster.

Chapter 5. FACILITATION SKILLS

1. Doyle, M. & Straus, D. (1976). *How to Make Meetings Work: The New Interaction Method*, New York, NY: The Berkeley Publishing Group.

2. Porter, L. & Sonberg, S., (1993, June) Group Facilitation: Practice, Practice, Workshop presented at the University Associates Consulting & Training Services, San Diego.

3. Mindell, Arnold (1992). *The Leader as Martial Artist*, San Francisco, CA, HarperCollins.

Chapter 6. CONFLICT AND NEGOTIATION

The chapter-heading photograph shows a team doing the All Aboard exercise. The members must figure out how to all stand together on a small "raft" without anyone's feet touching the floor.

1. Singer, Linda R. (1990). *Settling Disputes: Conflict Resolution in Business in Business, Families and the Legal System*, Boulder, CO: Westview Press.

2. Thomas (1977) *Five Conflict Resolution Styles*, Boston, MA: Academy of Management Review, page 487. (Also, see Thomas-Kilman Conflict Mode Instrument distributed by Xicom Inc.)

3. Kanter, Rosebeth (1983).*The Change Masters: Innovation and Entrepreneurship in American Corporations*, New York, NY: Simon and Schuster, page 157.

4. Fisher, Robert, & Ury, William & Patton, Bruce (1991). *Getting to Yes: Negotiating Agreement Without Giving In*, Boston, MA: Houghton Mifflin.

5. Brown, Warren & Swoboda, Frank (1993, January 31). GM Begins Painful Process of Reinventing Itself, *Washington Post*, page H1.

6. Mindell, Arnold (1992). *The Leader as Martial Artist*, San Francisco, CA: Harper Collins, page 53.

7. Hendricks, Gay & Hendricks, Kathlyn (1993). *Centering and the Art of Intimacy Handbook*, New York, NY: Simon & Schuster.

8. Covey, Stephen (1989). *Seven Habits of Highly Effective People*, New York, NY: Simon and Schuster.

9. The Mankind Project, New Warrior Training, conducted at Mar Lu Ridge Retreat Center, MD, in 1996.

Chapter 7. GROUND RULES AND AGREEMENTS

1. Gibb, Jack (1978). A Climate for Learning. In J. Denham (Ed.), *Human Relations Reader*, Mid-Atlantic Training Conference, Washington, DC.

For more information on this topic Tom Peters is an excellent source: Peters, Tom (1988). *Thriving On Chaos: Handbook for a Management Revolution*, New York, NY: Alfred A. Knopf.

Chapter 8. TEAM BUILDING ON-THE-RUN

The chapter-heading photograph shows a group member being "levitated" by his teammates. The exercise develops trust and the sense of interdependence between team members.

1. Covey, Stephen (1989). *Seven Habits of Highly Effective People*, New York, NY: Simon and Schuster.

2. Senge, Peter (1991). *The Fifth Discipline: The Art and Practice of the Learning Organization*, New York, NY: Doubleday.

3. Owen, Harrison (1988). *Spirit: Transforming and Development in Organizations*, Potomac, MD: Abbott.

4. Sher, Barbara & Gottlieb, Anne (1989). *Teamworks!*, New York, NY: Warner Books.

5. Kogan, Marcela (1993, September 14). The Workers' Party: Looking at the Positive Side of Office Celebrations. *Washington Post*, page B5.

For more ideas about office fun and celebrations take a look at this book: Hemsath, Dave; Yerkes, Leslie, (1997). *301 Ways to Have FUN at Work*, San Francisco, Berrett-Koehler.

Chapter 9. DECISIONS AND PROBLEM SOLVING

The chapter-heading photograph shows a team trying to decide how they are going to build a bridge. The bridge will allow them to cross the pit of "poisonous peanut butter" that stands between them and their destination. The exercise is called Canyon Crossing. It helps a team develop the related skills of problem solving and decision making.

1. Noone, Donald, J. (1993). *Creative Problem Solving*, Happauge, NY: Barron's Educational Services.

2. You can buy a booklet on Appreciative Inquiry by contacting: The Thin Book Publishing Company, Fax: 972-403-0065. Telephone: 972-378-0523

Why not use your PC to help the brainstorming process? IdeaFisher offers computer-based approach to enhance the creative process. IdeaFisher Systems, Inc, 222 Martin Street, Suite 110, Irvine, CA

92715, Telephone: 800-289-4332, fax: 714-474-811. Or you could just get the book: Fisher, Marsh (1996). *The IdeaFisher, How to Land That Big Idea—and Other Secrets of Creativity in Business*, Princeton, NJ: Peterson's/Pacesetter Books.

Chapter 10. ORGANIZATIONAL INTERVENTIONS

1. Burke, Warner (1982). *Organizational Development: Principles and Practices*, Boston, MA: Little Brown & Company.

2. Reilly, Anthony J. & Jones, John E. (1974). *The 1974 Annual Handbook for Group Facilitators*, San Diego, CA: University Associates.

To find out more about the Organizational Development Network, contact Chesapeake Bay ODN, 4227 46th Street, Washington, DC 20016. Fax: 202-686-8287, Web Site: www.concentric.net~Cbodn.

Chapter 11. DIFFERENT WORK STYLES

There are a number of books available on MBTI. One I like is: Kroeger, Otto & Thuesen, Janet, M. (1988). *Type Talk: The 16 Personality Types That Determine How We Live, Love, and Work*, New York, NY: Dell Publishing. Otto conducts courses for type certification in Fairfax, Virginia at Otto Kroeger Associates.

The people who keep track of the statistics on type are:

Center for Applications of Psychological Type, 2720 NW 6th Street, Gainesville, FL 32609.

Association for Psychological Type, P. O. Box 5099, Gainesville, FL 32602-5099.

For information on DISC you can call: Carlson Learning Company, Training Division, P. O. Box 59159, Minneapolis, MN 55439; Telephone: (612) 449-2868.

Chapter 12. ROPES COURSE

The person in the chapter heading photograph is jumping off the Pamper Pole. The name is derived from something you might need to wear just before you leap off.

1. Snow, Harrison (1992). *The Power of Team Building: Using Ropes Techniques*, San Diego, CA: Pfeiffer & Company.

2. ibid, page 68.

3. Bandura, Alfred (1979, Fall). Self-Efficacy: Toward a Unified Theory of Behavioral Change, *Psychological Bulletin*, pages 192–198.

4. Roland, Chris. (1985). Outdoor Management Training Programs: Do They Work?. *The Bradford Papers*, Vol. V. Bloomington, IN: Indiana University Press.

5. Favery, Mike (1988, October 3). Outside Antics, *The Wall Street Journal*, page 16.

6. Gordon, Jack (Ed.) (1991, May). Untitled article. *TRAINING: The Human Side of Business*, Saint Paul, MN: Lakewood Publications, page 48.

Chapter 13. WILDERNESS ADVENTURE

1. Gorman, Stephen (1993, Fall). Mountaincraft. *Summit*, page 93. Hood River, OR: Summit Publications. Quoted by Gorman from an article in "Outing," a popular magazine published in the 1920's which featured Sear's work.

2. Ewert, Alan, (1989). *Outdoor Adventure Pursuits: Foundations, Models and Theories*, Worthington, OH: Publishing Horizons, page 61.

3. ibid, pages 91, 70.

4. Csikszentmihalyi, Mihaly, (1998). *Finding Flow: the Psychology of Engagement with Everyday Life*, Basic Books, New York

5. Hale, A.H., (1988) Annual Review, International Safety Network, Bellefontaine, OH, page ii.

Chapter 14. CROSS-CULTURAL TEAMWORK

1. Casse, P. (1983). *Cross-Cultural Management Communication*, Englewood Cliffs, NJ: Prentice Hall.

2. Hofstede, Geert (1984). *Culture's Consequences*, Beverly Hills, CA: Sage.

3. Pfeiffer, John (1978, May). How Not to Lose the Trade Wars by Cultural Gaffes. *Smithsonian Magazine*, page 145–152.

4. Barker, Joel (1989). *Discovering the Future: The Business of Paradigms*, Videocassette produced and directed by Infinity Limited & Charterhouse Learning, 38 minutes.

5. Barrett & Bass (1973). In M. Dunnette (Ed.), *Handbook of Industrial and Organizational Psychology*, pages 1639–1678. Chicago, IL: Rand McNally College Publishing Company, Chicago, Editor, M. Dunnette.

The following are some of the organizations active in cross-cultural training

International Counseling Center, 300 Connecticut Avenue NW, Suite 138, Washington, DC 20008.

Society for Intercultural Education Training and Research (SIETAR), 733 15th Street NW, Suite 900, Washington, DC 20005.

For Culturgrams contact: Brigham Young University, General Editor, David M. Kennedy Center, 280 HRCB, Provo, UT; Telephone: 801-378-6528.

An excellent cross-cultural trainer is my associate, JoAnn Hinshaw. She can be reached by email at Jo_Ann_HINSHAW@umail.umd.edu.

Chapter 15. BENEFITING FROM DIVERSITY

1.Watson, Warren (1993). Cultural diversity's impact on interaction process and performance. *Academy of Management Journal*, Volume 16, Number 3.

2. Watts, Patti (1987, December). Bias Busting, Diversity in the Workplace. *Management Review*, page 51–53.

3. Malidoma Some, Ph.D. resides in Oakland, California, Telephone: (510) 639-7637.

A skilled trainer in the field of diversity is my associate, Tom Wootten. He can be reached directly by email at Teamalc@aol.com

Chapter 16. BUSINESS GAMES

1. Fluegelman, Andrew (1976). *The New Games Book*, page 55. Garden City, NY: Headlands Press, Dolphin Books/Doubleday.

2. Fluegelman, Andrew (1981). *More New Games*, Garden City, NY: Headlands Press, Dolphin Books/Doubleday.

3. Snow, Harrison (1992). *The Power of Team Building: Using Ropes Techniques*, San Diego, CA: Pfeiffer & Company.

A classic in this field is this book: Rohnke, Carl (1984). *Silver Bullets*, Project Adventure, Inc., 1984, Hamilton, MA

For indoor and outdoor activities another great book by yours truly is: *Indoor/Outdoor Team Building Games for Trainers* by Harrison Snow. You can order a copy from McGraw-Hill Business over the internet by emailing customer.service@mcgraw-hill.com or by calling 800-2mcgraw.

4. Sources for board games:

Compact Training Company, Telephone: 800-741-0011.

Quality Educational Development, Inc., New York, NY; Telephone: 212-724-3335.

Eagles Flight, Calgary, Alberta; Telephone: 888- 567-8077.

Workshops by Thiagi, Bloomington, Indiana; Telephone: 812-332-1478.

Leadership in Action Center for Creative Leadership Greensboro, North Carolina; Telephone: 336-288-7210.

A number of simulations, such as, Hurricane Disaster, Lost at Sea, and Wilderness Survival, are available from Pfeiffer & Company, 350 Sansome Street, 5th floor, San Francisco, CA 94104. 800-274-4434.

5. *TRAINING: The Human Side of Business*. St Paul, MN: Lakewood Publications.

6. *Training & Development Journal*. Alexandria, VA: American Society for Training and Development in Alexandria, VA, Telephone: 703-683-8100.

7. Sources for films:

CRM FILMS, 2233 Faraday Ave, Carlsbad, CA; Telephone: 619-431-9800.

Films Incorporated, 5547 N. Ravensworth Ave., Chicago, IL; Telephone: 312-878-2600.

Video Publishing House, 930 N. National Parkway, Schaumberg, IL; Telephone: 708-517-8744.

AMA Video, Nine Galen Street, Waterford, MA; Telephone: 617-926-4600.

Chapter 17. TEAM KILLERS

The chapter-heading photograph shows a team in the exercise called *Group Grope*. The blindfolded team members must find a nearby object without breaking the tape that keeps them together. Communication, coordination, and a sense of humor are essential.

1. Blotnick, Srully (1985). *The Corporate Steeplechase*, 1985, Penguin Books, New York.

2. Adapted from material presented in a workshop conducted by Jerry and Esther Hicks for the Abraham Series.

3. *Eight Verses for Training the Mind*, Buddhist Scriptural verses presented by His Holiness, the 14th Dally Lama at a conference at American University in Washington DC, November, 1998.

4. Adapted from material presented by Michelle Anderson and Richard Rylander, Master Angelic Work, Telephone 888-812-6435.

5. Fournies, Ferdinand, (1988). Why Employees Don't Do What Thy're Supposed to Do, And What to Do About It, McGraw-Hill Business, NY.

6. Applegate, Jane (1993, July 26). Advice for coping with disgruntled staff: Try a little tenderness. *Washinngton Post*, Business Section, page 10.

Chapter 18. MANAGING STRESS

The man in the chapter heading photograph is climbing the "Giant's Ladder." This high ropes activity involves two climbers who help each other up a "ladder" that has "steps" five or more feet apart.

1. Lew Childers, Doc, (1998). *Freeze Frame: Fast Action Stress Relief*, Planetary Publications, San Francisco.

Chapter 19. MANAGING CHANGE

The chapter-heading photograph shows a blindfolded team member being guided by her teammates as she walks along an elevated beam. The exercise fosters trust, communication and support among team members.

1. Dillard, Annie (1974). *Pilgrim at Tinker Creek*, page 28, New York: Perennial Library, New York. (Von Senden, Marius, Space and Sight, Methuen & Co.)

2. Lewin, Kurt (1951). *Field Theory in Social Science*, New York, NY: Harper & Row.

3. Machiavelli, Nicolo, *The Prince*, (1981), Bantam Books, New York

4. I have seen the Arbiter quote floating around for at least twenty years. But, the source of the quote has never enjoyed the same popularity. It could be a lot younger than it proposes to be.

5. Kubler-Ross, Elizabeth (1977). *On Death and Dying*, Los Angeles, CA: Jermey P. Tarcher Inc.

6. Liggett, Bill & Snow, Harrison (1992). *TQM and Team Building for GSA*, unpublished proposal.

7. Kanter, Rosabeth, (1983). *The Change Masters*, Simon & Schuster, New York.

8. Curtis, Charles, P. & Greenslet, Ferris (1962) *The Practical Cogitator, The Thinkers Anthology*, page 413. Boston, MA: Houghton Mifflin Company.

This book is worth reading for his views on the cycle of change that corporations go through: Want, Jerome, H. (1995). *Managing Radical Change: Beyond Survival in the New Business Age*, New York, NY: John Wiley & Sons.

Chapter 20. TEAM LEADERSHIP

1. Semler, Ricardo, (1993). *Maverick, the Success Story behind the World's Most Unusual Workplace*, Warner Books, New York.

2. Hershey & Blanchard, (1988). Management of Organizational Behavior: Utilizing Human Resources (5th ed.) (Prentice-Hall, Englewood Cliffs, NJ.

3. Margension, Charles; McCann, Dick, (1995). Team Management, Practical New Approaches, Management Books 2000, Ltd., London.

4. Bion, W.R. (1961). *Experiences in Groups*, New York, NY: Basic Books.

Chapter 21. STRUCTURAL REINFORCEMENT

1. Noonan, Tim, "The Agile Giant: How Hewlett-Packard Climbed To The Top," October, 1992, Hemispheres, United Publishing, Atlanta, pages 28–30.

2. Osborne, David; Gaebler, Ted, (1992). *Reinventing Government, How the Entrepreneurial Spirit is Transforming the Public Sector*, Penguin Books, New York, page 254.

3. Woodruff, David, Where Employees Are Management, Reinventing America 1992, Business Week Special Edition, Business Week, Washington DC, Page 66.

4. Jossey-Bass/Pfeiffer located in San Francisco, CA; Telephone: 800-274-4434.

5. The Wellness Council of America, 7101 Newport Ave. Omaha, NE 68152; Telephone: 402-572-3590.

Chapter 23. FORGING A VISION

The chapter-heading photograph shows a group of executives navigating their canoes through the Florida everglades.

1. Rosen, Robert (1991). *The Healthy Company*, Los Angeles, CA: Jermey P. Tarcher Inc.

Chapter 24. POSTSCRIPT

The chapter-heading photograph shows the author enjoying the winter view from the top of a peak near Aspen, Colorado.

1. Washington Business (*The Washington Post*), Power View, AES Has Plants Around the World but its Leaders Want to Talk About Values, Martha Hamilton, November 2, 1998.

For more comprehensive look at the new spirit in the workplace read the following article: *The Washington Post*, Spirituality at Work: Linking Joy, Meaning, Commitment and the Company's Bottom Line, April 15, 1997, Don Oldenburg.

HARRISON SNOW

Harrison Snow directs the activities of Team Building Associates. Since 1988 he has been conducting team building and leadership development programs for both Government and Fortune 500 clients using the techniques and programs described in this book. His background includes: military service as the team leader of a U.S. Army Special Forces "A" team, work as a marketing and operations manager for a technical services firm, and serving as an adjunct trainer for Outward Bound professional development programs. His previous books are *The Power of Team Building Using Ropes Techniques* (Pfeiffer) and *Indoor/Outdoor Team Building Games For Trainers* (McGraw-Hill Business). He is a member of the American Society for Training and Development and the Chesapeake Bay Organizational Development Network. Harrison is known for his skill in helping teams work through challenging issues. He lives in Falls Church, Virginia with his wife and son.

For more information on Harrison Snow's consulting and training services or to purchase copies of this book call 703-241-2421 or email:

Teambuilder@msn.com

You can visit our web site at:
www.geocities.com/teamtools